THE GRAND TETONS

THE
GRAND TETONS

The Story of the Men Who
Tamed the Western Wilderness

By
Margaret Sanborn

G.P. Putnam's Sons
New York

SBN: 399-12045-9

Library of Congress Cataloging in Publication Data

Sanborn, Margaret
  The grand tetons

  Bibliography: Includes index
  1. Teton Mountains—History. 2. Frontier and pioneer life—Wyoming—Teton Mountains. I. Title.
F767.T29S26   1978   978.7'5   78-15287

For Catherine
who shared the Teton adventure

By the Same Author

Robert E. Lee, A Portrait: 1807–1861
Robert E. Lee, The Complete Man: 1861–1870
The American: River of El Dorado
The Grand Tetons: The Story of the Men Who
    Tamed the Western Wilderness

Acknowledgments

I want to thank the following people for their interest, coop-
eration, and time, which have helped make this work possible:
Dwight C. Stone, Driggs, Idaho; Professor Robert C. Warner,
Journalism Department, the University of Wyoming, Laramie;
Dr. Gene M. Gressley, director, Western History Research
Center, the University of Wyoming, and David Crosson, re-
search historian, also of the Western History Research Center;
Dr. George C. Frison, head, Anthropology Department, the
University of Wyoming; Virginia Borland, librarian, Civic Cen-
ter Library, San Rafael, California, and reference librarians Jac-
quelyn Mollenkopf, Barbara Hughes, and Regina Jimenez; Sara
Monte, Marin County Library, Corte Madera, California; Alice
Susong, Yellowstone Library, Yellowstone National Park;
Annabelle McNamee, Western History Research Center, the
University of Wyoming; Mildred Goosman, curator, Western
Collections, Joslyn Art Museum, Omaha; Marie E. Keene, as-
sistant librarian, Thomas Gilcrease Institute of American His-
tory and Art, Tulsa; Dorothy Hinshaw, Belvedere, California;
James and Mary Skalet, St. Anthony, Idaho; Frances H. Stadler,
archivist, Missouri Historical Society, St. Louis; Gilda Turitz,
Bay Area Reference Center, San Francisco; Marguerite Her-
mann, University of California Library, Berkeley; Burke Davis,
Williamsburg, Virginia; Constance Karla, Greenbrae, California; Catherine Sanborn, Mill Valley, California; F. W. Thrane,
Orinda, California; William H. Williams, director, Wyoming

State Archives and Historical Department, Cheyenne; William H. Barton, research historian, Wyoming State Archives and Historical Department; Elizabeth Woolstenhulme, Driggs, Idaho.

I also wish to thank The Missouri Historical Society, St. Louis, for permission to quote from the letters of Sir William Drummond Stewart; The State Historical Society of Colorado, Denver, for permission to quote from the letters of Sidford Hamp; The Augustana Historical Society, Rock Island, Illinois, and Katherine A. Halverson, editor, *Annals of Wyoming*, for permission to quote from Thomas Moran's diary, transcribed from the original by Fritiof Fryxell, and published under the title *Thomas Moran's Journey to Tetons*.

MARGARET SANBORN

MILL VALLEY, CALIFORNIA
MAY 1978

CONTENTS

I	The Setting	13
II	Genesis	21
III	The Mysterious West	25
IV	Trail Through the Snow	34
V	"They Call Themselves Sho-sho-nies"	42
VI	The Wane of Shoshoni Power	54
VII	The Pilot Knobs	59
VIII	Fortunes in Fur	74
IX	Who They Were	80
X	Living Off the Land	96
XI	Saturnalia in the Tetons	103
XII	Pilgrim's Progress	108
XIII	The Battle of Pierre's Hole	117
XIV	Sacajawea's Son	125
XV	Peregrinating Peers	133
XVI	End of an Era	145
XVII	Washakie	151
XVIII	Continental Tea	166
XIX	The Great Surveys	177
XX	Conquering the Giant	186
XXI	Mystery of the Grand Teton	193
XXII	The Other Side of the Mountains	199

XXIII   Immortalizing the Tetons   210
XXIV   Six-Guns   216
XXV   Taming the Hole   226
XXVI   Riders   234
XXVII The Changing Mountains   247
AFTERWORD—Saving the Tetons   254
NOTES AND SOURCES
    CONSULTED AND QUOTED   263
BIBLIOGRAPHY   292
INDEX   312

TO THE READER

All quotations in this book are verbatim. With this understood, the reader is spared the distraction of having (sic) inserted after every error in spelling, grammar, and punctuation.

I
The Setting

In the northwest corner of Wyoming there is a chain of mountains called the Teton Range, a line of jagged peaks and spires forty miles long and fifteen miles wide. Flanking it on the east is a broad valley of infinite variety—sagebrush flats, wooded rises, meadows, marshes, cottonwood groves; stands of aspen, pine, and spruce; ponds, lakes, streams, and the mighty Snake River coursing through its center. From the floor of this valley, named Jackson's Hole for an early-day fur trapper, the Teton Range rises sheer and presents one of the steepest and most spectacular mountain fronts in the world.

The Tetons, unlike most ranges, are never static, but show constant changes in their outline, form, and setting with each slight shift in viewpoint. Peaks and pinnacles not visible before slip suddenly into place beside or behind other peaks, or rise unexpectedly above intervening ridges and gaps. Slopes become steeper or more gentle; and cirques, glaciers, gorges, and hanging valleys come into sight. The seasons, the weather, the time of day or night also bring change. Then the peaks may be shrouded in haze or clouds, veiled by rain, or be ghostly shapes behind a screen of falling snow. They may be purplish-blue and flat almost to formlessness; or clear-cut and sheeny gray, every gulch and crag, every facet of spire sharply defined. They may be rosy in early morning light, dazzling under a blanket of snow that softens and rounds the rugged crests, or gleaming and mysterious in moon or starlight.

There are rare times when the mountains seem to open and reveal what lies behind that steep front wall. On those days the air is sparkling clear, shadows are deep, and each peak stands apart. Canyons which segment the range, seen usually as mere lines, become broad chasms that lead into the heart of the Tetons, disclosing their substance—mountains within mountains—their core and strength.

Distant views give no hint of the Tetons' inner riches: the fragrant forests, the brawling cascades, the banks of flowers and ferns, the variety of birds, the alpine lakes and meadows, and the peaks themselves. Only within the mountains can one hope to learn something of their wonder.

The Tetons are dramatic from either side. From the west the peaks are fully as awesome and majestic as when seen from the east, and because the valley that spreads at their feet is in places two thousand feet lower than Jackson Hole, they soar correspondingly higher. Views are less spectacular, though, because the mountains do not rise sheer from the plain, but tower above the forested foothills and plateaus that form their foreground.

The west side has been long neglected, although it abounds in fine forests, waterfalls, streams, alpine meadows and lakes, permanent snowfields, and wilderness valleys. Yet, curiously, it was from the west that the Tetons were first recognized for their unusual beauty, and were first photographed and first painted. Pioneer photographer William Henry Jackson, approaching them from the west, observed that the line of mountains made "one of the most stupendous panoramas in America." Landscape painter Thomas Moran noted in his diary, while camped at the Tetons' western base, that they were doubtless the "finest pictorial range in the United States, or even N. America." It was on the west side that the first studies were made of their flora, fauna, and geology; that the mountains were first mapped; and that the first ascent of the Grand Teton was made by white men.

When seen from the west, the name Les Trois Tetons (The Three Teats) given by an early French trapper, becomes appropriate. Looming on the horizon across the Snake River plains of Idaho, their naturally sharp and jagged outlines, which reminded one old explorer of shark's teeth, are softened by distance.

Every season in the Tetons has its special charm, spring perhaps more than any other because of the abundance of wildflowers from mid-May until the first frosts touch the highlands. Since there are four life zones contained within less than fifteen miles, spring is a continuing season as it follows the receding snows to the heights.

Buttercups are the first to appear in mass as soon as the snow begins to melt in the valleys, turning newly bared patches of moist ground to shimmering gold. Spring beauty, shooting-stars, yellow fritillary, larkspur, paintbrush, and daisy follow quickly as the last snowbanks retreat. Along the lakeshores and streams, blue violets flower; the wet meadows are bright with yellow monkeyflower and purple, Rocky Mountain iris. In the forests bloom pinedrops, columbine, and fairybells.

Many of these valley flowers—glacier lily, daisy, and paintbrush—are mountain climbers that follow spring to the timberline and beyond. Other plants, such as Parry's primrose, sky pilot, and purple saxifrage, are strictly alpine and are found during their brief blooming season on bare rocky slopes ten to twelve thousand feet high. These flowers survive the harsh environment only because they spend more than half the year buried under immense snowdrifts which protect them from the blighting cold.

The purple saxifrage (*Saxifraga oppositifolia*) is a relic of the ice ages. This little plant that grows on the Tetons' talus slopes is identical with the saxifrage native to the Alps. Botanists believe that the continental ice sheets carried the plant south from the Arctic and, on receding left it isolated in these two widely separated localities.

The most common forest tree in the Tetons is the lodgepole pine. It owes its abundance in part to the fact that its tightly closed cones, which remain attached for years, are able to resist forest fires. After the parent tree has been consumed, many of the cones, only scorched, open as soon as the smoke clears. The seeds are then sown widely on the open ground, and a new growth immediately springs up out of the ashes. "Therefore, this tree not only holds its ground, but extends its conquests after every fire," observed John Muir.

Teton country supports a diverse and often unusual animal population. In the broken forests, and in willow thickets near ponds, there are moose, the world's largest antlered mammal. In the meadows graze herds of elk—properly wapiti, a Shawnee word meaning "light rump"—and a few buffalo or bison, the largest of the North American land mammals. On the plains there are occasional pronghorn antelope, fleet creatures, able to run up to sixty miles an hour, who are the only surviving members of a unique family, *Antilocapridae*, that evolved on this continent and is found nowhere else in the world.

In the streams live beaver, whose engineering projects benefit man by preventing erosion, and whose ponds create an environment that attracts swans, ducks, songbirds, deer, muskrats, and moose. Beside the waterways, in bank burrows, live mink and otter. Black bear (often cinnamon brown in color) and a small number of grizzly roam forests and mountain heights. A few bighorn sheep range the crags, and in the subalpine talus live marmot and pika. In the conifer woods there are porcupines that relish the succulent inner bark of these trees; and chipmunks, red squirrels, and snowshoe hares that feed on nuts, berries, treebuds, grass, and fungi.

Regal trumpeter swans, one of America's rarest birds, Canada geese, and mergansers frequent lakes and ponds and the quiet backwaters of the Snake River, which rises in the mountains of Yellowstone Park and winds through Jackson Hole on its way to join the Columbia. In the river's side channels there are speckled dace; in its swift waters, cutthroat trout.

Coyotes and badgers hunt the meadows for ground squirrels, voles, and mice, while overhead soar sharp-eyed hawks. In the alpine regions cliff swallows skim the snowbanks for insects, and rosy finches harvest the seeds of sedges growing along the lines of melting snow. Above the Tetons the eagle drifts down the wind, and surveys the entire range.

In spring and summer there is birdsong in every meadow, marsh, wood, and streamside grove—tanager, lark, robin, bluebird, redwing, grosbeak, and thrush. But the most unusual songbird in the Tetons is the water ouzel or dipper. What sets this, plump, slate-gray bird apart from others of its kind is its affinity for water, since it spends most of its days in or under it, being able to float on the surface like a duck, or walk beneath it along the stream bed in search of food. When singing, it prefers the accompaniment of rushing water to the chorus of other birds, and unlike other birds, it sings all year, even in the midst of winter storms. Its nest, "round and bossy in outline, with a neatly arched opening near the bottom, somewhat like an old-fashioned brick oven," is built almost entirely of green and yellow moss, interwoven and felted together. It is usually placed on a little rock shelf directly beside, or better still, behind a waterfall so that the drifting veils of mist keep it perpetually damp, and the mosses fresh and growing.

Men first came into the Teton valleys at least 10,500 years ago, when ice from the last glacial period still lay about in patches. Finding the land rich in new life, they stayed to gather the plants, roots, and berries; to harvest seeds that would be eaten fresh, roasted, or ground into meal; and to fish and hunt. Their hunting and gathering was attended by important rituals: prayers asking forgiveness for taking life; prayers of thankfulness to sun and earth, and supplications for the tribe's good fortune and health. These people made tools and weapons from the outcrops of obsidian and quartzite they found in the valleys and mountains, and bowls from the steatite they quarried on the Tetons' west slope, crossing the range from side to side over high passes and through canyons, marking out trails that are still in use. Artifacts fashioned from these materials reached the Ohio River basin, through trade, as early as 500 B.C.

Two and perhaps three groups of Indians came in each spring, from the south by way of the Green River valley, and from the north along the Snake River, and they stayed until the first falls of snow. Then, like most of the birds, they left for more sheltered wintering places. Later, Ute, Flathead, Shoshoni, Nez Percé, Crow, Gros Ventre, and Blackfoot, came into the Tetons to hunt buffalo or cross the range on their way to war. Still later, Shoshonis, unable to defend themselves against those tribes who had guns, found refuge among the Teton peaks. Here they lived furtively the year round in caves and secret glens.

White men did not discover the Tetons until the first decade of the 1800s. In search of furs, they found the streams rich in beaver and the valleys filled with grazing herds. But they did not stay long or explore extensively, for the American fur trade in the Far West was then in its infancy, and these men were its scouts. Traveling singly or two and three together, they had to be constantly on the alert for ambush by hostile Indians. They felt safest, they declared, in Jackson's Hole, because it was nearly inaccessible, an impenetrable fastness ringed by rugged and lofty mountains. In that more easily entered valley lying west of the Tetons, the biggest Indian battle in the history of the Rocky Mountain fur trade, was fought in 1832.

There is no record of any of these men remarking on the Tetons' grandeur or spectacular beauty. But it is known that they found the mountains useful. Since the peaks' peculiar shape could never be mistaken, and their height made them visible a hundred and fifty miles away, they were used as beacons. The Grand Teton became one of the most noted landmarks in the Rocky Mountains, watched for by every traveler to guide him on his way.

Not until the mid 1820s, when the Rocky Mountain fur trade was at its height, was Teton country thoroughly explored. Then the most famous of the mountain men—Kit Carson, Jim Bridger, Jedediah Smith, Old Bill Williams, Joe Meek, Bill Sublette, Black Harris, and Rube Herring—tramped every canyon and glade to set their beaver traps in the waterways, and roamed forests and plains in search of bear, buffalo, elk, deer, and antelope. They passed from valley to valley through the stream canyons and over the passes. Noblemen, artists, writers, physicians, and adventurers, taking advantage of the protection of the annual fur company supply caravans, rode with them into the mountains, where they hunted trophies, sketched and painted, described the country and the people they saw, or fought and scalped Indians. By 1840 the trade's best days were over, most of the big fur partnerships were dissolved, and Teton country was deserted except for those bands of nomadic Indians who rode in to hunt and fish, and the Shoshonis who lived secretly on the heights.

Twenty years went by before the first official explorers made their way through the mountains into Jackson Hole and crossed the Tetons to the west valley. With this company, led by Captain William F. Raynolds, was a young physician-naturalist, Dr. F. V. Hayden, who made the first reports on Teton fossils, geology, and mammals. But his observations were necessarily brief, for the captain was behind schedule and had to hurry on. Not until 1872 were comprehensive scientific studies made of the area. That year Dr. Hayden, then in charge of the government Geological Survey, sent a party that included geologists, topographers, botanists, zoologists, and a photographer into the Tetons. The copiously illustrated and highly readable reports which resulted were published the following year, and introduced the general public to a part of the Far West that was entirely unknown.

The years immediately following the Civil War were notable for widespread outlawry. Murderers, bank and train robbers, highwaymen, horse thieves, and cattle rustlers began appearing in Teton country. They had found that their trails were soon lost in the wilderness, and that lawmen were reluctant to follow them into the maze of mountains. Horse thieves drove their stolen herds from valley to valley over rugged passes that defied pursuit; hid them in secret canyons, or corralled them in the highlands. Up in Death Canyon, where there have been reports of ghost riders, there is a little meadow cut by a deep, narrow stream. Here for years stood an old drift fence that once penned stolen horses, safe from the posses which combed the valley below.

The outlaws built themselves stout cabins, well concealed in remote gulches and thickets, strongholds where they could resist attack should the sheriffs and their men ever overtake them. For over a quarter of a century, Jackson Hole was one of the most notorious outlaw resorts in the nation. It is said that the famed Butch Cassidy went there occasionally to allow the chase to cool, and that he hid some booty on Cache Creek. The valley lying west of the Tetons was not far behind in reputation, for it was a highly popular rendezvous with horse thieves who raided the Montana ranches.

By 1880 a good number of wealthy big-game and trophy hunters from the eastern states and from Europe (a few noblemen among them) had begun packing into Teton country in search of moose, elk, antelope, and bighorn sheep. Young

Owen Wister made the first of many such trips to Jackson Hole in the summer of 1887, to hunt and fish, and was so impressed by the beauty of the mountains he described them in his diary with each observed change in their color, form, and mood. Later he would use Teton country as a setting for some of his Western tales.

In the final decades of the nineteenth century white men came to the Tetons to prospect for gold; to mine silver, copper, and coal, drill for oil, and to lumber. Other men took up land and began raising cattle and horses, which they fed on the abundant wild hay.

With the establishment of ranches, the last of the colorful frontier characters found their way into Teton country: These were the cowboys who rode their sturdy ponies up the long trail from Texas, bringing with them their special skills learned from the Spaniards and Mexicans; their distinctive dress; their racy language; their stories full of atmosphere; and their songs—high-spirited, mocking, irreverent, or mournful and full of longing.

On the night of the Wolf Moon (the full moon of January), declared by old mountain men to be the most eerie night of the year, it is said that the clatter of hoofs is often heard in a Teton canyon where no horse has ever gone, and with it, trailed on the cold night wind, there are fragments of song—sad, almost sobbing—a cowboy song.

II
Genesis

The Tetons are still rising. Young geologically, these mountains are growing at the rate of about one foot every three to four hundred years. Jackson Hole, the valley at their eastern base, is meanwhile sinking.

Less than nine million years ago the Teton Range was uplifted when the earth's crust broke along a north-south fracture, or fault, within the Rocky Mountain chain in northwestern Wyoming. Although upthrust was rapid, it was intermittent rather than continuous, and was accompanied by violent earthquakes.

Two adjacent earth blocks were displaced at the same time on opposite sides of the fault. The block on the west was pushed up to form the Tetons, while the one to the east was dropped, resulting in the valley known as Jackson Hole. Since uplift was greatest next to the fault, where a displacement of over seven thousand feet was involved, and decreased toward the west, both mountain range and valley took on a marked westward tilt. Because subterranean forces are still active—small earthquakes are recorded frequently, sometimes daily, throughout Teton country—the mountains continue to rise, and Jackson Hole to sink and tilt.

The Tetons, whose needlelike peaks now tower from nine to nearly fourteen thousand feet in elevation, rose as a gentle, plateau-like block forty miles long. As it pushed up it took with it a part of the hardened floor of that ancient, shallow sea that in Paleozoic times repeatedly inundated western North America, and as often withdrew, leaving behind each time vast deposits of sediments containing entrapped marine plants and animals. Today, coral reefs in fossil form stand nearly two miles above sea level on the Tetons' west face. There are also trilobites and brachiopods exposed on canyon walls. Most interesting are the large calcareous mounds of algal heads lying at over ten thousand feet elevation on the divide between North and South Leigh creeks—marine plants from the Cambrian sea that drowned the Teton site about five hundred million years ago.

Erosive forces started shaping the Teton block as soon as it began to rise. Stream courses formed throughout it, and as it gained height, their channels became straight and parallel, extending from the crest down the east and west slopes. With continued elevation there came a time when air currents were forced to rise so high to pass over the range, their moisture condensed. Rain and snowfall increased, and the streams, gaining in volume and speed, cut deep, narrow canyons that notched the ridge, creating its first domes and gaps.

About a million years ago the ice age began. In the Tetons and other high Western ranges the climate grew so cold there came a time when the summer sun no longer melted the seasonal snows. Vast banks, therefore, collected about the peaks. Turning into crystalline ice, the snow masses, compacted by their own weight, became glaciers. Ice rivulets from these glaciers felt their way into the stream canyons and began creeping down the slopes, wiping away stands of trees, grinding and scouring the canyon walls, and deepening the gorges as they went. Many moved as much as several hundred feet a year and pushed beyond the canyon mouths to join the great glaciers in the valleys east and west of the range.

There were at least three periods of intense glaciation. The most extensive took place two hundred thousand years ago. Then a vast river of ice that was in places three thousand feet deep moved southward through Jackson Hole, shaping the terrain as it inched along. But it was the final period, the Pinedale, that was chiefly responsible for the Teton landscape we know today. Although of lesser scope than the other glacial periods, it was during this time that the peaks were completely carved, and the chain of lakes along the east base was created. Pinedale glaciers pushed down Cascade, Garnet, Avalanche, and Death canyons and out onto the valley floor to form the moraines which now ring Jenny, Bradley, and Phelps lakes. Ice from Leigh Canyon, with contributions from canyons to the north, formed a large sluggish field in the area of present Jackson Lake. It completely encircled Signal Mountain, leaving only the upper few hundred feet towering islandlike above the frozen mass.

Then, a relatively few thousand years ago the climate moderated, and the glaciers began to melt. Those which filled the canyons retreated slowly to the heights where in deep gulches on shady north slopes they defied the passing millennia, and continued their erosive work long after it was finished in other parts of the range. As a result, most north-facing walls are steeper and more intricately sculptured.

Today there are nearly two dozen glaciers in the Tetons—Mount Moran alone has five—supposed by some geologists to be survivors from the Pinedale period, by others to be of later origin. They are all found on the east slope at altitudes of 10,000 to 11,500 feet, and range from half a mile to nearly a mile in length. The largest is Teton Glacier on the north slope of the Grand Teton. This moving ice mass, like the others, continues its work of cutting back the sheer walls and sharpening the peaks.

With the passing of the Pinedale period, "plants and animals, biding their time, closely followed the retiring ice, bestowing quick and joyous animation on the new-born landscape," wrote John Muir. "Pine-trees marched up the sun-warmed moraines in long, hopeful files, taking the ground and establishing themselves as soon as it was ready for them; brown-spiked sedges fringed the shores of new-born lakes; young rivers roared in the abandoned channels of the glaciers. . . . The ground burst into bloom with magical rapidity, and the young forests into bird-song; life in every form warming and sweetening and growing richer as the years passed."

The Teton Range was profoundly changed by its glacial experience. Prior to the ice ages, wind, snow, frost, streams, and rock slides had stripped the surface strata in those alpine regions where uplift had been greatest, laying bare the mountains' silvery core of Precambrian crystallines, more than two and a half billion years old. These Archean rocks, the oldest in the world, record about seven eights of *all* geologic time.

Although these rocks are among the hardest and least porous known, they proved susceptible to glacial sculpturing. Individual peaks, attacked by ice from many sides, were cut into a complexity of spires and pinnacles, no two alike, and the skyline transformed into the most jagged on the continent. Connecting ridges were cut back to knifelike sharpness and worn down so as to isolate each mountain. The old narrow gorges were widened into sheer-walled canyons, some so deep they segmented the range. There were hanging valleys, and giant stairways down which cascades and waterfalls now plunge. In the highlands, dozens of basins, quarried and polished by the down-pulling action of the ice, filled with snow-water and became lakes.

As Muir observed, "Nature chose for a tool not the earthquake or lightning to rend and split asunder, not the stormy torrent or eroding rain, but the tender snow-flowers noiselessly falling through unnumbered centuries . . . Laboring harmoniously in united strength they sculptured, fashioned, modeled all the range, and developed its predestined beauty."

III
The Mysterious West

Eighteenth-century knowledge of the trans-Mississippi West was based chiefly on hearsay, travelers' reports, and Indian accounts. The wonders were many. There was a lake in which lived "a monstrous amphibious animal . . . with horns like a Cow." There was a cavern capable of tearing apart anything that might fall into it—a man, a tree—and toss the pieces out high in the air. There was a mountain of solid rock salt, a hundred and eighty miles long and forty-five miles wide; and a nation of mysterious people who had "blue & gray eyes & light colored hair." Mammoths grazed on the shoulder-high grasses of the tablelands, and on the Upper Missouri a large volcano erupted regularly. There was a second lake whose waters attracted stone as a magnet does iron, so that the country around was bare of rocks while the lake bottom was covered with them. There were Indians who spoke Welsh, descendants of intermarriage with a colony supposed to have been settled in the twelfth-century by Prince Madoc of Wales. Somewhere among the red men of the West lived the Lost Tribes.

A formidable range, known as the Stony, Shining, Snowy, Rocky, Missouri, or Mexican Mountains, soared twenty-five thousand feet north and south along the divide of waters, preventing those who went overland from reaching the Pacific shore. Some reports stated that it was a single chain; others that it was five ridges deep. Indians said that it made "a great noise," but could offer no explanations.

Of the many men who urged exploration of this vast, unknown region, Thomas Jefferson was the most prominent and active. For more than twenty years he had gathered information about the West and made three attempts to organize an expedition. But not until he became president did he succeed in launching one.

As a man of science, Jefferson was interested in the geography of the West. As a statesman, he recognized the economic necessity for pushing the frontier westward and discovering the potential wealth that lay there. He was also aware of the benefits of a transcontinental trade route for interoceanic commerce, and wanted to establish a claim to the territory before the British could do so. As early as 1783 he was worrying about an English proposal to explore the territory extending from the Mississippi to California, which appeared to him to be a first step toward colonization there.

Since mapmakers of the day lacked accurate information about the West, they resorted to guesswork. Those maps which Jefferson consulted showed the headwaters of the Missouri and Columbia lying but "a single portage" apart. He therefore considered these rivers a possible route for transcontinental trade. In his January 1803 message to Congress, he included a proposal to send an exploring party—a Corps of Discovery—organized as a military detachment, to trace the Missouri River to its source, to "cross the highlands, and follow the best water communication which offered itself thence to the Pacific Ocean." Congress approved the plan and voted twenty-five hundred dollars to finance it.

Jefferson chose as the expedition's leader, a twenty-nine-year-old army captain and fellow-Virginian, Meriwether Lewis, who had been living at the White House for nearly two years, as his private secretary. He considered Lewis better qualified than anyone else he knew to head the exploring party. He was courageous and resolute, resourceful and hardy; kindly, yet firm in the maintenance of discipline, Jefferson wrote. He had an agile and retentive mind, and was so exact in his observations that "whatever he should report would be as certain as if seen by ourselves." Although without formal training in the sciences, he had through a keen interest in them acquired a fund of accurate information in several fields.

To enlarge his specific knowledge Lewis went to Philadelphia in the spring of 1803 to make some concentrated studies in botany, zoology, anatomy, Indian history, and methods of specimen collecting. His instructors were the most prominent men in those fields: Dr. Benjamin Smith Barton, Dr. Robert Patterson, and Dr. Caspar Wistar.

The distinguished physician Dr. Benjamin Rush gave him training in diagnosis and treatment of the sick. He furnished Lewis with eleven rules for maintaining health, recommended the drugs and medical equipment to be taken on the journey, and supplied him with fifty dozen pills of his own formula—a powerful purgative known familiarly as "Rush's thunderbolts." The doctor also gave Lewis a list of questions pertaining to the medical history, morals, and religion of the Indians. With the Lost Tribes in mind, he asked him to watch carefully for resemblances between Indian ceremonies and those of the Jews. At Lancaster, where Lewis was assembling supplies, Andrew Ellicott, astronomer and civil engineer, coached him in the use of the sextant, chronometer, and artificial horizon.

By June 19, Lewis, well-prepared for the work ahead, was back in Washington. That day he wrote to his friend and fellow officer, William Clark, giving details of the expedition, and asking him to join as co-captain. In accepting, Clark replied: " . . . My friend I do assure you that no man lives whith whome I would perfur to undertake Such a Trip &c. as your self . . . "

In October 1803 the United States bought from Napoleon that vast tract of land called Louisiana, which comprised the western half of the Mississippi drainage basin. With its purchase the national territory was increased by a hundred and forty percent. No one knew for sure where its exact boundaries lay or just what it contained. The government was anxious to have the tract explored, and Thomas Jefferson's Corps of Discovery suddenly took on a new importance.

The president's instructions to Lewis were comprehensive

and detailed. Beyond the main objectives, the explorers were to make a thorough study of the Indians, listing their tribes and number, reporting on their relations with other tribes, their languages, food, dress, houses and "domestic accommodations." They were to note in addition, traditions, monuments, arts, and warfare; prevalent diseases and remedies, and those articles of trade the Indians might furnish or need. "In your intercourse with the natives," Jefferson advised, "treat them in the most friendly & conciliatory manner which their own conduct will admit."

The explorers were also to describe all plants and animals, paying particular attention to those kinds unknown within the United States; to look for "the remains or accounts" of creatures "rare or extinct"; report on mineral deposits, soil, and all evidences of volcanic action, and keep statistics on the weather. "Great pains & accuracy" were to be taken with astronomical observations in order to map the region. Multiple copies were to be made of all notes, charts, tables, and maps in case of accident or loss. Jefferson suggested that one copy of everything be made "on the paper of birch, as less liable to injury from damp than common paper."

A third of December 1803 had passed before the party was ready to start. A winter encampment was therefore set up a short distance from St. Louis. There the time was spent in disciplining the men, weeding out the misfits, recruiting additional members, assembling stores, and gathering information from fur traders and hunters familiar with the Upper Missouri, and the Yellowstone River.

At four o'clock on the afternoon of May 14, 1804, the Corps of Discovery embarked aboard a fifty-five-foot keelboat that carried a square sail. William Clark noted that a number of people who lived nearby gathered to see them off and watch the boat proceed "under a gentle brease up the Missourie."

It took the entire summer and much of the fall to breast the swift current of this treacherous river with its shifting sandbars, hidden snags, and collapsing banks. By the end of October the cold weather and low water drove the expedition into winter quarters near Bismarck, North Dakota, then the country of the Mandan Indians, a peaceful people well advanced in the arts. There the explorers put up a group of log huts, surrounded

them with a stockade as a protection against marauding no-
mads, and called the encampment Fort Mandan.

Not until April 1805 was the Missouri sufficiently thawed to
allow a start on that part of the journey that would take the
expedition to the Pacific Coast. On the afternoon of April 7,
once again at four o'clock, the explorers left Fort Mandan.
They were now traveling in six small canoes and two large pirogues. The keelboat in which they had come was being sent
back to St. Louis, laden with letters and reports, Indian artifacts, and plant and animal specimens (many of the latter living) for Thomas Jefferson.

As Lewis wrote in his journal, "we were now about to penetrate a country at least two thousand miles in width, on which
the foot of civilized man had never trodden . . . and
these little vessells contained every article by which we were
to expect to subsist or defend ourselves."

In addition to the two captains and twenty-six enlisted men,
most of whom were experienced Kentucky hunters and frontiersmen, there were two French-Canadian interpreters,
Clark's black servant York, a Mandan peace emissary—and
Lewis' hundred-and-twenty-five-pound Newfoundland, who
proved an excellent watchdog and hunter.

One of the interpreters, Toussaint Charbonneau, was bringing his young Shoshoni wife, Sacajawea. Both captains were
pleased with her addition to the party, certain that when the
time came, she would be able to help them bargain with her
people for those horses needed to take the explorers across the
mountains. As it proved, Lewis and Clark were grateful for her
presence throughout the long journey, for she was resourceful,
provident, and wise in woodcraft. In her home territory she
was able to act as their guide. Her amiable disposition made
her one of the best-liked members of the expedition, while her
fortitude in times of hardship set everyone an example. The infant son, Jean Baptiste, whom she carried in a cradleboard on
her back, soon became the pet of the camp, and the special favorite of the kindly William Clark.

The party followed the Missouri to the foot of its Great Falls,
where it became necessary to make a portage of eighteen miles.
Two crude carts were constructed for transporting the canoes
and baggage, and everything that could be spared was cached.

The load was considerably lightened by leaving behind the cumbersome swivel-gun and carriage, as well as Lewis' field-desk.

It was in this region that the party first noticed those unaccountable noises the Indians had told about. Clark wrote that they resembled "precisely the discharge of a piece of ordinance of 6 pounds at the distance of 5 or six miles." He had paid little attention at first, thinking it was thunder. The following day, however, as he walked along under a cloudless sky and heard it again distinctly, he stopped to listen carefully and take notes. His pocket compass fixed the direction of the sounds as nearly west. Their recurrence was irregular, "sometimes heard once only and at other times several discharges in quick succession. It is heard at different times of the day and night. I am at a great loss to account for this Phenomenon."

Lewis was equally puzzled, but one of their men had the answer: The explosive noises were caused by the bursting of the rich silver mines these mountains were known to contain. Later travelers would also hear the boomings in various parts of the Rocky Mountains and be equally baffled.

After completing the portage, which took twenty-five days, and making two dugout canoes—for the pirogues were no longer practicable—the party pushed on by water to the Missouri's Three Forks. At this point they were about a hundred and twenty-five miles northwest of the Teton Range, and less than seventy-five miles from the thermal curiosities of present Yellowstone Park. But the discovery of these wonders was reserved for one of their men, two years later.

Lewis and Clark named the three streams which form the Missouri's headwaters the Madison, the Gallatin, and the Jefferson. Since the Jefferson flowed westward, they launched their little fleet of eight canoes and followed it to that point where it was no longer navigable.

Passage of the mountains then faced them, but the Shoshonis from whom they must get horses were not to be found. On August 8, Sacajawea recognized a landmark, known to her people as the beaver's head, which was not far from that valley where the Shoshonis usually summered. She assured the captains they would find the tribe along a river just beyond the mountains.

Taking three men, Lewis set off on foot the next day to look for the Indians. On the twelfth he and his little band crossed the Continental Divide, and soon after Lewis stopped beside a stream for his first taste of "cold Clear water" from the Pacific slope.

In the valley beyond they found the Shoshonis, preparing to cross the mountains east on a buffalo hunt. Lewis convinced them of his peaceful intentions and persuaded the chief, Cameahwait, to return with him for a meeting with Clark. The Indian took with him two subchiefs, a number of warriors, and a party of women and children.

The captains found the meeting between Sacajawea and her people touching. She was at the head of Clark's party, which was just arriving at the appointed rendezvous. As soon as she saw the Indians with Lewis, she "danced for the joyful sight and . . . made signs to me that they were her nation," Clark wrote. Later in the day, when she was called on to interpret at a council, she recognized Chief Cameahwait as the brother she had not seen since her capture in this region five years before by a band of raiding Hidatsas. The war party had taken her to their home on the Plains and kept her as a slave until Toussaint Charbonneau had bought her or acquired her by trade.

Now she ran up to her brother, hugged him, and threw her blanket over him, "weeping profusely: the chief himself was moved, though not in the same degree. After some conversation between them, she resumed her seat, and attempted to interpret for us, but her new situation seemed to overpower her, and she was frequently interrupted by her tears."

About two weeks later the explorers were ready to move on, for Lewis and Clark with Sacajawea's help had bargained with the Shoshonis for twenty-nine horses and two guides. This part of the journey, the portage between the Missouri and the Columbia, formed the basis of Jefferson's plans. It was this part, too, that was to prove the most difficult. In order to continue their westward march toward the Columbia, it was necessary to first make a detour north, nearly two degrees of latitude, through the rugged Bitterroot Mountains. The journey consumed nearly a month's time. Game was scarce, for winter had already set in. There was rain and sleet. Heavy snowfalls blotted out the Indian trail and froze feet that were shod only in thin moccasins. Then food supplies ran out, and the party ate candles and bear grease, and boiled the roots of plants with which they were unfamiliar. Digestive problems became rampant. Clark wrote that not only was he feeling very sick, but all of the men including Lewis were complaining of "a *Lax* & heaviness in the stomack. I gave rushes Pills to several." Others he dosed with "Salts & Tarter *emetic.*"

Once out of the mountains and beside a navigable river again—the Clearwater—they made dugout canoes from pitch pine for the final push to the Pacific. Since most of the men were still very weak, they burned out the logs, Indian fashion, to lighten the labor. The rushing Clearwater, winding through deep, mountain gorges, first south, then north, and finally west, took them to its junction with the Snake River at today's Lewiston, Idaho. Embarking on the Snake, which was bringing with its waters the melt of Teton snows, they meandered through the high, treeless plains of present Washington to meet the Columbia.

On November 7, 1805, Clark wrote in his journal: "Great joy in camp we are in view of the Ocean . . ." It was then too late in the year to consider a return home, so once again they built a group of log huts inside a stockade and named the encampment for their nearest Indian neighbors, the Clatsops. Fort Clatsop, close to present Astoria, Oregon, was the first American settlement west of the Continental Divide.

It was a miserable winter—rainy, foggy, cold, and perpetually damp, with much sickness among the men and never enough to eat. On Christmas Day William Clark noted that he and Lewis had been wakened at dawn by the sounds of celebration: a volley of small arms fired under their windows (a southern custom), followed by "Shouts and a Song." After breakfast there was an exchange of gifts. Lewis gave him some welcome "fleece hosrie," a shirt and drawers. From one of the men Clark received a pair of moccasins; from another, a small Indian basket. As for Sacajawea, she had for him two dozen white ermine tails. To those men who smoked, the captains gave tobacco; for those who did not, there was a handkerchief apiece.

". . . we would have Spent this day . . . in feasting, had we any thing to raise our Sperits or even gratify our appetites. our Diner concisted of pore Elk, so much Spoiled that we eate it thro' mear necessity, Some Spoiled pounded fish and a fiew roots."

During the winter Clark completed a map of the country through which they had traveled, and both he and Lewis continued to fill their notebooks with observations on the Indians of the region, the animals, birds, plants, weather, and other scientific data.

On March 23, 1806, the homeward trip was begun, and on September 23, the party reached St. Louis after an absence of two years, four months, and nine days. They had covered some eighty-five hundred miles by boat, foot, and on horseback through country that was always challenging and often hostile. This they had accomplished with the loss of but one man, early in the journey, whose symptoms suggest a ruptured appendix which would have been fatal anywhere at the time.

In the history of American exploration no other expedition has ever been so productive. Lewis and Clark brought back important and extensive collections and reports in botany and zoology (among the latter many fossil as well as living creatures); in geology, geography, and linguistics. Their information on the Indians of the West and their collection of Indian artifacts was exhaustive and permanently important. In addition, they located, described, and mapped mountain ranges and major river systems, made known the width of the continent, and established a claim to the Columbia River.

They had found no amphibious monsters with cow's horns, no magical lakes and caverns, no native race with light eyes and blond hair, no spouting volcanoes on the Upper Missouri. But they had established the West as a reality.

Their discovery that the short portage between the Missouri and the Columbia was actually a two-hundred-and-twenty-mile trek across rugged mountains blasted Jefferson's dream of an easy transcontinental trade route. But this disappointment was offset by their reports on the territory's almost limitless potential for every kind of American enterprise.

The most important immediate result of the Lewis and Clark expedition was the opening of the Rocky Mountain fur trade, which in turn led to the discovery of the Teton Range.

IV
Trail Through the Snow

Crusaders, admiring the Saracens' lavish use of fur in their dress, introduced the fashion to the west. It was immediately popular, and fur came to be worn so extravagantly that the kings of France and England thought it necessary to pass laws against its use. But little attention was paid to these edicts, and the demand for fur continued among all classes of people in Britain, France, and the rest of Europe.

At first, Siberia supplied most of the pelts: bear for coats, robes, and caps; ermine, marten, sable, squirrel, and red fox for hats, linings, edgings, and muffs. But years of uncontrolled hunting finally depleted the furbearers. The search for pelts crossed the Atlantic to North America, which was to prove the richest and most extensive field in the world for collecting fine furs. Beaver fur, because of its thick, velvety softness, was one of the most valued, and since the animal was so numerous in the waterways of the north woods, its fur became the staple of the American trade.

On his return from the Pacific Coast, Meriwether Lewis reported to Jefferson: "We view this passage across the Continent as affording immence advantages to the fur trade . . . The Missouri and all its branches from the Chyenne upwards abound more in beaver and Common Otter, than any other streams on earth, particularly that proportion of them lying within the Rocky Mountains."

This report, which was widely circulated, had the effect of a major gold discovery. Foreseeing quick riches, friends hastened to form partnerships, buy traps, guns, ammunition, and canoes, and set off up the Missouri. Merchants organized companies and advertised for hunters and trappers. Men flocked to the call for, as one St. Louis youth who joined the ranks recalled, Lewis' words had stirred up "a spirit of trafficking adventure among the young men of the West."

But before any of them could get away, John Colter, one of Lewis and Clark's own hunters, who had been frequently selected by the two captains for special duty on the cross-country journey, was already leading a trapping party into the wilderness. This party is credited with marking the opening of the western fur trade.

On the morning of August 12, 1806, the returning explorers, traveling along the Missouri above the Mandan villages, came on the camp of two trappers, Joseph Dickson and Forrest Hancock. These were the first white men they had seen, aside from their own party, in sixteen months. Dickson and Hancock told Lewis that they had been working their way up the Missouri since the summer of 1804, trapping beaver and hunting, and although not particularly successful, they were determined to continue to its source, where, they had been told, beaver was plentiful. They were reluctant to risk it, however, without a guide.

The idea of leading the trappers appealed to John Colter. He talked it over with Dickson and it was agreed that if he could get his discharge, he would guide them to rich beaver grounds in return for a share in the profits.

He received his discharge for, as Clark wrote, the offer was an advantageous one, and he could be spared. Further, he and Lewis were "disposed to be of service to any of the party who had performed their duty as well as Colter had." They gave him his pay and fitted him out with traps, tools for building canoes, powder, lead, and enough other necessary supplies to last two years, "which they are determined to Stay untill they make a fortune," a comrade observed.

That fall and winter the partners trapped along the Yellowstone River, but for Colter there was no fortune. The following spring saw him alone in his canoe, making his way through the broken ice of the Yellowstone, heading for the Missouri and St. Louis. What happened to the partnership no one knows. Most likely there was a quarrel that prompted him to take his share of the furs and start for home.

Soon after entering the Missouri he met a keelboat carrying a large party of hunters and trappers, a company that had been organized by the St. Louis merchant Manuel Lisa. Lisa hailed Colter, asked where he was from and where bound, then told him that he was going to push into the wilderness and establish posts among those Indians who had yet no contact with American traders. Since Colter was fresh from the very country Lisa was heading for, would he be interested in acting as his guide?, the merchant asked.

Once again Colter seized the opportunity to return to the wilderness life he seemed to prefer. Packing up his equipment (known in trapper vernacular as "possibles" or "fixens") and his furs, he set his canoe adrift and climbed aboard the keelboat where he was greeted by three former members of the Lewis and Clark expedition.

At the junction of the Bighorn and Yellowstone rivers, on a site recommended by William Clark, Lisa built a fortified post. This was the first American post of the western fur trade, and the first building within what is now Montana. When it was finished, Lisa asked Colter if he would be willing to take word of the new post to the Crows, Cheyennes, and Shoshonis, and encourage them to bring in their pelts to trade. Colter was willing, even though winter had already begun.

"He was . . . five feet ten inches in height, and bore an open, ingenious and pleasing countenance of the Daniel Boone stamp," a comrade described Colter. "Nature had formed him, like Boone, for hardy endurance of fatigue, privations and perils."

The thirty-one-year-old Virginian was no illiterate backwoodsman. He came from a family of Shenandoah Valley landowners, possibly prosperous and certainly long-established, among whom there were judges and physicians. John himself had some schooling, for he could read and write, and among the few possessions found at the time of his death were three books.

In November 1807 he set off on foot and alone from Lisa's fort, carrying "a pack of thirty pounds weight, his gun and some ammunition," to penetrate a region wholly unknown to white men.

From the fort he traveled west along the Yellowstone River until he came to Pryor's Creek. There he turned south to follow that stream to its source and cross the mountains into the valley of the Bighorn River, then the home of the Crows and Shoshonis.

Colter's progress through the valley was unhurried. He would have made frequent stops at Indian camps to win their goodwill by gifts of vermilion, beads, awls, tobacco, and knives; to smoke with them and urge them to bring their furs to Lisa's trading post.

Coming to a river that flowed from the west—today's North Fork of the Shoshone—he followed it until he reached a large, boiling sulphur spring. It was a region that was "often agitated with subterranean fires"; underground rumblings and "frightful" explosions were frequently heard, wrote an early traveler. "The sulphurous gases which escape in great volume from the burning soil infect the atmosphere for several miles. . . ." Because of the smell, Colter called the river the Stinking Water, a name it bore for nearly a hundred years. The thermal region itself came to be known as Colter's Hell.

Where he went from this point, from the summit of which pass he first saw the Teton Range, by what route he entered Jackson Hole, and how he reached present Yellowstone Park have long been debated. On his return to St. Louis in 1810, he told the story of his travels to William Clark who traced them on the map he had drawn to accompany the expedition's report; he labeled the broken line he used to indicate it, "Colter's Route in 1807." But because the map contains some topographical errors in those parts with which Clark was personally unfamiliar, the route is subject to several interpretations.

However, since a network of Indian trails ran through the

Bighorn valley in all directions, Colter would have logically asked the Indians for help in plotting his westward course. They would no doubt have suggested that he follow that well-traveled route which led from the buffalo hunting grounds near Heart Mountain to the Owl Creek Mountains, where it crossed a low divide near present Washakie Needles and led down to the "big bend" in the Wind River.

At the Wind River he would have come upon another well-used trail that was part of the old Shoshoni trade route. This led to the stream's source, then turned west and crossed the divide that the Indians called "the summit of the world," by way of today's Togwotee Pass. This pass, named over half a century later for a noted Sheep Eater medicine man and guide, remained the favorite Indian route because it was direct and of unusually easy passage.

At the head of Wind River there was an alternative trail Colter could have taken that led over the mountains above present Union Pass. In view of the fact that this route was considered by early explorers to be extremely difficult and is crossed now only by trail, it is likely he would have chosen the obviously better-traveled Shoshoni route. After his return to St. Louis he also told the story of this trip to the traveler-author Henry M. Brackenridge, who remembered Colter stressing the fact that "a loaded wagon would find no obstruction in passing" over the route he followed across the divide.

Presuming that he took the Shoshoni trail, Colter would have had his first sight of the Tetons from the summit. A turn in the path led out of the aspen groves and forests of lodgepole pine into the open. Suddenly, there was almost the entire range banking the horizon. He may have marveled at the rugged beauty of the line of peaks so unlike any he had seen before— peaks the Shoshonis called "hoary-headed fathers." More certainly, like all the mountain men who followed in his trail, he saw the Teton Range as a challenging barrier to travel.

He scanned the plains below for the smoke of Indian fires but would have seen none, for the valley that was a hunting and fishing ground for several tribes in summer and fall was too exposed for winter encampment.

Observing that the range grew lower at the south end, he rejected the idea of following a fork of the trail that led north to Pacific Creek; instead, he went on down the slope into Jackson Hole. Hoping to find friendly Indians on the west side of the range, he snowshoed over the valley, crossed the Snake River at the Indian ford, and followed still another Indian trail that led to the pass.

From the summit of the pass he saw that a broad valley also flanked the Tetons on the west, and he took note of its river system. On Clark's map, a stream labeled Colter's River is shown meandering with others through what came to be known as Trou à Pierre or Pierre's Hole (to the mountain man a deep valley was a "hole"), named for an Iroquois trapper, Pierre Tivanitagon, who discovered it in the early 1800s.

On the transcontinental expedition Colter learned the importance of recording information. The fact that he was aware of the passing months suggests that he now kept a diary. He no doubt also drew a map, for it would have been nearly impossible to otherwise retain the details of mountain and river systems, the locations of hot springs, and the names and positions of Indian villages and their populations.

The Indian trail Colter followed along the Tetons' west side kept to the heights as such trails usually did for better observation of the surrounding country. As he traveled northward, he could see there were no Indian encampments here either, for this was another open valley, exposed to every blast of winter wind from north and west.

At this point Colter left an important piece of evidence that proves his presence west of the Teton Range. One night he made camp in a sheltered spot some distance from the main trail. Close by was an outcrop of rhyolite, and among some fallen pieces he noticed one that roughly suggested a man's head and profile. With his knife he cut away the soft, volcanic rock to emphasize the resemblance. When he was through, he carved his name in capitals on one side of the head, and on the other, the year 1808. He left the stone behind when he broke camp.

For nearly a century the rock lay in the open, and the carvings and lettering became deeply weathered and chipped away through exposure. In time, it was buried by natural means, and a quarter of a century more passed before Colter's handiwork was discovered by two homesteaders who were ploughing near South Leigh Creek in Pierre's Hole.

Colter's trail took him through mixed forests of lodgepole pine, Engelmann spruce, and aspen. On the open slopes were mountain ash, serviceberry, and wild orchards of chokecherry. In season scarlet gilia, paintbrush, harebell, larkspur, and asters of several kinds bloomed there.

Near the head of Henry's Fork he found his first Indians, a village of Shoshonis, noted on William Clark's sketch map as Po-nah Snakes. After presenting these people with gifts and telling them about Lisa's post, he was ready to cross the Tetons to the east. Here again he had a choice of routes. He may have followed the Indian trail along Bitch Creek that led to the north shore of Jackson Lake with its clumps of willow and its aspen stands. This rough, remote trail later became a favorite route for outlaws and was known to ranchers as Horsethief Pass. Or he may have taken the more northerly and easier Conant Trail that also led to Jackson Lake, not far from where the Snake River enters it.

Once in Jackson Hole again he traveled north along the Snake, past Lewis Lake to West Thumb Bay. He then continued along the shore of Yellowstone Lake to its head. Here he followed the course of the Yellowstone River winding through today's Hayden Valley, to Tower Fall, crossing the river by the ford that was part of the great Bannock Trail. This important Indian route led from Henry's Lake, Idaho, over the Gallatin Range to Mammoth Hot Springs in Yellowstone Park, where it joined the trail Colter had been following from the south, a trail that today's highway parallels.

Again there was a clue to his route, for the sulphur beds at this ford are also shown on Clark's map and labeled Hot Springs Brimstone, a name Colter probably gave them.

Although nomadic Bannocks, Crows, and Shoshonis fished the area's lakes and streams and hunted in the broad, grassy valleys for buffalo, elk, and deer, they avoided the thermal regions as being the abodes of evil spirits. Many tribes were reluctant even to talk about them. Colter, therefore, would have had no hint of the unusual sights he was to discover there.

After crossing the Yellowstone, he followed the Bannock

Trail east, along the Lamar River winding through its open valley. At Soda Butte Creek he turned down a fork in the trail that led him to the Stinking Water, and from there retraced his outbound path up Pryor's Creek, reaching Lisa's post sometime during the spring of 1808. He had successfully completed a solo journey of five hundred miles, most of it in the dead of winter, through some of the West's most rugged and confusing mountains.

His discovery and exploration of new territory made an important contribution to knowledge of the West, for he was the first white man to pass through the valley of the Bighorn, the first to penetrate the Absaroka Mountains and cross the passes at the head of Wind River. He was the first to travel through Jackson Hole and Pierre's Hole, to find the sources of the Snake, and to discover many of the thermal curiosities of Yellowstone country. He was the first white man to see the Teton Range and cross it twice.

V
"They Call Themselves Sho-sho-nies"

The meaning of the word has been lost to the Shoshonis themselves. Some time after 1668 French traders and explorers began hearing about Indians on the Plains whose tribal sign was a serpentine motion of the hand. The French interpreted this to mean *snake,* and called them *Gens du Serpent.* Later, English and Americans called them Snakes. It is thought, however, that the gesture was not meant to indicate the reptile but the in-and-out movement used by the Indians in weaving their grass and bark lodges. At the beginning of the nineteenth century these members of the Uto-Aztecan family began to be identified by their linguistic name, Shoshoni.

Before the Shoshonis ventured east across the Rockies into the mountain parks and plains of Wyoming and Montana, they were a poor people whose lives were spent in the endless task of finding enough to eat. Since plants and game were scarce in the semidesert Basin where they lived, they were kept constantly on the move, afoot, in search of food. Their diet consisted chiefly of seeds, roots, insects, birds, and rabbits, with an occasional bighorn sheep or antelope.

Clothing and shelter were also minimal. Most of the year the men wore only a breechcloth, and the women a double apron usually made from pounded sagebrush fibers. In winter both men and women wore rabbit-skin robes, although not everyone was so fortunate as to have the forty pelts it took to weave this garment. Those who had only a few skins used them to protect their feet and legs.

Summer houses were circular shelters made of sagebrush, temporary and easily transported during the food-gathering season. In winter they lived partially underground in moundlike earthen structures which had a top opening used both as a smoke hole and an entrance.

Toward the end of winter food supplies often ran out and many people starved. Each spring, it was said, the Utes, who were active in the Indian-Mexican slave trade, would raid the Shoshonis, knowing they were too weak from hunger to resist or run away. They killed many of the men and carried off large numbers of women and children whom they fattened and then sold into slavery.

The desperation of hunger gave the Shoshonis the courage to cross the Rocky Mountains. Some ethnologists think this migration took place as early as the 1500s, others that it was not until the middle of the next century. They agree that most, if not all, lived for a time in the mountains before entering the Plains.

This was not, however, a mass migration, for many remained in the Basin. But by 1730 the Shoshonis appear in old records as the most important tribe on the Plains. Their number was large and their territory vast. Within their holdings was the Teton Range.

There is no evidence that they lived on the Plains all year. They seem to have gone there only to hunt buffalo and send out raiding parties (for warfare was a way of life on the Plains), then having laid in a lasting supply of meat and defeated their enemies, they retired to the sheltered mountain parks.

The Shoshonis would not have wintered in either of those valleys flanking the Tetons, for they are too exposed. But they hunted the big game which ranged there at other seasons, and the wild sheep that lived on the crags. They fished the lakes and streams, and their women harvested in their big burden baskets the abundant crops of fruit: serviceberries, heavily sweet; currants, "black, white, yellow, and red . . . large as cherries"; thimbleberries, huckleberries, and chokecherries, growing on slopes and streamsides and in the pine woods.

Berries were eaten fresh or dried to make cold drinks or teas. Some were pounded into a meal that was mixed with jerked meat, or shaped into flat cakes which were baked. With pointed sticks the women dug the potato-like camas root, a staple of Indian diet. This was boiled, baked, dried, or eaten raw. The roots of the yampa (resembling parsnips in flavor), the elk thistle root and stalk (tasting like artichoke), bitterroot, balsamroot, and the corns of yellow fritillary were also relished. Aster leaves were eaten boiled, as were the flowers and leaves of beeplant. Seeds of giant hyssop, evening primrose, and yellow pond lily were parched with hot coals before being eaten, while the oily seeds of the blazingstar were roasted and ground into flour. Bistort was gathered to flavor soups and stews, and yarrow for medicinal use.

The Shoshonis were still walkers, but this was no handicap in hunting or war. They used the buffalo trap and the antelope surround which enabled them to round up and kill large numbers of animals with relative ease. An early traveler observed, that the individual hunter wrapped himself in the dressed skin of a wolf or buffalo calf, "the head and legs left attached," then "with his short bow and a brace of arrows ambles off into the very midst of the herd. When he has selected an animal as suits his fancy, he comes close alongside it, and without noise, passes an arrow through its heart. One arrow is always sufficient, and it is generally delivered with such force, that at least half the shaft appears through the opposite side. The creature totters, and is about to fall, when the Indian glides around, and draws the arrow from the wound lest it should be broken. A single Indian is said to kill a great number of buffaloes in this way, before any alarm is communicated to the herd."

Shoshoni warriors made long expeditions on foot to raid enemy camps in surprise, predawn attacks, killing many in the confusion and capturing women and children. At other times they met their enemies on the plains, and fought in battle array, two lines of men seated on the ground, facing one another and shooting arrows from behind the shelter of leather shields. The Shoshonis were so well equipped that their buffalo-hide shields formed a solid wall, while their opponents' line showed gaps and one shield often had to cover two men.

The Shoshonis' shorter bows were made of better wood—cedar or pine, bound with buffalo sinew for strength and suppleness; or they might be fashioned from a single piece of elk or mountain-sheep horn, made pliant by soaking in a hot spring and reinforced with sinew and glue. Horn bows were prized and highly ornamented.

Their slender arrows, often made from serviceberry wood and tipped with quartz or obsidian, carried four feathers six to seven inches long, placed opposite but turning gently on the shaft, "to give it a spiral motion, which prevents it from wavering, and enables it to cleave the air with less resistance," an early chronicler noted. Shoshonis rarely dipped their arrow points in the lethal combination of rotted antelope liver mixed with rattlesnake venom.

Their warriors wore leather armor, consisting of a sleeveless shirt made from many folds of dressed antelope skin held together by sand-and-fishbone glue spread between the layers.

A young Cree warrior recalled how his party's iron-tipped arrows failed to pierce Shoshoni shields. This was because their shamans had been successful in imparting arrowproof properties to the hide.

The two lines of warriors sat and fought until dark. A few men might be killed or wounded on either side, but no scalps were taken. Occasionally Shoshonis charged the enemy lines with clubs and lances to make them run. But these big war parties were chiefly for a display of might and arms to humiliate their foes. It was the surprise attacks on individual camps that really counted.

By 1740 the Shoshonis were well mounted on Spanish horses obtained from their Comanche kinsmen in the Southwest. Then, riding bareback or using a small leather pad stuffed with hair, Shoshoni fighting men ranged as far north as the Saskatchewan River and as far east as the Black Hills, fighting their interminable quarrels, avenging and revenging without respite. They would ride "swift as a deer" into the villages of their enemies, crushing skulls with well-aimed blows of their long-handled pogamoggans, then were off again before arrows could be nocked.

Groups of mounted hunters encircled great herds of buffalo that scouts had located and killed as many as they needed. Men on swift horses took elk and antelope with ease. Large trading expeditions traveled south as far as Mexico along a trail that started at the Missouri's Three Forks and passed just east of the Tetons. The Shoshonis were lords of the Plains.

However, they never became typical Plains Indians, even though they assimilated many aspects of Plains culture: decorative arts, sacred ceremonies (the most important of these was the Sun Dance), shelter, dress, and arms. The Shoshonis were unique in that they showed the influence of three definite cultures—Basin, Plateau, and Plains.

In the Basin they had scant clothing, but after they gained wealth they dressed in all the finery of Plains fashion: robes, shirts, leggings, moccasins, fur tippets, feathers, earrings, necklaces, and gorgets.

Their knee-length robes, worn loosely about the shoulders, fur side in, were made from buffalo, antelope, bighorn, beaver, or marmot skins: elk was used for summer wear. These robes were left open at the sides but in winter were belted for warmth. Shirts, which reached halfway down the thigh, were of dressed antelope, deer, or bighorn hide, without hair, the side seams cut into fringe and the whole decorated with porcupine quill embroidery in several colors.

Each legging, that reached from ankle to waist, where it was tucked under a girdle, took an entire antelope skin. The tail of the animal was worn upward, while the neck, deeply fringed and ornamented with colored quills, dragged on the ground behind the heels. Outside seams were fringed and often decorated with tufts of hair taken from slain enemies.

Moccasins of deer, elk, or buffalo hide were made like those of the Mandans, with a single seam on the outer edge and one up behind. These were also decorated with colored quill embroidery. Dandies often covered theirs with the skin of a polecat, letting the striped tail drag at their heels. In winter everyone wore buffalo-skin moccasins, the fur side inward.

Women had the same articles of dress as men: Only the shirt was longer, reaching below the calf, and was more heavily embroidered around the neck and down the front.

Meriwether Lewis reported that the Shoshoni tippet was

"the most eligent peice of Indian dress I ever saw." It was cut from the back of an otter pelt, "the nose and eyes forming one extremity and the tail the other." The center was decorated with "the shells of the perl oister," and the outer edge sewn with a fringe made from several hundred small rolls of ermine which fell down over the shoulders nearly to the waist to form a short cloak.

Women and children wore necklaces of elk teeth, and gorgets of seashells obtained in trade. Bone beads and triangular pieces of abalone shell were hung in the ears. Men wore strings of fish vertebrae around their necks, and collars of plaited sweetgrass embroidered with quills. But necklaces of bear claws were valued most and worn with pride, for to have killed a grizzly was an achievement equal to having slain an enemy.

Men tied the wings and tails of birds—eagle feathers were protective and flicker, curative—in their front hair. Some wore bandeaux of fox, weasel, or otter skin which also possessed special properties. Face and body paint were usual, red being preferred.

For housing they adopted the tipi. "Their lodges are spacious and neatly made of dressed Buffaloe skins, sewed together and set upon 11 or 13 smooth poles." An average-sized tipi took from fifteen to nineteen hides, for, as with poles, an odd number was traditional.

The hides were fleshed and tanned by the women who also sewed the skins together, set up the framework, put the covering in place, and pegged it tightly to the ground. The fire pit, where coals were always kept alive, was in the center of the lodge, and smoke escaped through the top where the poles joined.

The tipi cover was provided with two moveable flaps of hide sewn near the smoke hole and attached to two poles outside the general framework. By moving these extra poles it was possible to regulate the outlet of smoke whenever the wind veered, or to close the hole entirely in bad weather. This was a distinctive feature of the Plains tipi.

A man was the sole proprietor of his daughters and wives (polygamy was general) "and can barter or dispose of either as he thinks proper," Meriwether Lewis noted. Infant daughters were frequently promised in marriage to older men either for themselves or for their sons. It was customary for a young man to apply to the parents of a chosen girl; if they approved of him, a price was set, to be paid in horses. If he agreed to the price and promised to deliver the horses, then the marriage was considered consummated and he was invited to sleep with the girl in her father's lodge. If a young woman was unacquainted with a suitor, she was consulted by her mother before any agreement was made. If she had objections, these were usually respected. In the absence of religious sanctions a marriage could be easily dissolved, yet separations were not common.

From the white man's viewpoint Indian women were condemned to a life of endless drudgery. Actually it was a division of labor according to a primitive pattern, with the women digging the wild roots, harvesting the berries and edible or medicinal plants, drying meat, grinding meal, cooking, hauling wood and water, dressing hides and tanning them; making clothing and moccasins, with sinew taken from the back and loins of elk, deer, and buffalo as their only thread; caring for the children, making baskets, painting geometric designs on hide, and manufacturing a variety of soft leather pouches used as work bags for themselves or to hold ceremonial articles—a series of duties not unlike those of pioneering white women in the early days of the northern colonies or on the frontier. In spite of their countless tasks Shoshoni women still had time to take part in ceremonials and dances, and to play games. While engaged in communal work, they often sang in chorus.

Basketry (a relic of their Basin culture), quill—and later bead—embroidery in which designs were diverse and complex, the making of leather containers in a variety of shapes, and painting on rawhide all called for skill and imagination. Doubtless, these tasks brought Shoshoni women the satisfaction that accompanies creativity.

A man's chief occupation was war. He also hunted, butchered game, fashioned weapons, and bone and stone implements. He looked after the horses, and painted figures and realistic forms on tipis, shields, and robes.

Men were also responsible for government, but among the Shoshonis government lacked unity. The sentiment of egalitarianism was prevalent in their culture and thought. Each individual was his own master, the chief having no real power.

His advice and commands had no effect on those not inclined to obey. The only deterrent to wrongdoing was fear of reprisal through force or magic. The chief's position was acquired mainly through his valorous deeds in battle, and his shadowy authority often decayed with his personal vigor, or was transferred to some current hero. Not until 1830, with the rise of Washakie, were the Shoshonis united under a strong leader.

There were firm bonds of affection between parents and children, especially boys, who were seldom corrected and never whipped; as a Shoshoni explained to Meriwether Lewis, it "cows and breaks the spirit . . . and . . . he never recovers his independence of mind after he is grown."

"Cheerfulness and gayety, approaching even to wittiness, are prominent traits of the Shoshoni character," it was observed. "With their liveliness of temper they are fond of . . . all sorts of amusements."

Hand was the favorite game of chance with both women and men. Football was a strenuous contest in which some forty men and boys on a side ran as fast as they could, kicking two hide balls stuffed with animal hair toward a goal that was often several miles from the starting point; betting on the outcome heightened the excitement. There were also dart games, archery and hoop-and-pole contests, foot and horse races, and secular dances.

On winter nights there was storytelling by the old people. Coyote, who was father of their tribe, was both benefactor and trickster, and the hero of countless tales in which he and other animals spoke and acted like human beings.

There were frightening stories about NunumBi, those irascible dwarfs who lived in the mountains and shot invisible arrows into any who doubted their existence or otherwise displeased them. Inside the tipi it was safe to talk about these little people for they were unable to enter a lodge.

Tales that explained natural phenomena were common. Those Shoshonis who lived in the Wind River valley could account for the low roaring noises heard in the bottom of the gorge where Bull Lake lies.

Once long ago, they said, an old Shoshoni hunter was chasing a gray bull buffalo whose prized hide he wanted for a robe. On and on they raced until he and the buffalo came at length to the rim of a steep, rocky bluff. Horse and rider stopped, but the buffalo went on over the edge and down to a lake in the canyon bottom. The hunter followed, but as he caught up, his quarry rushed into the water. The old man went after him, but suddenly buffalo, horse, and rider vanished together. Those roaring sounds one hears are the gray buffalo's dying groans.

Since individualism was a strong Shoshoni trait, and with it often a critical skepticism of dogma, religious beliefs were basically an individual matter. Most, however, believed in a supreme being, Tam Apa (Father or Sun Father), in an afterlife, and a pervading supernatural power. All seem to have placed great faith in their shamans and prophets, who were endowed with their powers, instructed in the mysteries of their profession, and guided by supernatural patrons.

The Sun Dance was the most important Plains religious ceremony adopted by the Shoshonis. Indian tradition holds that the first version came to them possibly as early as 1726 when one of their people, named Grass Hut, had a dream in which a buffalo gave him instructions for a ceremony to be held at the time of the summer solstice.

"You will call it *Dagoo Winode,*" the buffalo said. "It is a dance in which you do not eat or drink for three days and nights. You only worship. If you pray for your people, the sick ones . . . will get well."

In the vision Grass Hut saw a brush structure in which four men were dancing. Two old women sat with bunches of willow twigs in their hands on either side of the center pole, and as the dancers passed they brushed away the footprints in the dust. Shoshoni tradition states that the first dance was held in either the Green River valley or the Bighorn Mountains.

Around 1790 Yellow Hand, a Comanche who was acquainted with the Kiowa Sun Dance and had also acquired some knowledge of Christian concepts through the Spaniards, had a vision. A man appeared to him and said: "You are looking for great power. I'll tell you what to do. Get a center, forked cottonwood tree and twelve poles; build them like a tipi. Get willows and lean them against the poles. The center pole will represent God; the twelve posts, God's friends.

"Get a two-year-old buffalo; face it west. Get an eagle, face it east. If anyone sick goes in, the buffalo will help him, with good power from the Sun. So will the eagle. . . . "

Some ten years later Yellow Hand moved north, joined the Shoshonis, and became a noted chief, shaman, and Sun Dance leader. During the nineteenth century other influences, mainly Arapaho and Crow, modified the Shoshoni Sun Dance. As the result of a series of loans and developments, with the addition of a number of features that were their own, the Shoshonis evolved a reasonably stable ceremony.

During the winter the dance leader would announce that he had been ordered through a dream to hold the ceremony. As summer approached, messengers were sent out to tell all Shoshoni villages and friendly related tribes about the coming dance.

After the scattered groups had ridden in and were camped in a rough circle on the dance field, the leader would put up his tipi in the center and begin practicing the dance with the participants. He would also teach them songs which had been dreamed during the past winter, or ones he had composed especially for the ceremony.

Some two days before the start of the dance proper there was a ceremonial buffalo hunt to secure the head for the center post. Although a number of hunters went out, only one was allowed to kill the selected animal. This was an honor reserved for some noted warrior. The only ritual here was a prayer spoken by the chief hunter when the buffalo was first sighted:

"I at this moment, am praying to you for that which will be killed . . . You will bless from above those who are here. That is ended."

The selection and cutting of trees for the lodge poles, particularly the center pole, was attended by ritual and ceremony. Soon after the center pole was brought in, the Sun Dance director lashed a bundle of willows in the fork—that was Thunderbird's nest. Around the tree itself, warriors noted for bravery painted broad bands of black—one for each coup counted. The center pole was then raised, accompanied by song, and the side posts put up and the rafters laid, the first one set exactly west to east. When the lodge was finished, a man climbed the center pole to place in the fork, the buffalo head painted with yellow clay, and the eagle. Finally, the Sun Dance doll, carved of wood each time for the ceremony, was hung on the center pole.

As the day neared its end, the dancers gathered in the leader's tipi to paint their hair and their upper bodies with white clay. They then hung around their necks single-hole whistles made from an eagle's humerus, and tied eagle-down plumes to their little fingers.

At dusk the singers took their places around a large drum in the southwest corner of the dance lodge. Women helped with the singing and waved sagebrush branches in rhythm to the beat, but did not drum. By this time the dancers were ready and, blowing their whistles, they filed over from the director's tipi. Before entering the lodge they circled it clockwise from two to four times. Once inside they took their places at the west end.

The shaman then stepped to the center pole to pray for success in war, relief from sickness, longevity, and good health and fortune. When the prayer was done the singers began, and the dancers came forward. The steps were simple—merely rising to the toes and lowering the foot, in place, up and down in time to the drumbeat, all the while blowing their whistles through which their prayers were being breathed, prayers asking that this earth be as clean as the skies where Thunderbird soars. Throughout the dancing the participants kept their eyes fixed on the buffalo head or the Sun Dance doll in order to obtain a vision. Once or twice a day they stopped dancing, and an old woman came up and brushed away their footprints with a leafy branch or an eagle feather, just as Grass Hut had seen in his dream so long ago.

Around midnight a fire was built just east of the center pole by a noted warrior who afterward recited his bravest deeds in battle. Just before dawn the dancers lined up facing east. Then as the rim of the sun appeared above the horizon they stretched their arms toward it in greeting, blowing long blasts on their eagle-bone whistles. After welcoming the sun, the dancers sat down around the fire and sang four sacred songs in low voices, breathing their prayers through their whistles at the end of each song.

Following this ritual, singers and audience left the lodge to eat, but the dancers continued their fasting and thirsting. During this interlude they repainted their bodies any color their visionary guardian suggested. They then purified themselves with cedar smoke, the singers and spectators returned to the lodge, and the dance began again, to continue in the same pattern.

The third day was ritually the most important. On that day one's fate in battle could be foretold in dreams and visions, spectators were prayed for, and those who were sick could have their illnesses brushed away with an eagle wing in the shaman's hand. During this day some of the dancers fell into a trance, or fainted. This was interpreted as a form of receiving power or gaining protection from the supernatural.

The dance ended on the afternoon of the fourth day. Old men brought containers of water mixed with clay to the lodge, the shaman blessed the water, and the dancers drank for the first time. The ceremony was now over except for the feast of buffalo tongues prepared by those women who had taken part in battle. After the feast, the dancers went to the stream to bathe, and the musicians and spectators started for home.

Since restraint was a dominant Shoshoni trait, their version of the Sun Dance lacked those features of self-torture, fasting to the point of death, and intense emotional climax during ritual which were present in other Plains interpretations.

Since 1880 the Sun Dance has seen a marked lessening of war-centered elements within the ceremony, and a growth of Christian concepts. Still it remains the most important religious ceremony among the Wind River Shoshonis and their neighbors. As an essential emotional and cultural force, it binds together a proud and intensely individualistic people who, in looking eastward toward the Black Hills and westward to the Tetons, recall those days when their fathers were masters of the Plains.

VI
The Wane of Shoshoni Power

It was the gun that brought Shoshoni power to an end. In 1755 these Indians met their first serious defeat when a party of Crees and Assiniboins, armed with guns, joined a Blackfoot camp. It was an encounter of the old kind, fought from behind the shelter of shields. Lying on the ground, their guns out of sight, and each man holding two balls in his mouth for rapid reloading, the Blackfoot allies fired at the Shoshoni line as quickly as they could, killing and wounding many. Terrified by this mysterious weapon, the Shoshonis fled, leaving their shields standing to cover their retreat.

By 1772 their enemies were well equipped with guns and ammunition obtained from British traders in the north. But the Shoshonis, whose main trade channels were through the Spaniards in the southwest, were unable to get guns, for Spain refused to arm the Indians. Instead of being able to send out strong raiding parties as they had been accustomed to do, they were faced with the prospect of being surprised in their camps by bands of warriors armed with a weapon against which they had no defense.

Late in the 1790s most of the once-powerful Shoshonis had

been driven from the Plains; many had by then even lost their horses. Some went south and joined their Comanche kinsmen; others settled along the Green River. These became known in historic times as Wyoming Shoshonis.

Most, however, fled into the mountains to the west. But here their enemies followed and forced them over into the Plateau region, where they were to assimilate aspects of yet another culture. But they were not safe there either, for as in olden times, their camps were subject to periodic raids by tribes, now often armed with guns, who crossed the ranges to kill their men and capture their women and children. It was during such a raid that Sacajawea had been taken by the Hidatsas. Gradually the Shoshonis became scattered and impoverished, forced to keep to lonely rivers and mountain streams, and to subsist chiefly on salmon.

But this would not be, Chief Cameahwait assured Meriwether Lewis, "if we had guns; we could then live in the country of the buffalo and . . . not be compelled to hide ourselves in these mountains and live on roots and berries as the bear do." They had no fear of their enemies "when placed on an equal footing with them."

Those who had been able to escape with their horses kept much of their former bold spirit, and after a time, gaining numerical strength through an alliance with the Flatheads, they began making annual fall excursions across the mountains to their old buffalo hunting grounds. An early fur trader reported seeing "at least five hundred warriors armed and equipped for action . . . keeping watch upon hill tops, while about fifty were hunting in the prairies." Once they had collected and dried sufficient meat to last until the salmon ran again in the rivers of the west, they started back, crossing the Tetons and other ranges by those well-traveled trails that led over passes and through canyons.

One trapper, whose party was joined by such a band bound for a buffalo hunt, wrote that there were "three thousand horses of every variety of size and colour, with trappings almost as varied as their appearance, either packed or ridden by a thousand souls from squalling infancy to decrepit age." Faces were painted with vermilion and yellow ocher, and dress was elaborate—scarlet cloaks, blankets of every color, buffalo robes painted with human figures, and shirts, leggings, and moccasins decorated heavily with colored porcupine quills, beads, hawk's bells, and human hair.

He also noted the sounds: the constant rattle of hundreds of lodgepoles dragged by packhorses; the screaming of children, the scolding of women, the howling of dogs, the yip and whoop of Indian boys dashing across the plains full speed. He saw frightened horses run away with a clatter, scattering their loads over the prairie, and bands of horsemen, as many as a hundred in a group, giving chase to antelope herds. He observed crowds of ravenous dogs running in every direction after rabbits and other small game.

Once over the mountains they found the plains "alive with buffalo, of which we killed great numbers, and our camp was . . . once more graced with piles of meat." The Indians, who were close to starvation, ate greedily, and men, children, and dogs "lay sprawling about, scarcely able to move . . . the squaws alone were busy," slicing meat, flaking the choice cuts for pemmican, gathering fuel, and setting up the drying racks. After the meat was hung, they cracked the bones to extract the marrow which they put into a kettle with the best of the tallow and rendered over a slow fire.

When the flakes were dry they were usually mixed with berries and pounded on a flat stone to the consistency of mincemeat. This was then spread into a layer some two inches thick and smoothed with a buffalo horn or a bird claw. It was then covered with the melted fat and marrow. The whole process was repeated until the required amount was made. Trappers found one pound of pemmican equal to five pounds of meat.

Some Shoshonis became so demoralized by the frequent raids of their enemies that they withdrew to the mountains permanently, and took to living in caves and on inaccessible crags and cliff tops in the Tetons east and west, and other mountain ranges in the area. Limited food supplies did not allow dense settlement, so they broke up into small, widely scattered family groups. They often drove off raiders by rolling boulders on them from above. But their best defense lay in keeping hidden, and they grew so furtive they even covered their conical shaped shelters with grass, brush, or unstripped branches to make them resemble shrubbery or stands of saplings.

Because they became heavily dependent on the bighorn sheep for food, they were known to other Shoshonis as *Tuka-düka* or Sheep Eaters. This animal became as important to them as the buffalo had been, supplying not only meat but skins for clothing and containers, and horn for bows and other utensils. They hunted the mountain sheep all year, using light snowshoes in winter.

In the Basin and on the Plains the Shoshonis had excelled in basketry. The Takadüka now added to this skill by making nicely shaped steatite cups with bases, and bowls for cooking and eating, quarrying the stone on the west slope of the Tetons.

Their existence was seminomadic. When it was safe to do so, they ventured into such secluded areas as Jackson Hole and Pierre's Hole, and remote valleys in Yellowstone country, to hunt and fish and harvest plants, seeds, and berries. Large dogs of a now extinct breed were used to drive some of the bigger game into corral-shaped traps of log or stone. Bears were caught in pitfalls, while ground dwellers were smoked out of their burrows. After the hunt the butchered game was packed in sheepskin bags and loaded on travois which were pulled by these dogs.

In historic times mountain men often came on traces of these people, saw the smoke of their fires curling up from some distant crag, but rarely saw the Sheep Eaters themselves. In the summer of 1835 a small trapping party came on a group in a mountain valley north of the Tetons. The Indians immediately ran off to the heights, but the trappers succeeded in convincing them they were friendly, and persuading them to return and encamp with them. One trapper noted that as soon as their fears were conquered, the Sheep Eaters seemed to like the white men's company, and eagerly traded furs for axes, awls, kettles, and tobacco.

"Give us whatever you please for them, we are satisfied," he remembered them saying as they threw the pelts at their feet; "we can get plenty of skins but we do not often see the Tibuboes" [white men].

He saw that they were dressed in deer- and sheepskins of the best quality, but that their personal possessions were few. They had one "old butcher knife nearly worn to the back," two shattered fusees, "long useless for want of ammunition," a little stone pot, and some thirty dogs, which they used as pack animals. They were all well armed with bows made from mountain sheep, buffalo and elk horn, reinforced with deer and elk sinews, and decorated with porcupine quills, in the style of the Plains Shoshonis.

They were very alert, he found, and possessed an exact knowledge of the topography of the surrounding country. One of them drew a map with a piece of charcoal on a white elk skin; it showed where the trappers could find passes, and in what directions the rivers flowed. He also gave them a detailed description of the terrain and its chief obstacles to travel.

The Sheep Eaters remained in their Teton strongholds and other mountain fastnesses until around 1879 when they went to join those Shoshonis who were already settled on reservations in Idaho and Wyoming. Again their way of life changed radically, for they had horses once more and could hunt the buffalo and go on long trading expeditions. Togwotee, a noted Sheep Eater medicine man, became a subchief under the great Shoshoni leader Washakie. Like most Shoshonis, Togwotee was friendly to white men and was employed frequently as a guide for explorers and for troops in the Indian wars.

Today, relics of the only Indians who ever had permanent homes in the Tetons are still found on remote cliff tops or in alpine valleys: the skeletal remains of Sheep Eater wickiups, old fire pits, piles of arrowhead chippings, and the rock and log remnants of game traps.

VII
The Pilot Knobs

Three years after John Colter discovered the Tetons, white men went into that country again. Early in March 1810, a party of trappers and traders left Manuel Lisa's fort on the Yellowstone to set up a post at the Missouri's Three Forks. The party included two of Lisa's partners, Andrew Henry and Pierre Menard, and two Lewis and Clark veterans, George Drouillard, a Shawnee-French interpreter and hunter, and John Colter, who was again the guide.

Some twelve days later they came to a place where Colter had fought the Blackfeet two years before and narrowly missed death. They stopped to look at the site—"skulls and bones were lying around on the ground in vast numbers," one trapper noticed—and to hear Colter's account.

He was on his way back to Lisa's fort, he told them (that was the year Lisa had sent him out to spread the word of his new trading post among the Indians), and he was traveling with a band of Crows who were bringing in their furs to trade. Suddenly a Blackfoot war party, numbering fifteen hundred, attacked them "with fury." The Crows fought "with great spirit" and defended their ground "manfully." Colter, who was in the thick of it, was badly wounded in the leg but managed to crawl into the underbrush, and "there loaded and fired while sitting on the ground." The Crows were of course overwhelmingly outnumbered, but their "desperate courage saved them from a general massacre," and the Blackfeet were finally driven back.

On April 3 the party Colter was now leading reached the Three Forks. Here, on a point between the Madison and the Jefferson, they began building a fort. They were in the heart of Blackfoot country, and nearby was the scene of another of Colter's hairbreadth escapes. He had a tale to tell again and led some of his companions to the spot.

Since the encounter had taken place just that last fall, he was able to describe "his emotions during the whole adventure with great minuteness," a comrade wrote. "As we passed over the ground . . . and listened to his story an undefinable fear crept over us all. We felt awestruck by the nameless and numerous dangers that evidently beset us on every side."

A hunter named Cheek, who was there, admitted: "I am afraid, and I acknowledge it. I never felt fear before, but I feel it now." To his friends he seemed melancholy, and "serious almost to sadness."

But thoughts of the fortunes to be made in this rich beaver country cheered them, and they were soon organizing parties to set traps. Then, on the morning of April 12, a party of eleven trappers working along the Jefferson was ambushed, and five of the men were killed. Among the dead was Cheek.

The Blackfeet took all their beaver and most of the traps, guns, horses, and ammunition. An old chronicle adds that "hats, knives, dirks . . . and a number of bank notes" were taken as well.

"This unfortunate incident has quite discouraged our hunters," partner Pierre Menard wrote home. "They are unwilling to hunt here any more."

John Colter was one of the party and had just missed death again. When he had been in his last tight spot not many months before, he had "promised God Almighty that he would never return to this region . . . if he were only permitted to escape once more with his life." He had come through, but here he was back again. "Dangers . . . seemed to have for him a kind of fascination," one of his fellows recalled.

Now he came into the fort and, throwing his hat on the floor, said:

"If God will only forgive me this time and let me off I *will* leave this country day after tomorrow—and be damned if I ever come into it again!"

He left, with two companions who shared his feelings, and reached St. Louis safely before the end of May, although not without having one more brush with the Blackfeet and death.

Just a few days after Colter's departure there was another surprise attack during which several more trappers were killed. Pierre Menard, deciding the place was untenable, announced he was returning to St. Louis. But before he could get on his way, the Blackfeet struck again, this time killing three trappers. One of them was George Drouillard whom Meriwether Lewis characterized as "a man of much merit," who had taken part in "all the most dangerous and trying scenes of the voyage" and "uniformly acquitted himself with honor."

This attack had taken place within range of help, but a high wind had kept those inside the fort from hearing the shouts and the firing. From the appearance of the ground where Drouillard's mangled body lay, it was obvious he had put up a good defense, fighting in a circle on horseback, and killing some of his attackers before he and his mount were fatally wounded.

By this time Menard had a considerable following. Taking with them the season's packs of beaver, he and his party reached St. Louis without incident.

There were a number of hunters, among them three Kentucky frontiersmen, Edward Robinson, John Hoback, and Jacob Reznor, who decided to stay on with partner Andrew Henry. But before the end of summer all were convinced the post would have to be abandoned. Aside from the constant threat of Indians and the menace of grizzly bears, (for these were plentiful and a number of trappers were badly mauled), there was the economic aspect. Since the fort had to be strongly manned to resist attack, the number of trappers in the field was limited. For safety's sake, those who went out had to band together and did not dare venture beyond six miles. Such restricted operations made it impossible for the enterprise to be profitable.

Early that fall Henry and his men packed up and moved

south across the Divide. While going through the mountains they lost a band of horses, not to the Blackfeet this time, but to the Crows. Coming on the North Fork of the Snake they followed it into a pleasant valley, well watered and abounding in beaver. Here, directly west of the Tetons, they built a fortified post consisting of several small log buildings. Henry's Fort was the name they gave this first American trading post west of the Divide. Still closer to the Tetons, near today's Drummond, Idaho, they evidently had another encampment, for they left clues. Several inscribed stones, very like the one John Colter carved, have been found in the area. One reads "Camp Henry Sept 1810"; another has among a list of names those of A. Henry and J. Hoback, as well as a face cut in profile.

Here they were no longer troubled by Indians or grizzly bears, but they came close to starving to death. Game was scarce for winter was closing in, and when it came, snows piled deep. The party kept alive by eating their horses. Before the drifts had melted they were reduced to boiling the hides for soup.

With the arrival of spring the discouraged party dispersed. Andrew Henry returned to Lisa's post with the packs of beaver fur, but the others scattered in many directions. The three Kentuckians, Hoback, Reznor, and Edward Robinson, who had in his youth been scalped and always wore a kerchief tied around his head to cover the scar, set off on an Indian trail that took them south into Pierre's Hole. There they followed the windings of the river and trapped along its willow-lined tributaries fed by snows from the heart of the Teton peaks. Deer, elk, and moose had returned to the valley and were feeding on the spring herbage in the lush meadows, and on the tender new shoots in the thickets and groves.

At the south end of Pierre's Hole they took a trail that led over the range. In Jackson Hole they forded the Snake and set their traps in its leafy backwaters. They explored the valley at least as far north as Buffalo Fork, for in going east they left by way of Togwotee Pass. In the annals of the western fur trade these three Kentuckians are credited with being the first to trap the Teton valleys commercially.

Lewis' report on the abundance of furbearers in the country that he and Clark had explored fired the New York fur merchant John Jacob Astor with the ambition to carry out Jefferson's plans for transcontinental and interoceanic trade. Astor saw how he could monopolize the western and China fur trade by establishing a line of posts along the Missouri, Snake, and Columbia rivers, and a large trading house on the Pacific Coast, near the Columbia's mouth. Early in 1810 he organized the Pacific Fur Company as a western branch of his American Fur Company and prepared to send out two parties. One party would go overland, open the route, decide on the best places for posts, and trap and hunt along the way. The other would go by sea with the stores and personnel to set up the coast trading post that was to be called Astoria.

To act as his chief agent and head the overland party Astor chose one of his partners, twenty-seven-year-old Wilson Price Hunt. Hunt was described as "a person of great probity and worth." He was, however, entirely ignorant of both the fur trade and the wilderness and had no acquaintance with the West beyond St. Louis, where he had been a merchant.

On October 21, 1810, Hunt's party, traveling aboard three keelboats, left St. Louis for the Upper Missouri. A month later, finding further navigation impossible, they went into winter camp at the mouth of the Nodowa River. Over the next few months Hunt began hearing so many reports from passing travelers about the warlike character of the Sioux, he grew uneasy and decided to return to St. Louis, hire an interpreter, and recruit more hunters and trappers who could double as fighting men.

When he left the city for a return to his winter camp, Hunt took with him an assortment of people: there was the half-breed interpreter Pierre Dorion, his Sioux wife, and their two small children; a number of hardy voyageurs; Sacajawea and Toussaint Charbonneau who were on their way to the Mandan villages; the jurist-author and inveterate traveler Henry M. Brackenridge; and two British botanists, Thomas Nuttall and John Bradbury, who wanted to study flora along the Missouri.

Bradbury, described as "a man of mature age," had been sent out by the Liverpool Linnean Society to collect American plants. Nuttall, who was just twenty-four, had undertaken the study of native flora only two years before, on settling in Philadelphia, but would soon achieve wide recognition as both a botanist and ornithologist, and receive a professorship at Harvard. Now a new world was opening for him in the prairies. "No sooner does the boat touch shore than he leaps out," Henry Brackenridge observed, "and when his attention is arrested by a plant or flower everything is forgotten." Frequently when the boat was ready to go on, he was nowhere in sight, and someone would have to hunt for him. "At such times he would be found far off in the prairies, or up the course of some . . . stream, laden with plants of all kinds."

This preoccupation was incomprehensible to the voyageurs and furnished them no end of amusement. "*Le fou,* the fool, is the name by which he is commonly known," Brackenridge continued. "*'Où est le fou?'* (Where is the fool?)" was a frequent inquiry, to be answered with, "*'Il est après ramasser des racines.'* (He is gathering roots.)"

One morning while the party was still ashore at breakfast, they had a visit from John Colter, who had turned farmer. He stayed with them until noon giving advice on how best to avoid clashes with the Blackfeet, and recounting his experiences with them. As he talked, John Bradbury took notes.

In the fall of 1808, Colter said, he and John Potts, another Lewis and Clark veteran, were trapping in the Three Forks country, just where Andrew Henry had put up his first post. He and Potts were aware of their danger, so they set their traps at night, took them up before dawn, and kept in hiding during the day. However, sunrise caught them one morning while they were still inspecting their catch along a small tributary of the Jefferson. Suddenly they were conscious of a trampling sound. Colter was sure there were Indians close by and advised immediate retreat, but Potts was just as certain that what they heard were buffalo coming to water.

Before they could do anything five to six hundred Blackfeet appeared on the shore and made signs for them to land. "As retreat was now impossible," Bradbury wrote, "Colter turned the head of the canoe to shore." When it touched, he jumped out, but Potts, thinking he could escape, pushed back into the stream. Just then an arrow struck him.

"'Colter, I'm wounded!'" he cried, and "instantly levelled his rifle at an Indian, and shot him dead on the spot." The air was then thick with arrows, and, as Colter said, poor Potts "was made a riddle of."

The Blackfeet then waded into the creek, pulled the canoe ashore, and hacked Potts' body to pieces. "They now seized Colter, stripped him entirely naked, and began to consult on the manner in which he should be put to death. They were first inclined to set him up as a mark to shoot at; but the chief interfered, and seizing him by the shoulder, asked him if he could run fast." Colter told him in the Blackfoot tongue that he was a very poor runner, "although he was considered by the hunters to be remarkably swift."

The chief then ordered his men to stay where they were and led Colter out some three or four hundred yards into the prairie. Releasing him, he said: "Go—go away. Save yourself if you can."

As he began to run across the six-mile plain, covered thickly with prickly pear, he heard a loud whoop and knew the Indians had started after him. He ran with a speed that surprised himself, he said. Not until he was halfway across did he dare look back. Then he saw that the main body was greatly scattered and still some distance away. But he also saw that one man, armed with a spear, had outstripped the others and was not more than a hundred yards behind him. Still, he felt escape was possible, and this spark of hope gave him the strength to go on. Blood now gushed from his nostrils and covered the front of his body.

When about half a mile from the Jefferson he heard the footsteps coming closer, and turning his head saw that the single Indian was now not twenty yards away. Determined to escape the expected spear thrust if he could, he stopped suddenly and faced his pursuer with outspread arms.

The Indian, surprised by this unlooked-for action, tried to stop short and hurl his spear, but fell and broke it. Colter instantly snatched up the spearhead and "pinned him to the ground."

Although close to fainting, he ran on, reached the river, and plunging in swam a short distance down to an island to look for cover. There, lodged against the bank, he found a large mass of driftwood that formed "a natural raft." Diving under the raft he found a place where he could keep his head above water and still remain hidden.

He waited anxiously, and soon the Indians came up "screeching and yelling like so many devils," he said. During the rest of the day they were constantly passing and repassing the raft, and even climbed on it in their search.

Not until nightfall could he relax; then, "hearing no more of the Indians he dived from under the raft and swam silently down the river to a considerable distance, when he landed, and travelled all night."

Daytime found him crossing the prairie, naked under a scorching sun, the soles of his feet covered with prickly pear spines. He was hungry but had no means for killing game. Lisa's fort, which was his only hope, lay about two hundred miles east as the crow flies.

"These were circumstances under which almost any man but an American hunter would have despaired," Bradbury observed. "He arrived at the fort in seven days, having subsisted on a root much esteemed by the Indians of the Missouri, now known by naturalists as *Psoralea esculenta*," or breadroot.

Now Colter was strongly tempted to join Hunt's expedition. Only the fact that he had recently been married kept him from going. "He reluctantly took his leave of us," Bradbury added. Three years later John Colter, adventurer and exploreer extraordinary, the first white man to see the Tetons, was dead from jaundice. He was just thirty-eight.

By April 21 Hunt's whole party, which by then numbered sixty and included five partners, was ready to start off from winter quarters. They were traveling in four boats, one of which was mounted with a swivel and two howitzers. Nights were spent ashore "on some beautiful bank, beneath spreading trees, which afforded . . . shelter and fuel. The tents were pitched, the fires made, and the meals prepared by the voyageurs, and many a story was told . . . and song sung round the evening fire," Bradbury remembered.

Another morning when the party was still ashore, someone noticed two canoes slipping downstream along the opposite bank. With the aid of a spyglass they saw two white men in one canoe, and a third in the other. A gun was fired to attract their attention, and the boatmen seeing the party, crossed over. They turned out to be the Kentuckians Hoback, Reznor, and Robinson, on their way to St. Louis with a load of beaver fur.

Would they want to join him? Hunt asked. The sight of the large, well-equipped expedition was tempting. After they learned it was bound for the Pacific Coast, "home and families and all the charms of green Kentucky vanished from their thoughts." They cut loose their canoes and "joyfully enlisted in the band of adventurers."

Hunt had intended to follow the Lewis and Clark trail, but the three recruits persuaded him to go by the route they had just taken: south of the Little Missouri, across the Powder River, into the valley of the Bighorn, then along the Wind River, and so avoid the dreaded Blackfeet. They would guide the company over the Divide by an easy pass, Togwotee. The country was well watered, and game was plentiful. At the village of the Arikara Indians, just a few days' travel away, Hunt would be able to trade for horses and abandon his boats. He was convinced.

At the Indian village he parted with Thomas Nuttall who was returning to St. Louis with his large plant collection. Bradbury and Brackenridge had already left for St. Louis with a passing party from Lisa's fort. By July 18 Hunt had bartered for horses and was ready to move on.

A little less than two months later the travelers had reached the Wind River. Their guides had intended to follow the Shoshoni trade route at the river's head, but an unexpected shortage of game sent them hurrying over the mountains by way of present Union Pass into the valley of the Green, in the hope of finding buffalo.

At the summit they stopped to look at the "almost boundless" view, and one of the Kentuckians pointed out "three immensely high and snow-covered peaks," which he said rose "above a fork of the Columbia River"—the Snake. Because these "remarkable peaks" were to remain in sight for many days and serve the party as guiding landmarks, Hunt named them the Pilot Knobs, although they were already known to travelers as the Tetons, or simply the Teats or the Paps.

On reaching the valley of the Green River the party spent five days along its grassy banks, about twenty-five miles south of Jackson Hole, resting the men and horses. In preparation for the long journey ahead, their hunters killed numbers of buffalo and dried the meat. Nearby was a band of Shoshonis who had crossed the mountains on their fall hunt. "Their camp was full of jerked meat, all of the choicest kind," Hunt wrote. To assure an adequate supply for his men, Hunt traded with them for about two thousand pounds.

Following the river that was to be called the Hoback, flowing between the Gros Ventre and Wyoming ranges, the Astorians came to its junction with the Snake, known to some as the Mad River, because of its turbulence. Here they made camp. A few miles away towered Hunt's Pilot Knobs, newly mantled with snow.

Spirits rose when Hoback now told them they had reached headwaters of the Columbia. Should they abandon their horses, take to this swift and impetuous river, and let it lead them to the main body of the Columbia? A vote taken among the partners was unanimous for embarkation. Only Hunt seems to have had some doubts, for he sent three men to explore the river downstream "a distance of four days' march." Meanwhile the rest of the party began cutting trees for the canoes.

One morning two Shoshonis came into camp. Seeing the men at work on the boats, they shook their heads and by other signs made it understood that the stream was not navigable. Then the scouts returned with reports that the river grew narrow and winding and was blocked by numerous falls and rapids. Although keenly disappointed, all agreed they must go on by land and look for another river.

The Kentuckian guides then stepped forward to suggest that the party go on to Henry's Fort, on "an upper branch of the Columbia," just west of the Tetons. That river was less turbulent, and there were many trees suitable for canoes. The Shoshonis, learning their destination, offered to guide them over the Tetons and north through Pierre's Hole.

It then began to storm, and the travelers rode toward Jackson Hole through new-fallen snow. At the south end of the valley they forded the Snake; Hunt noted that the water was "up to the horses' bellies." After covering only four miles, the party encamped at the foot of Teton Pass. The next morning they made the crossing "by an easy and well-broken trail."

As they rode north through Pierre's Hole, Hunt noticed "numerous bands of antelope," and thickets of "wild cherries . . . the size of ordinary red cherries . . . not yet ripe." Roses were in hip along the stream banks, and purple asters and yellow salsify bloomed in the meadows. On October 8 they reached the welcome shelter of Henry's Fort. There had been flurries of snow all day and a biting wind blowing strong from the west.

Hunt now committed his greatest blunder by giving in to pressures from the company to abandon land travel and take their chances with the river. In the morning he ordered cotton-wood trees to be felled and work begun on the canoes.

He decided to turn Henry's Fort into a trading post for Astor's hunters and trappers who would be working in the area. He explained its use to the two Shoshonis, urged them to get their people to bring in furs to trade, and outfitted a party to trap beaver. Included in the party were those veterans Hoback, Robinson, and Reznor. Partner Joseph Miller, who was by this time disgusted with Hunt's leadership, decided to relinquish his share in the company and join the trappers.

By the eighteenth, fifteen canoes were finished, and the next day the Astorians set off by water. The current bore them along rapidly, and the voyageurs, in their element again, made the valley echo with song. John Bradbury translated a favorite one:

> Behind our house there is a pond,
> 　　Fal lal de ra.
> There came three ducks to swim thereon,
> All along the river clear,
> Lightly my shepherdess dear,
> 　　Lightly, fal de ra.
>
> There came three ducks to swim thereon,
> 　　Fal lal de ra.
> The prince to chase them he did run,
> All along the river clear,
> Lightly my shepherdess dear,
> 　　Lightly, fal de ra.
>
> The prince to chase them he did run,
> 　　Fal lal de ra.
> And he had his great silver gun,
> All along the river clear,
> Lightly my shepherdess dear,
> 　　Lightly, fal de ra . . .

Verse upon verse.

They came at last to the Snake itself, wide and swift. Hunt

noticed its beautiful light green color. Cottonwood groves and willow thickets lined its banks. Close to shore he saw flocks of ducks and geese feeding, while others passed overhead in south-flying wedges. For two days the river paralleled the mountains, the summit of the Grand Teton always in sight.

Twenty miles, then another twenty, and the character of the river suddenly changed. Rock walls compressed it to less than thirty feet in width, the waters forming "a whirling and tumultuous vortex" which the boatmen called the Devil's Scuttle Hole.

On the morning of October 8 the lead canoe slipped safely by, but the one following struck a midstream rock. The craft split and overturned. Astor partner Ramsay Crooks and another passenger swam ashore. The steersman, Antoine Clappine, and the others clung to the wreck which was shortly hurled against another rock. Two of the men scrambled onto it and were rescued later, but the impact flung Clappine—"one of the most valuable of the voyageurs"—into the rapids. He was swept downstream and drowned. The Scots in the party named this stretch of the river Caldron Linn—a linn being a torrent—a name it still bears.

Hunt and three companions now scouted the Snake by land for thirty-five miles, only to find that it continued to twist through the narrow gorge and was frequently intersected by falls. There was no recourse but to go on by land. "Our situation had become very critical," Hunt noted in his diary. "We had food for not more than five days."

Three parties started off in different directions. Partner Robert McClellan and his men elected to stay near the river; partner Donald McKenzie was to strike north across the desert in the hope of locating the Columbia, while Ramsay Crooks agreed to retrace the trail to Henry's Fort and bring back the horses left in the Shoshonis' care. If, within a reasonable distance of the main camp, any of the parties found Indians with whom they could barter for horses and provisions, they were to come back; otherwise, they should continue west and fend for themselves.

Three days later Crooks and his party returned. They had decided it would be impossible to get to Henry's Fort and back with the horses before winter set in.

Hunt resolved to delay no longer. He cached everything that could be spared and divided the remaining provisions—dried buffalo meat, parched corn, "grease," and "bouillon tablets"—between the two parties he formed. On November 9 they started on their way. Hunt, with twenty-two persons, kept to the north side of the Snake, while Crooks, with nineteen others, traveled along the opposite bank. The Tetons, the Pilot Knobs, so long a familiar landmark, were left behind. The travelers were letting this wild river lead them through a country no known white man had ever entered.

Hunt's party reached Astoria on February 15, 1812, after eleven months' travel, some of it retrograde, much of it confused, and all of it difficult. They found the McKenzie and McClellan parties already there; both had come in more than a month before after "suffering incredible hardships."

All of the travelers had experienced alternate plenty—when they came on scattered Indian camps and traded for salmon, horse, and dog—and famine, when they crossed the wastes and were reduced to eating boiled beaver hide or nothing. At these times sound men lost their reason and went raving into the wilderness, never to be seen again, or in their madness flung themselves into the river and drowned. Of the partners, only Crooks had been unable to keep up, and Hunt had left him behind with a hunter, John Day, equally weak, to travel as they could. They did not reach Astoria until May.

But now with Hunt's arrival a day was set aside to celebrate. "The colors were hoisted; the guns, great and small, were fired; there was a feast of fish, of beaver, and venison . . . a genial allowance of grog was issued . . . and the festivities wound up . . . with a grand dance at night, by the Canadian voyageurs."

That summer Hunt sent a small company east, six men in all, under young Robert Stuart, who had come to the Pacific by ship with despatches for Astor. Crooks and McClellan, tired of the venture, were going with him. They intended to follow Hunt's route in the belief that it would be easier at this time of year. They soon found that every season had its hardships in that rugged country.

By August 20 they had reached the sagebrush plains paralleling the Snake River. It was a sultry day, and the party climbed down to the river for water. Here to their surprise they found a white man sitting under some willows, fishing. It was John Hoback. Stuart wrote that an instant later, Miller, Robinson, and Reznor, "who had been similarly employed . . . joined us." Their "haggard looks and naked condition" told much. A recital of their adventures included theft of all their horses, traps, and pelts, and near-starvation. They decided to join Stuart and return to St. Louis.

At Caldron Linn they stopped to open Hunt's caches. Six had been robbed, but three were intact, and from these Stuart took what was needed. As soon as the three Kentuckians realized they could be outfitted for another trapping expedition from the stores, they forgot their recent troubles and voted for a return to the wilderness to recoup their fortunes. Former partner Miller was not tempted; he admitted that his curiosity about the Indians and life in the wilderness was fully satisfied.

October 1 found Stuart's party in Teton country. They camped three days beside the Teton River waiting for Crooks to recover from some ailment for which Stuart dosed him with castor oil. The rest of the men feasted on elk, for one of their hunters had killed five, and they dried as much of the meat as they could carry.

As soon as Crooks was strong enough to travel they crossed the marshy meadows of Pierre's Hole, added the meat of a grizzly bear to their stock, and on October 7 climbed the Indian trail to the summit of Teton Pass which they found covered with fresh snow.

They left Jackson Hole the next morning, traveling south into the valley of the Green, and skirting the Wind River Mountains. October 21 and 22 were spent in crossing the Continental Divide by way of South Pass. They were the first known white men to use this crossing that became so important in later overland travel and exploration.

On April 30, 1813, Robert Stuart made the final entry in his travel journal: "This day . . . we a little before sun set reached the Town of St. Louis, all in the most perfect health, after a voyage of ten months from Astoria, during which we underwent many dangers, hardships, & fatigues. . . ."

With the departure of Stuart's party from Jackson Hole in October 1812, thirteen years were to pass before white men went there again. War with England had been declared in June of 1812, and Astoria was surrendered that December to the British Northwest Company. There was the threat of a general Indian uprising among the tribes of the Upper Missouri, owing to agitation by the English. Traders consequently withdrew from their posts in that area, trapping was sharply curtailed, and fur prices fell.

For the time, men thought no more about those imposing landmarks, the Three Tetons or Pilot Knobs, nor their beaver-filled streams and valleys teeming with game. These were left to the undisputed possession of their rightful proprietors, the Indians.

VIII
Fortunes in Fur

On February 13, 1822, the following notice appeared in the *Missouri Gazette & Public Advertiser:*

TO

Enterprising Young Men

The subscriber wishes to engage ONE HUNDRED MEN, to ascend the river Missouri to its source, there to be employed for one, two or three years.—For particulars, enquire of Major Andrew Henry, near the Lead Mines, in the County of Washington, (who will ascend with, and command the party) or to the subscriber at St. Louis.

Wm. H. Ashley.

This advertisement marked the birth of the fur company that was to revolutionize the trade and discover some of the richest beaver-trapping grounds in the country. Many able men who were to figure prominently in the history of the West answered Ashley's call for recruits at this time, and later—Jedediah Smith, David Jackson, the Sublette brothers, Etienne

Provost, Jim Bridger, Tom Fitzpatrick, Jim Beckwourth, Joe Meek, and James Clyman.

In their search for beaver these fortune hunters opened a vast new territory. As one of them observed in 1840: "Not a hole or corner in the . . . wilderness of the 'Far West' but has been ransacked by these hardy men. . . . The beaver-hunter has set his traps in every creek and stream. All this vast country, but for the daring enterprise of these men, would be even now a *terra incognita* to geographers . . . these alone are the hardy pioneers who have paved the way for settlement of the western country."

An early historian agreed: "*They* were the 'pathfinders' of the West, and not those later official explorers whom posterity so recognized. No feature of western geography was ever *discovered* by government explorers after 1840 . . . "

The mountain men not only discovered, but gave names to the rivers and mountains, the landmarks and valleys: the Bear River, the Ashley, the Sweetwater, Black's Fork, Horse Creek, Chimney Rock, Independence Rock, Scott's Bluffs. In Teton country Ashley's men were the first to explore closely every stream, slough, lake, and marsh in those valleys lying east and west of the range, and to name Jackson's Hole and Jackson's Little Hole.

The company dealt almost exclusively in beaver fur, and its records show that during its short career it shipped to St. Louis more than a thousand packs in all valued at over half a million dollars.

The founder of this lucrative enterprise was forty-four-year-old William Henry Ashley, a Virginian who had settled in St. Louis in 1808 and had engaged variously in mining, real estate, and the manufacture of gunpowder. He helped organize the state militia and rose through its ranks to become a general. In 1820 he was elected the first lieutenant governor of Missouri.

His experience in the mountain fur trade, and his phenomenal success, added stature and an aura of romance to a figure already admired for public spirit and business acumen. Keelboats and steamboats were named for him, and "Ashley beaver" came to denote the finest quality fur. He was considered an authority on all matters relating to the fur and Indian trade, and his opinions, which were frequently sought, carried weight. In

1831 he was sent to Congress to fill out the unexpired term of Spencer Pettis who had been killed in a duel and was re-elected twice. Next to Senator Thomas Hart Benton, General William Ashley was the most influential man in Missouri.

He chose Pennsylvania-born Andrew Henry, who had also been engaged in mining, as his associate in the fur business. As Manuel Lisa's partner in the Missouri Fur Company, Henry had gained much valuable experience, especially as a wilderness trader. He had been the first American to carry the business to the Pacific slope of the Rocky Mountains.

Little is known about Henry's career beyond his fur trade years, spent chiefly in the wilderness where he bore the brunt of the Blackfoot troubles. He was remembered as a man of "intelligence and enterprise," who played the violin expertly and was "fond of reading." In appearance he was said to have been tall and slender, "yet of commanding presence"; his hair was dark, and his eyes "inclined to blue."

Ashley and Henry were to make some decisions that would effect a radical change in the American fur trade. Instead of depending on Indians to supply the pelts, as British and French traders did, they resolved to send out their own trappers into the field. As a result, there evolved a new type, the mountain man, described by an early trader as "hardy, lithe, vigorous, and active; extravagant in word . . . thought, and deed; heedless of hardship; daring of danger; prodigal of the present, and thoughtless of the future." There also came into existence a novel kind of mart, the annual rendezvous, that combined country fair, marketplace, and bacchanal.

In the fall of 1824 Ashley decided to abandon the Missouri River valley and carry his operations into and beyond the Rocky Mountains where, it was said, there existed "a wealth of furs not surpassed by the mines of Peru." The voyageur and his canoe gave way to itinerant parties of hunters on horseback, and accessible mountain valleys, where traders and trappers could meet to exchange and sell furs for goods, largely replaced the fixed trading post on the riverbank. Although this system had been used by others before him in a limited way, Ashley perfected it and established it on a large scale and a regular basis. He is also credited with being the first to call the annual meeting a *rendezvous*.

In the summer of 1824 Tom Fitzpatrick tried the system experimentally on the Sweetwater, but the first general gathering was held by Ashley himself the next year in the Green River valley. Eight hundred Indians were said to have brought in their furs, but the number of white trappers was small. Aside from Ashley's men there were only two dozen—all deserters from the Hudson's Bay Company. But the following summer signs were posted along the important trails, inviting all free trappers (men who worked for themselves in just the finer furs) to bring their pelts to Cache Valley, near the Great Salt Lake.

For the next fifteen years the summer rendezvous was an important annual event, not only as a mart, and a meeting place for old friends and comrades, but as a place where company business was transacted as well. There partners came to decide policy and fix the site of the next rendezvous, for the location was changed from year to year to accommodate the trapping parties which were constantly working new territory.

Many papers in the company files were headed "Pierre's Hole, Under the Three Teton Mountains," for this was the site of two general rendezvous. None was ever held, however, in that valley soon to be named Jackson's Hole for, ringed by mountain ranges, it was considered too inaccessible.

In 1824 Andrew Henry retired from the trade, and Ashley chose a new partner from among his hired men: Jedediah Strong Smith, in whom he saw great promise. At the Cache Valley rendezvous two years later, Ashley announced his decision to sell. He had already made around eighty thousand dollars. The ablest of his lieutenants, Jedediah Smith, David Jackson, and William Sublette, were the buyers. Residence in St. Louis was a necessity for the politically ambitious Ashley, but he would still look to the mountains for continuing riches. By the articles of sale he was to supply the new firm of Smith, Jackson & Sublette with merchandise and Indian trade goods, dispose of their furs, and act as their banker. He left the rendezvous that summer with one hundred and twenty-three packs of beaver fur valued at around fifty-nine thousand dollars.

After the business was finished, Smith set off with a party on the first of those long and perilous journeys for which he became noted. His trail took him by Utah Lake, across the Sevier valley, along the Virgin, Colorado, and Mojave rivers, and finally over the mountains into California where he investigated the fur potential and trapped the principal streams.

Not until 1827 did the partners spend time trapping the waterways in Teton country. That year William Sublette led a party north through Pierre's Hole to Henry's Fort (harassed by Blackfeet all the way), then crossed the Tetons into Jackson Hole. There he and his men explored the Snake's countless snowfed tributaries and its calm side channels (sloughs they called them); its marshes green, russet, and gold; its reedy ponds, willow coppices, and fine cottonwood stands in search of the precious beaver.

They followed the Snake to its headwaters and crossed the mountains to the Yellowstone's source, described by a trapper as "a large freshwater lake . . . as clear as crystal," with "hot and boiling springs" along its south shore. They were the first white men to see Yellowstone country since its discovery by John Colter nineteen years before.

The partners reaped a bountiful fur harvest in the Tetons over the next three years, and few of their secrets remained hidden. In going from valley to valley they penetrated the very heart of the mountains, by way of Indian trails that led east and west through deep-cut canyons and over passes. Here they found unexpected falls and cascades, alpine meadows and tarns. They saw ancient picture writing on smooth rock walls, and on the west slope the ruins of a strange stone structure with doorway facing east. They came on the haunts of grizzly bear, bighorn, marmot, and pika, and heard the distant cry of the eagle drifting above the peaks.

It was during these years that the valley lying east of the Teton Range became David Jackson's favorite haunt. For this reason his comrades began calling it Jackson's Hole. It is not known whether its awesome beauty played any part in its attraction for him; but it is known that he felt reasonably secure from Indian ambush in this valley that was so difficult to enter.

At the 1830 rendezvous, held in the Wind River valley, Smith, Jackson and Sublette, having each made a fortune, were ready to sell. Jim Bridger, Tom Fitzpatrick, Milton Sublette, Henry Fraeb, and Baptiste Gervais, gave their note for $15,132, and bought the business. They called their partnership the Rocky Mountain Fur Company.

Immediately after the sale was completed, Smith and his partners left for St. Louis, taking with them one hundred and ninety packs of beaver worth eighty-four thousand dollars.

The *St. Louis Beacon* heralded their arrival on October 10:

> We understand that these gentlemen have done well . . . and are richly rewarded for their perils and enterprise. . . . Mr. Smith has been out five years, and has explored the country from the Gulf of California to the mouth of the Columbia. We hope to be able to give a more particular account of the extraordinary enterprise of these gentlemen, and of the country which they have explored.

Smith had this in mind. Soon after his return he began arranging his notes and journals and filling in those parts which had been lost along the way. He intended to publish an account of his travels and explorations and an atlas that would embody his discoveries and correct prevailing misconceptions about the geography of the West.

But this work was never completed, for seven months later Jedediah Smith was killed by Comanches.

IX
Who They Were

Men of all types and from all walks of life joined the fur brigades. There were a few French aristocrats from Louisiana—Lucien Fontenelle was said to have been of royal lineage—and members of the British gentry. There were New England merchants and runaway apprentices; and there were scions of Southern first families—Joe Meek was kin to President Polk, while Jim Bridger's mother was a sister of John Tyler. There were preachers—Old Bill Williams was one—and ne'er-do-wells. There were those who could neither read nor write, but there were also graduates of Harvard, Dartmouth, West Point, and European academies. There were a few desperate characters and some who were escaping the law, but the majority were men of probity.

Most of them signed on in the hope of making a fortune, although some were attracted by the promise of adventure, and others went in search of health.

About half of them were French Creoles from Canada and Louisiana, mostly former voyageurs, "mild in disposition, mercurial in temper, obedient, willing, and contented, ever ready to undergo the most severe hardships."

One mountain man observed that "rain or shine, hungry or satisfied, they are . . . generally carolling in honor of some St. Louis Creole beauty, or lauding the soft skies . . . of La Belle France, occasionally uttering a *sacré* or *enfant de garce*, but suffering no ill humor to overshadow them but for a moment." They were recalled as being "full of anecdote and song, and ever ready for the dance" around the evening campfire. Their yarns stretched credibility to the limit. One told of chasing an antelope for a week "without intermission or food, over a spur of the Wind River Mountains, and another of riding a grizzly, full tilt, through a village of Blackfoot Indians."

Their speech was a French patois, embroidered with Indian and English words and expressions; their dress was described as being half-civilized, half-savage, a style which American mountain men soon copied.

It became a point of pride with the trapper from the States to discard everything that bore the stamp of civilization and adopt Indian manners, habits, gestures, and walk, even. "You cannot pay a free trapper a greater compliment than to persuade him you have mistaken him for an Indian," it was remembered. Trapper and Indian shared the same "wild, unsettled, watchful expression in the eyes; the same unnatural gesticulation in conversation, the same unwillingness to use words when a sign, a contortion of the face or body or movement of the hand" would suffice. When the trapper talked, it was in the quiet, even tones of the Indian.

Even his singing and dancing took on Indian character. A favorite drinking song included the hi, hi-a, hi-a, he-a, he-a, hay-o-hay chant. When he danced in a ring around the campfire, to the accompaniment of fiddle or banjo, or in the settlements at public balls, he was seen to include Indian steps, and was heard whooping occasionally with "unearthly cry" as he did them.

Through constant exposure to weather the mountaineer's skin became the color of the red man's. His uncut hair hung about his shoulders Indian fashion or was worn in braids, "tied up in otter skins, or particolored ribands." Because Indian dress was most practical he adopted that too, adding some touches of his own. In summer the most popular shirt was a light-blue coarse cotton or one of "ruffled calico of bright dyes." Over this he wore the Indian's short-sleeved leather tunic hanging to the knees. Long deerskin leggings, the outer seams sewn with scarlet strings, hair, fringes, and a profusion of hawk's bells reached from hip to ankle, meeting moccasins decorated with quills, beads, and fringe.

The trapper shared the Indian enthusiasm for fringe, not solely for decoration but also for practical use. He found that the long leather strips were handy for mending moccasins and packsaddles, tying bundles, serving as tourniquets, or any other purpose to which his ingenuity might put stout buckskin whangs. As a result, his sideseams were often nearly stripped bare.

At his heels he wore iron spurs of large proportions and Spanish make, with tinkling drops attached to the rowels: their jingle he found comforting on long, lone rides. The spurs were attached to his moccasins by a beadwork strap, four inches broad, running over the instep.

In winter he put over his leather suit a heavy capote of blanket cloth, usually green. Or he made himself a poncho by simply cutting a slit in the center of a Mackinaw blanket. Whenever there were deep rivers to work in or long marches in the rain, he cut off the lower half of his leggings and substituted scarlet wool. He had learned that wet leather would shrink on drying to an uncompromising tightness. Many a man going to sleep in wet moccasins and leggings wakened in the night with the horrifying impression that he had somehow been caught in a working fur press. He would then stumble on numbed feet to the nearest water and soak his legs and feet to get relief. For this reason moccasins made from used tipi covers were in demand, for hides well seasoned with smoke did not shrink.

Hats were of "white wool, with round crowns, fitting tightly to the head, brims five inches wide, and almost hard enough to resist a rifle ball." Or they might be of the mountaineer's own manufacture, from cloth or leather. Whichever he wore, he decorated lavishly with ostrich plumes, turkey quills, bunches of wild bird feathers, often a fox's brush. Sometimes a cap was made from the entire pelt of a small animal, the tail left to dangle over the right shoulder; or from a wolf's head with a flap of skin hanging down the back. This type of hat was also useful as a disguise when the hunter, afoot, approached a buffalo herd.

The powder horn, and bullet pouch in which he carried his "balls, flint and steel, and odds and ends of all kinds," hung from a strap passed over the left shoulder and below the right arm. In his belt was stuck "a large butcher-knife in a sheath of buffalo-hide, made fast . . . by a chain or guard of steel." Suspended from the chain was "a little buckskin case containing a whetstone." Attached to the belt was a small bottle made from the point of an antelope horn, scraped transparent, which contained the "medicine" or castoreum used to bait beaver traps. A tomahawk was likewise standard equipment.

Most mountaineers had what they called "coats of mail," made from the heavy hide of blacktail deer. These were worn over the leather shirt and covered the body to the thighs. Before going into an Indian fight, the coats were soaked in water and then wrung out. "It was impossible for an arrow, whether iron or flint-pointed, to penetrate buckskin so prepared," it was remembered.

The rifle was lavishly decorated by the owner with brass tacks and vermilion, and often had a buckskin case that was fringed and tied with feathers. The most celebrated mountain rifles were those made by the St. Louis gunsmiths Jacob and Samuel Hawken. One hunter described the Hawken as being "of heavy metal, carrying about thirty-two balls to the pound, stocked to the muzzle, and mounted with brass, its only ornament being a buffalo bull, looking exceedingly ferocious, which was . . . engraved upon the trap in the stock."

There were two classes of trappers, hired and free. Hired trappers received regular wages which ranged from three to four hundred dollars a year, paid in goods priced five to six hundred percent over original cost. They were outfitted by the company and bound not only to trap and hunt for them, but to turn their hand to anything else that was asked for.

Free trappers, or freemen, the most daring and dashing in the calling, were envied by all less adventuresome company men. "They come and go when and where they please; provide their own horses, arms, and other equipments; trap and trade on their own account, and dispose of their skins and peltries to the highest bidder."

They were vain of their appearance, proud of their position, their hardihood and courage, and were boastful of their recklessness and profligacy. Each claimed to own the best horse and most reliable gun, to have had the most hairbreadth escapes, to have scalped the greatest number of Indians, to have killed the most grizzlies, to have downed the largest amounts of liquor at a time, to be the favorite among Indian belles, and to have the most beautiful woman. If any of his listeners were inclined to doubt him, he was ready to prove his superiority by racing him on horseback, beating him at cards, besting him in a shooting match, or fighting him, if that was preferred.

. The freeman selected his horse for speed, spirit, sagacity, and endurance. Since he was often his master's only companion for months at a time, the animal stood high in his estimation, "second only to himself," and was decked fittingly with a bridle and crupper heavily decorated with beads and cockades. His head, mane, and tail were tied with eagle plumes that fluttered in the wind, and his body was painted in stripes or spots with white clay, ocher, or vermilion, whichever contrasted best with the animal's natural color.

French Creole mountaineers were the first to appreciate the worth of Indian women and take them as wives, and Rocky Mountain hunters followed the example even though they kept up a constant warfare with most of the tribes.

Many of the best known traders and trappers were squaw-men—Manuel Lisa, Lucien Fontenelle, Kit Carson, Jim Bridger, Joe Meek, Milton Sublette, Bill Williams, Joe Walker, Edward Rose, William Bent, Jim Beckwourth, and, it would seem, Captain Bonneville.

Some had several Indian wives simultaneously if they could afford them, or in sequence, for mortality was high among these women who were exposed to the same perils as the mountaineer. Others, traders in particular, who divided their time between the wilderness and the settlements, had both Indian and white wives and families, the one for mountain living, the other for town, each woman unaware of the other.

Frequently these alliances were political, created to assure the trader or trapper the goodwill of those tribes in whose territory he traveled or hunted. Then he bargained with the chief for a daughter, or the daughter of an important warrior or medicine man, and married her according to Indian custom. Often he paid as much as six hundred dollars for his bride, in the legal tender of the mountains: blankets at forty dollars each; guns at one hundred dollars apiece; red flannel at twenty-nine dollars a yard; tobacco at two dollars the pound, and vermilion at three, going deeply into debt. Often the trapper would have to pledge himself to one of the companies to turn in all his pelts for several years to pay for the bride and her outfit.

For the Indian girl, marriage to a white trader or trapper, especially a freeman, represented status. Although she was expected to do her share of work about the lodge and on the trail, this rise in rank freed her from the endless chores of a communal life and allowed her to travel with her man from place to place. Of even more importance, she was able to indulge a natural taste for finery, since it was a point of pride with the mountain man to fit out his woman extravagantly. Nothing pleased him more than to find all eyes turned toward her admiringly, enviously even, as she rode with him into camp or rendezvous.

Her horse, wrote one mountaineer, was no "jaded, sorry, earth-spirited hack" such as an Indian husband would have allotted her, but "the most beautiful animal she can lay her eyes on."

Joe Meek's Shoshoni wife had a dapple gray named All Fours that cost him three hundred dollars. The price of the bridle was fifty dollars, and the saddle, crupper, and breastbands cost a hundred and fifty more, for these were all embroidered with quills and "fine cut glass beads," and hung with clusters of thimbles and little hawk's bells that tinkled with every step.

The dress of the trapper's woman was never of common buckskin, but of the best quality broadcloth, most often green, scarlet, or bright blue. Her leggings were of softest doeskin, kept white with chalk, or of scarlet wool; moccasins were of only the finest make. There were earrings, bracelets, necklaces, and finger rings, as many as she could wear, and more which she carried with her in two leather bags hung on either side of her saddle.

On her head she either tied a square of scarlet silk, hood fashion, or wore a hat stuck all about with clusters of wild bird plumes. A blanket of fine weave and bright color, usually scarlet, completed her outfit. This she draped over her shoulders.

Some of these women were beautiful, and like beauties

everywhere they could afford to be flirtatious and demanding, refusing all offers but those from partisans, traders, or free trappers of note.

The mountain man who had such a woman had to guard her carefully and indulge all her fancies or he might return to his lodge one day and find that in a fit of pique at some real or imagined wrong she had ridden back to her home village; or, as sometimes happened, she had been won and carried off by some other trapper.

In general, Indian women who followed the fortunes of white hunters and traders were noted for loyalty and affection, virtues not always shared by their men. Many mountaineers had no scruple about deserting their women on slight pretext or none at all, just "whenever the fancy takes them to change their harems." Some, on leaving the mountains permanently, simply abandoned their wives and children without a thought.

However, there were many white men in the Rockies who were genuinely attached to their Indian wives. Some took them to the settlements to legalize the marriage with a church or civil ceremony, and if there were children, to have them baptized. Many were concerned about these children's education and placed them in mission schools, or boarding schools in the States. And if these men ever returned finally to civilization they were not ashamed to bring their families with them.

Of all frontier callings, the trapper's, especially the freeman's, was the most perilous. He was subject to ambush as he worked, ate, smoked by his campfire, or slept. For this reason a number of freemen would sometimes band together when in dangerous territory. One of them told about Indians disguised in white wolf skins gliding noiselessly into their camp at night: "Two of the wolves were shot in the head and proved to be Bannocks. Other wolves were seen departing."

But it was not only Indians against whom he must be on guard. The successful trapper was sometimes murdered for his catch by a fellow hunter. Indians were always blamed for the disappearance, and revenge taken by killing the first Indian who was met. Since mountain men also scalped—raising or lifting hair, they called it—it was not always easy to tell whether a murdered man was the victim of white or Indian—an intentionally equivocal act on the part of the killer.

However, the Indian menace was genuine. The Blackfeet and allied tribes were implacable. But, as one man wrote in 1834, "this determined hostility does not originate solely in savage malignity, or an abstract thirst for the blood of white men; it is fomented and kept alive from year to year by incessant provocatives on the part of white hunters, trappers, and traders, who are at best but intruders in the rightful domains of the red man. Many a night have I sat at the campfire and listened to a recital of bloody and ferocious scenes, in which the narrators were the actors, and the poor Indian the victims, and I have felt my blood tingle with shame, and boil with indignation, to hear the diabolical acts applauded by those for whose amusement they were related." He felt these tales were responsible for turning many a man into a murderer and thief, inciting him to kill the first solitary Indian trapper he met and rob him of his packs of beaver fur.

Still, there were many mountain men who maintained they had turned against the Indians only after having seen a comrade hacked to pieces, and his heart, liver, and bowels torn out and flung to waiting dogs.

Wherever the fault lay, the necessity existed for the white trapper to try to outwit his enemies. "His nerves must be ever in a state of tension, and his mind ever present to his call," one of them wrote. As a result, he became a master of woodcraft and guerilla warfare. His "eagle eye sweeps round the country, and in an instant detects any foreign appearance. A turned leaf, a blade of grass pressed down, the uneasiness of wild animals, the flight of birds, are all paragraphs to him written in nature's legible hand and plainest language."

Many mountain men became so skilled in this type of detection they could recognize an Indian's tribe by the imprint of his moccasins, and, happening on the trail of a party, could tell how many were in it, whether it was a war party or had squaws and children along, and how many days ago it had passed.

"There are in the mountains many hunters who have become so practiced in this species of discernment as to be acknowledged by Indians as equal to themselves; though the Indians, in this respect are inferior to none," observed a trapper.

This need for constant vigilance gave the American mountaineer an air of solemnity; to some he appeared taciturn, gloomy, and brooding, even. It also kept him strictly sober in the field. Only in groups could he relax his watchfulness somewhat, and only at rendezvous did he dare allow himself complete abandon.

Although the death rate was high among trappers, some managed to attain a respectable age by practicing extreme caution with regard to Indian *sign*. Bill Williams was one of these. He spent forty years in the mountains, growing "as tough as the parfleche soles of his moccasins . . . On occasions when he had been in company with others, and attacked by Indians, Bill invariably fought manfully, with all the coolness that perfect indifference to death or danger could give. . . . His rifle cracked away merrily and never spoke in vain. . . ." But at those times when he saw anything that convinced him there were more Indians about than they could handle, he would say:

" 'Do 'ee hyar now, boys, thar's sign about? this hos feels like caching;' and without more words, and stoically deaf to remonstrances, he would forthwith proceed to pack his animals, talking the while to an old, crop-eared, raw-boned Nez-Percé pony, his own particular saddle-horse. . . .

" 'Do 'ee hyar, now. This niggur sees sign ahead—he does; he'll be afoot afore long, if he don't keep his eye skinned—*he* will. Injuns is all about, they ar'; Blackfoot at that. Can't come round this child—they can't, wagh!' "

He would then ride off and nothing was seen or heard of him again for months. But come rendezvous and there was Old Bill Williams with "galore beaver," and all his horses safe.

Next to the threat of ambush from Indian or white was the menace of the grizzly bear, *Ursus horribilis*, known to mountain men as Old Ephraim. These were the only animals the trapper considered dangerous.

"They were everywhere—upon the plains, in the valleys, and on the mountains," a hunter wrote. "I have killed as many as five or six in one day."

They were seen most often when wild fruits were ripe, and it was not unusual then to come on as many as a hundred in a day's travels. At these times they usually fed in groups, and at a distance were frequently mistaken for buffalo—until they stood erect. Many a mountaineer in need of meat found himself in the unenviable position of being surrounded by twenty or thirty grizzlies instead of the buffalo he thought he was stalking.

By nature the grizzly was not pugnacious. Once wounded, however, his strength and rage were terrible. He would rush toward the spot where he saw gunsmoke, and as one trapper warned, if the hunter "has not already secured his safety, he will hardly have an opportunity."

The bear attacked from a standing position, first with a blow of the forepaw, then by snapping and tearing with teeth and claws. When it is remembered that a weight of five hundred pounds was common, and that the average grizzly measured six feet from nose to tail, but that nine feet was not unusual, there is small wonder the Indian and mountain man regarded him as formidable. Still, rare was the white hunter who could resist the temptation to kill a grizzly, and many lost their lives in the attempt.

When on his way to the Rockies in 1823, Jedediah Smith was mangled by a grizzly but not killed. Three ribs were broken and one ear torn away with a part of his scalp. In this case Smith roused the bear while pushing his way on foot through a brushy river bottom. The startled animal ran into the midst of the cavalcade, throwing it into confusion, then turned again toward cover. Smith, in attempting to reach open ground where he could see to take aim, broke through the thicket just as the bear was entering it. There was no time to raise his rifle before the animal attacked. Only quick action on the part of some of his men saved him from death. After Smith's wounds were dressed, the grizzly was skinned, and Jedediah later took the hide home with him to St. Louis.

In Pierre's Hole especially, it was rattler-snakes, as he called them, of which the trapper must be wary. Once when caught in a violent thunderstorm there, Joe Meek took cover under a rock shelf, and then watched with horror as hundreds of rattlers—the ground was "literally alive with them," he insisted—sought their holes in this same cliff. The trapper, who never quailed before a grizzly, was completely unnerved by the rattler's buzz, and nothing was more abhorrent than the thought that one or more might crawl in to share his bed. To prevent this, each man before going to sleep at night encircled his buffalo robe with a hair rope.

During the rendezvous of 1833 twelve men were bitten by a rabid wolf that attacked during the night. One man, George Holmes of New York, young and well educated, who had joined the fur brigade for adventure, was badly bitten about the face and ears while he slept.

When the rendezvous broke up, his party started for the Bighorn valley, and were not many days on the way before Holmes began acting strangely. Whenever he came to a stream he would refuse to cross and had to be covered with a blanket and led over; two men were always ordered to stay with him until the fit had passed. Finally tiring of this duty, they one day left him to come on by himself. When he did not appear, the leader sent back for him, but he was nowhere to be found. His clothing, which he had torn off in his madness, lay scattered over the ground. He had run naked into the wilderness and was never seen again. Nearly all those who were bitten that night died horribly during the next few months.

"We little know how much wildness there is in us," wrote John Muir. "Only a few generations separate us from our grandfathers that were savage as wolves. This is the secret of our love for the hunt. Savageness is natural, civilization is strained and unnatural." Turned loose, and given a few centuries, he felt, we would return to "killing and bloody barbarism."

It took but a short time for that wildness to assert itself in the mountain man, and he shortly earned the reputation for being bloodthirsty. Men whose lives are constantly endangered come to place little value on life itself and will destroy it as freely as they expose their own. As the mountaineer saw it, life was reduced to a question of mine or yours, and he acted accordingly.

To the outsider he seemed a paradoxical composition of goodness and evil. Beyond the savagery he was found to be steadfast in friendship, kind and obliging, frank and open in his manners, and generous in his disposition. "Sit and eat" was the never-failing invitation to strangers with whom he was ready to share his last morsel. This openhandedness, without thought of repayment, extended to everything he owned.

"Take nothing which does not belong to you without the owner's consent," was the prevailing rule in the mountains, an old trapper wrote. Any man who failed to live by it "would be fined about all he possessed, besides being ostracized. Far better to be dead than in that condition. He would never be allowed in a trapper's camp. His act would in a short time be known throughout all the camps."

In the fraternity a man's word was respected. In business dealings trappers and traders trusted one another and written agreements were rarely required.

Those who were there insist that crimes were fewer than in places where there was established law, and punishment more just and swift. Disputes between individuals were usually settled by some form of duel. Rifles at twenty paces were popular. In this case "the fall of one or the other combatant is certain, or as sometimes happens, both fall to the word 'fire.' "

Still, the solitary, roving life favored the criminal, and the culprit's trail was often lost in the rugged high country. David Jackson's Hole, with its secret canyons leading through the Tetons, remained for years a favorite hiding place for fugitives.

During the long winter encampment, or around the night fire when on the trail, men who had no schooling often taught themselves to read and write. Joe Meek was one of them. He remembered that there was reading aloud nights for the benefit of those who were not literate. Shakespeare, Scott, and Byron were favorite authors in the mountains. Another trapper told about the frequent debates that were held in the winter, and of how much he and his fellows learned in what they called the Rocky Mountain College.

Storytelling was another popular winter pastime. Many related their own hand-to-hand encounters and narrow escapes with Indians and grizzly bears, or the adventures of such noted mountain men as Old Bill Williams, Joe Walker, Rube Herring, and Moses (Black) Harris. Throughout the telling there was usually a running commentary from the listeners: "He had true grit in *him!*"; "he was *some*, now!"; or, "he'd take the gristle off a darned painter's tail—wagh!", and so on.

Others told stories of a marvelous cast that struck awe and silence in the audience—accounts of natural phenomena unexplained, places that were "bad medicine," and encounters with the devil whose works were manifest throughout the Rockies.

There was the November night—the year Joe Walker went to California—when the sky was covered thick with flaming meteors. Some exploded in midair, others were dashed to pieces on the ground, so terrifying the party's horses that they tried to stampede. Men were frightened, too, thinking the world's end had come.

Then there were those strange, unnatural echoes at that inlet on Jackson Lake, when the report of a man's gun sounded like "condensed thunder" and charged up the "great glacier channel in a hollow deep growl giving consecutive reports which bounded from cliff to cliff," reechoed far up the canyon, then came back like the rattle of musketry. If several men shouted in chorus, they were answered by "a hoarse mob of voices in accumulating thousands from the great gorge." These, on retreating, "called to each other and back at us till the multiplied voices mingled in a harsh jargon of weird and wild receding . . . sound, ending in a long moaning sigh and a rustle as of falling leaves" among the Teton spires.

To many mountain men those steaming, bubbling springs along the Snake River, in the Tetons west, and in Yellowstone country, which smelled strongly of brimstone, were the vents of hell where the devil and his helpers surfaced for fresh air. Most trappers disliked camping near them, and some, like Old Bill Williams, didn't relish going into areas where they were concentrated, for they had a reputation of being bad medicine. But there were times when certain mountaineers, hounded by persistent misfortune, visited some spring secretly to "make medicine" and rid themselves of those imps who dogged their trail.

Whenever John Hatcher was present, he was always asked to tell about the time he met two "black critturs . . . with tails, an' red coats (Injun cloth, like that traded to the Navyhoes), edged with shiny white stuff, an' brass buttons," who escorted him to hell, where the devil, "a kind-lookin', smallish old gentleman, with a black coat an' briches, an' a bright, cute face, an' gold spectacles," greeted him cordially, offered him a chair, and gave him a cigar.

But John wasn't comfortable on that chair. "I squared myself on it, but a ten-pronged buck wasn't done sucking, when I last sot on a cheer, an' I squirmed awhile, oneasy as a gut-shot coyote. I jumps up an' tells the old gentleman them sort of 'state fixins' didn't suit this beaver, an' he prefers the floor."

After they had finished their cigars the devil took him on a tour of his domain, and Hatcher had much to tell about what he saw and which old comrades he met, and how they were getting on. It was a tale that took half the night to tell.

Nearly every mountaineer had seen the Phantom Horse somewhere, at some time, and had something to tell about him. He was milk white in color, of perfect form and marvelous beauty. In speed, endurance, fire, and canniness he was unmatched by any horse known. He was always alone—too fine, too proud to keep company with other wild horses, they said. Large sums had been offered for his capture, but he "tired down not less than three race nags, sent expressly to catch him." He was never known to gallop or trot, but could "pace his mile in less than two minutes, and . . . keep up this pace until he had tired down everything sent in pursuit." He was of course never caught, and continued to roam the prairies for years, to be seen fleetingly, now here now there, and then vanish again.

But of all the natural wonders encountered in the Tetons, in Yellowstone country, and in other Rocky Mountain areas, fossils and petrifactions were the most marvelous. To the trapper there seemed to be a kind of magic in giant trees and tiny creatures from long ago being turned to stone, and his imagination was fired. Jim Bridger told many stories about a mountain where every living thing was petrified, cursed by a great Crow medicine man, he said; and of a prairie where the bushes and trees bore precious jewels instead of fruits.

Bridger's tales have often been repeated by those who heard him tell them, but never in Jim's words. A young Englishman, who spent a good part of a year with the mountain men, chronicling their way of life and their picturesque and vigorous speech, now extinct, set down a tale of petrifaction as told by Black Harris in a St. Louis tavern.

Harris had just come in from Laramie, after more than three years in the mountains. A woman at the inn opened a conversation with him by saying she had heard he was a great traveler and had been "over a sight of ground."

"A sight, marm, this coon's gone over . . . I've trapped beaver on Platte and Arkansa, and away up on Missoura and Yaller Stone; I've trapped on Columbia, on Lewis Fork, and Green River . . . I've trapped in heav'n, in airth, and h———; and scalp my old head, marm, but I've seen a putrified forest."

"La, Mister Harris, a what?"

"A putrified forest, marm, as sure as my rifle's got hindsights, and *she* shoots center. I was out on the Black Hills, Bill Sublette knows the time—the year it rained fire—and every body knows when that was. If thar wasn't cold doins about that time, this child wouldn't say so. The snow was about fifty foot deep, and the bufler lay dead on the ground like bees after a beein'; not whar we was tho', for *thar* was no bufler, and no meat, and me and my band had been livin' on our moccasins (leastwise the parflesh), for six weeks; and poor doins that feedin' is, marm, as you'll never know. One day we crossed a cañon and over a divide, and got into a peraira, whar was green grass, and green trees, and green leaves on the trees, and birds singing in the green leaves, and this in Febrary, wagh! Our animals was like to die when they see the green grass, and we all sung out, 'hurraw for summer doins.'

" 'Hyar goes for meat,' says I, and I jest ups old Ginger at one of them singing birds, and down come the crittur elegant; its darned head spinning away from the body, but never stops singing, and when I takes up the meat, I finds it stone, wagh! 'Hyar's damp powder and no fire to dry it,' I says, quite skeared.

" 'Fire be dogged,' says old Rube. 'Hyar's a hos as 'll make fire come'; and with that he takes his ax and lets it drive at a cotton wood. Schr-u-k—goes the ax agin the tree, and out comes a bit of the blade as big as my hand. Young Sublette comes up, and he'd been clerking down to the fort on the Platte, so he know'd something. He looks and looks, and scrapes the trees with his butcher knife, and snaps the grass like pipe stems . . .

" 'What's all this boy?' I asks.

" 'Putrefactions,' says he, looking smart, 'putrefactions or I'm a niggur.' "

"La, Mister Harris," says the lady, "putrefactions! why, didn't the leaves, and the trees, and the grass smell badly?"

"Smell badly, marm! . . . would a skunk stink if he was froze to stone? No, marm, this child didn't know what putrefaction was, and young Sublette's varsion wouldn't shine no how, so I chips a piece out of a tree and puts it in my trap-sack, and carries it safe to Laramie. Well, old Captain Stewart, (a clever man was that, though he was an Englishman), he comes along next spring, and a Dutch doctor chap was along too. I shows him the piece I chipped out of the tree, and he called it a putrefaction too; and so, marm, if that wasn't a putrefied peraira, what was it? . . ."

The following morning one of the St. Louis dailies announced the recent discovery of a stand of petrified trees with every twig and leaf perfect. Along the branches sat birds with their beaks open, having been transformed to stone in the midst of a song.

A journalist had also been having his dinner in that tavern.

X
Living Off the Land

Except for supplies of coffee, tea, and sugar bought from the trader at rendezvous or at the occasional post, the mountain man lived exclusively on game, chiefly buffalo, which was most plentiful and the favorite with nearly all. Some rated painter flesh first in "delicacy of flavor, richness of meat, and other good qualities"; while others chose beaver tails, lynx—and dog.

About dog, the Indian breed, there was a sharp division of opinion. To some it tasted like mutton, and for this reason was relished. Others considered the flavor "delicate," and preferred it to "sucking-pig, which it nearly resembles."

One man, however, spoke for many when he said that "whether cooked or barking, a dog was still a dog everywhere." The objection was chiefly one of scruple, as a mountaineer who ate it under the name of terrapin proved. It was delicious until that moment when a companion asked:

"Well, hos! how do you like dogmeat?"

The victim recalled: "A revulsion of opinion, and dogmeat, too, ensued, for I could feel the 'pup' crawling up my throat." But deciding that it would be unwarranted prejudice to stop, he quickly stuffed in another piece, and "ever after remained a stanch defender and admirer of dogmeat."

A large number of his fellows agreed, and for all Indians in the Rockies, except Shoshonis, dog was choice eating.

"Nothing comes amiss to the mountaineer," one of them observed, "from buffalo down to rattler, including every quadruped that runs, fowl that flies, and every reptile that creeps."

"Meat's meat" was a common saying in the mountains.

One man felt that this variety of fare "would excite the envy of the most fastidious gastronome. From the 25th of August to the 10th of September . . . we killed to supply our wants, as we journeyed on, three fine buffalo cows and two large bulls, (only to obtain the tongue and marrow bones); two large deer as fat as we could have wished; three goats . . . a bighorn or mountain sheep, two fine grey bears, and a swan—to say nothing of pheasants, fowls, snipe, ducks, and geese. . . ."

Most men drew the line at human flesh. There are records of cannibalism, but these were all instances when desperation drove them to eat those companions who had already died from starvation. There are, however, some grisly tales about certain mountain men suspected of having killed and eaten their comrades.

In these times of famine one mountain man recalled: "I have held my hands in an ant-hill until they were covered with ants, then greedily licked them off." They had a pleasant acid taste. "I have taken the soles off my moccasins, crisped them in the fire and eaten them." And large black crickets: "We used to take a kettle of hot water, catch the crickets, and throw them in, and when they stopped kicking, eat them. That was not what we called *cant tickup ko hanch* (good meat, my friend), but it kept us alive."

Horses and mules were standard fare when there was nothing else. The meat was lean, stringy, and often tough, and the flavor reminded some of stale sweat.

When there was neither food nor water, horses and mules were often bled, about a pint taken from each one. This furnished nourishment and *relief* from thirst—it did not quench it. Men with squeamish stomachs found it hard to drink the blood, and still more difficult to keep it down.

But of all the game of the plains and mountain valleys, buffa-

lo was the mainstay. Its flesh, especially that of what the trapper termed "fat cow," was considered far superior to beef, a superiority he felt was due to the fact that each spring there was a
complete renewal of flesh and fat after the leanness of winter.
From the end of June until September bull meat was "rank and
tough, and almost uneatable, while the cows are in perfection,
and as fat as stall-fed oxen." Not only was their flesh delicious
and nourishing, but men who had gone several days without
food found they could eat "prodigious quantities" without dis-
tress.

"It is true we have nothing but meat and good cold water,
but it is all we desire; we have . . . no dyspepsia, clear heads,
sharp ears, and high spirits, and what more does a man require
to make him happy," a physician traveling into Teton country
with a fur brigade wrote in his journal. "We rise in the morning
with the sun, stir up our fire, and *roast* our breakfast, eating
usually from one to two pounds of meat at a morning meal. At
ten o'clock we lunch, dine at two, sup at five, lunch at eight,
and during the night-watch commonly provide ourselves with
two or three 'hump-ribs' and a marrow bone, to furnish em-
ployment and keep the drowsy god at a distance."

Wrote a trapper: "We . . . live upon it solely, without bread
or vegetables of any kind, and what seems most singular, we
never tire of it." Nor was there any nutritional deficiency from
the all-buffalo diet. In the literature of the Rocky Mountain fur
trade there are no mentions of scurvy which abound in the
writings of men who lived entirely on salt beef and pork.

The buffalo provided a variety of parts that could be broiled,
roasted, baked in ashes, or stewed; made into soup, sausage, or
dumplings; dried, smoked, or eaten raw. In times of scarcity
everything was used—even the blood, which was boiled with
marrow to make a thick soup.

The mountaineer was indebted to the Indian for his knowledge of how best to prepare and eat the buffalo parts. He
learned from him that the liver was most delicious when eaten
raw and warm from the freshly killed animal. Then a little gall
was sprinkled over it, "by way of relish," and the result tasted
very much like a raw oyster.

He learned the value of *dépouille* or fleece which was peculiar to the buffalo. "It is a fat substance that lies along the back-

bone, next to the hide, running from the shoulderblade to the last rib, and is . . . from seven to eleven inches broad, tapering to a feather edge on the lower side," one trapper described it. "It will weigh from five to eleven pounds, according to the size of the animal." Before being eaten fresh it was "dipped in hot grease for half a minute." The provident hung it inside the lodge to smoke for twelve hours. Then it would keep indefinitely and was used as a substitute for bread, "but is superior to any bread that was ever made. It is eaten with the lean and dry meat, and is tender and sweet and very nourishing. . . ." Indians going on the warpath always took fleece with them.

He also learned that the intestines, or *boudins*, were not to be discarded. "On slaughtering a fat cow," says a mountaineer, "the hunter carefully lays by as a tid-bit for himself, the 'boudins' . . . which are prepared by being inverted and partially cleaned (this, however, is not thought indispensable)," tied at either end to prevent the loss of fat as it liquifies, then laid over the embers to brown. When pronounced done, the sundry yards were "taken off the hot coals, puffed up with the heat and fat, the steam escaping from little punctures, and coiled on the ground or a not particularly clean saddle blanket, looking for all the world like a dead snake. . . . The fortunate owner shouts 'hyar's the doins, and hyar's the coon as savvys "poor bull" from "fat cow"; freeze into it, boys!' and all fall to, with ready knives. . . ."

Another method of preparing *boudins* was to stuff them, after cleaning, with strips of tenderloin seasoned with salt and pepper. The whole was then cut and tied like small sausage, skewered with sticks, and set to roast before the fire.

One trapper described a kind of "French dumpling," made from minced buffalo meat, rolled into little balls and covered with dough, then fried in marrow.

French Creoles were noted for their ability to live for long periods on the traditional Hudson's Bay Company ration of a rabbit track and a cartridge, and were equally renowned for being able to devour incredible quantities of meat at a meal. American mountain men were close rivals. One of them recalled a time when after a day or more of empty stomachs, there had been a successful buffalo hunt, and his party had "throw'd the meat cold" (indulged their appetites).

At first in their ravenousness they ate everything raw. Once the initial keen edge of hunger was dulled, and spitted roasts began to be done, they ate more slowly and with greater relish. When rib after rib of tender hump had been picked clean and the bones flung to waiting wolves; when piece after piece of juicy and delicate fleece and yards of well-browned boudins had been downed, when every man, sure that nothing of super excellence remained, was wiping the greasy knife that had done such good service, a hunter was seen chuckling to himself as he raked the deep ashes of the fire and drew out a pair of tongues "so admirably baked, so soft, so sweet, and of such exquisite flavor" no man could resist. Knives were quickly put to work again, and the feasting continued well into the night.

One of the party remarked that after having eaten nearly his weight in meat he felt as comfortable as if he had "lightly supped on strawberries and cream."

This dependence on game added yet another element of uncertainty to the mountain man's existence. Since he could never rely on buffalo, elk, and deer being in a certain place at a particular time, he fluctuated constantly between plenty and want. Eating to excess on "fat cow" one week, he would be reduced to boiling his parfleche soles the next. This might have been easily avoided if he had looked to the future, as the Indians did, and smoked or dried meat when it was abundant. Of, if he had paid some attention to migratory patterns and their close connection with weather, water, and browse, the supply of meat would have been more constant. Instead, he seems to have preferred simply to take his chances. Providence was never a strong point with the mountaineer.

He also looked to the land for needs beyond food. As a tobacco substitute he used the dry leaves or bark of manzanita, *Arctostaphylos uva-ursi*, or the inner bark of red-osier dogwood, *Cornus stolonifera*, which he called by the Indian name *kinnikinnick*. These were either mixed together or smoked separately according to taste. The bark was prepared for smoking by being scraped off in thin, curly flakes from the shrubs, crisped before the fire, then pulverized between the palms and stored in leather pouches. Those unused to smoking dogwood alone found it had a highly narcotic effect.

For cuts and wounds, salve made from bear fat, or beaver oil and castoreum, was applied after the parts had been soaked in salted water. For coughs, the leaves of gumweed, *Grindelia squarrosa*, were chewed as an expectorant. The botanist John Bradbury learned that the voyageurs drank a decoction of *Rudbeckia purpurea* or *Houstinia longifolia* roots as cure for "the Venereal." Those in search of relief for an "irritated or ulcerated stomach" found nothing better than buffalo-gall bitters. One-fourth of a gill of gall was mixed with a pint of water. "You will then have before you," writes a trapper, "a wholesome and exhilarating drink. . . . Upon the whole system its effects are beneficial."

"A handful of beaver fur" was used to stanch the flow of blood. Fieldmint, crushed, was rubbed on the face and hands to discourage the attacks of mosquitoes and black gnats.

For rattlesnake bites, the warm flesh of the freshly killed snake was laid over the wound to draw out the poison. Whiskey used externally (but far more often internally) was considered an excellent antidote. Many trappers, however, put their greatest faith in gunpowder. Then the puncture was "slightly creased above and below, and a small portion of powder was burnt upon it four or five times in succession, which completely destroyed the effects of the poison," one of them reported. This same treatment was used successfully on their horses.

For some sicknesses and accidents nature was allowed to take its course. For embedded arrowheads and bullets, for shattered bones, and for gangrene, the mountain man was forced to rely on his own crude ministrations or those of his comrades.

After Jedediah Smith was attacked by the grizzly, his men were at a loss as to what should be done, and Smith had to direct them himself. He told someone to get water and wash the wounds. Then he spoke to James Clyman, asking him to get a needle and thread and sew up the cuts around his head. Clyman found that the bear had taken Smith's head "in his capacious mouth close to his left eye on one side and clos to his right ear on the other and laid the skull bare to near the crown of the head leaving a white streak whare his teeth passed one of his ears was torn from his head . . . after stitching all the other wounds in the best way I was capabl and according to the captains directions the ear being the last I told him I could do nothing for his Eare O you must try to stich up some way or other said he then I put in my needle stiching it through and through and over and over laying the lacerated parts together as nice as I could with my hands. . . ."

When Clyman had finished, Smith was able to mount his horse and ride a mile to camp. The ear adhered and the other injuries healed rapidly. As Jim Bridger once observed: "In the mountains the meat never spoils." This now classic reply was given someone who asked Jim whether the iron arrowhead he had embedded in his shoulder for three years, "had been long suppurating."

XI
Saturnalia in the Tetons

They came into Pierre's Hole from all directions, singly and in groups of two to ten, free trappers and company men. They came from the Three Forks region, Yellowstone, Bighorn, Bear, and Green River country, and over the Tetons from Jackson Hole. Some came with many packs of beaver, others came with few, and more than one came empty-handed and afoot, having lost both animals and peltry to theft along the way. Those who had squaws brought them, dressed in all their finery, dazzling in reds, blues, and greens, and tinkling with hawk's bells and thimbles.

Some of the most noted trappers and traders in the mountains—Smith, the Sublette brothers, Jackson, Williams, Carson, Bridger, Walker, Fitzpatrick, Herring, Meek, and Harris— were soon gathered in that grassy, well-watered valley, teeming with game. In 1832 merchant Nathaniel Wyeth, and his little band of New England colonists bound for the Pacific Coast, were there, as was Baptiste Charbonneau.

And Indians: Shoshonis, Bannocks, Flatheads, and Nez Percés, as many as three thousand, come in by villages to trade furs and horses. Chiefs, medicine men, warriors, women, chil-

103

dren, and dogs—hundreds of dogs, eternally famished, who raided white men's camps to devour everything within reach, "even to the bull-hide thongs with which we fastened our horses," recalled one trapper. "We were compelled to keep guard by turns or risk the entire loss of our baggage." Even so, they made off with over forty dollars' worth of furs from one man's pack, and a Frenchman insisted that "the scoundrelly dogs"—*sacré*—had eaten up his axe.

Each rival company tried to reach rendezvous ahead of the others, for the first partisan to open his packs of tempting trade goods and supplies of coffee, sugar, tea, chocolate, tobacco, liquor, guns, blankets, and other wares had the best chance of getting the greatest number of choice furs from Indians and free trappers. The caravans usually started from Independence, Missouri, the "prairie port," as soon as the plains greened. After about a month of travel, they arrived at the appointed meeting place. In addition to supplies they brought the long-awaited mail, newspapers, and magazines from the States.

Pierre's Hole was shortly teeming with men and animals and bustling with activity. A settlement had risen as if by magic. Hundreds of hide tipis, brush bowers, and canvas tents were scattered over the valley, and immense herds of grazing horses and mules. The smoke of countless cooking fires, driven by the prevailing wind, veiled the Teton foothills.

"We are now lying at rendezvous," a newcomer to the mountains reported; "our camp is crowded with . . . visitors. The principal of these are Indians . . . who come with the furs and peltries . . . they have been collecting . . . to trade for ammunition, trinkets, and 'fire water.'" In addition there were "white men, French-Canadians, half-breeds, &c., their color nearly as dark, and their manners wholly as wild, as the Indians with whom they . . . associate. These people, with their obstreperous mirth, their whooping, and howling, and quarrelling . . . the mounted Indians, who are constantly dashing into and through our camp, yelling like fiends, the barking and baying of savage wolf-dogs, and the incessant crackling of rifles and carbines, render our camp a perfect bedlam."

By this time traders had opened their bales of goods, set up their tent saloons, and broached the casks of rum, and the flat kegs of raw alcohol from Turley's distillery, a "fiery spirit" known to New England mountain men as "O be joyful." A spree of buying ensued—it was "an absolute mania," one trader remembered. Everyone, white and red, was engaged in bartering, haggling, and cheating.

"The beaver went briskly, six dollars being the price paid per lb. in goods,—for money is seldom given in the mountain market, where 'beaver' is cash. . . . In a short time peltries of every description had changed hands."

Free trappers traded their fur for supplies, goods and trinkets for their wives and women—and drink. Company men charged their purchases against their wages. In these transactions the company's gross profit was reckoned at two thousand percent over the original cost. Men, tempted to buy beyond their means, were soon deeply in debt to the trader or the company.

Not realizing the value of their furs, many Indians exchanged them at great disadvantage. Unscrupulous traders saw to it that they drank until they could no longer drive any kind of bargain, and were ready to give up everything for another cup of liquor. As the Indian's senses became fuddled, the trader would begin to dilute the drinks more and more until he was finally selling him plain water.

Meanwhile, as a trapper remembered, men resorted to every expedient to pass away their time. They played cards, raced their horses, wrestled, and practiced target shooting. The excitement of every activity was heightened by drink, and the gathering shortly turned into "one continued scene of drunkenness . . . brawling, and fighting." Some men became so drunk "their senses fled them entirely, and they were therefore harmless." But most were just drunk enough to be quarrelsome and aggressive. "We had 'gouging,' biting, fisticuffing, and 'stamping' in the most 'scientific' perfection; some even fired their guns and pistols at each other, but these weapons were mostly harmless in the unsteady hands which employed them."

When they staggered into line for target shooting, sober men (and there were some) threw themselves on their faces to avoid the bullets that went "careering through camp."

Gamblers sat cross-legged around the fires, with a blanket spread before them, playing poker, euchre, and seven-up, the popular mountain games. The stakes were beaver, "and when the fur is gone, their horses, mules, rifles, and shirts, hunting-packs, and *breeches* are staked. Daring gamblers make the rounds of camp, challenging each other to play for the trapper's highest stake,—his horse, his squaw . . . and, as once happened, his scalp."

"There goes hos and beaver!" was said whenever a loss was large; "and, sooner or later 'hos and beaver' invariably find their way into the insatiable pockets of the traders. A trapper often squanders the produce of his hunt, amounting to hundreds of dollars, in a couple of hours."

Competition for the attentions of Indian women caused many a quarrel at rendezvous. Kit Carson's noted duel with Shunar, "the great bully of the mountains," came about through rivalry for the same girl. Shunar, full of liquor, picked up his loaded rifle, got on his horse, and rode from camp to camp to challenge "any Frenchman, American, Spaniard, or Dutchman, to fight him single combat." Carson, anxious to settle matters with him, told him if he wished to die, he would accept the challenge. He took up his pistol, swung on his horse, and galloped up to meet him. "Our horses were touching," Carson recalled. He then asked Shunar if he was the one he wanted to shoot.

"He said no, drawing his gun at the same time so he could have a fair shot at me. I was prepared and allowed him to draw. . . . We both fired at the same time, and all present said that but one report was heard. I shot him through the arm and his ball passed my head, cutting my hair and the powder burning my eye, the muzzle . . . being near my head when he fired."

Carson, furious, went for another pistol, and tradition holds that he killed Shunar. In his own account Kit merely states: "During the remainder of our stay in camp we had no more bother with this French bully."

Meanwhile, sober leaders and traders in the rival companies were keeping close watch on one another in attempts to forestall plans and movements for the coming hunt. They hired away the best trappers by promising "inflation" wages; and they contrived to supplant their competitors in the goodwill and custom of those Indians at rendezvous. Just as soon as they learned where a rival was planning to work in the season ahead, they tried to beat him to those grounds. If they could not learn his destination, they trailed him secretly.

Only after the liquor kegs ran dry and credit was exhausted did the uproar begin to subside. Then the caravans laden with fur started back to Missouri, and men turned their thoughts to the fall hunt. Parties of company trappers were organized and despatched, and freemen got their equipment together and set out for the beaver grounds.

Most of these men were returning to the wilderness practically impoverished. Many were so deeply in debt it would take them years to pay what they owed. It was a system that kept company men in virtual slavery. Even freemen were but little better off since they had to equip themselves each year at inflated mountain prices. Although the mountain man could have curbed his spending, it was a point of pride and a convention of the fraternity to squander earnings.

A French trapper, who had been in the mountains since his youth, told how at the end of each hunting season he resolved to return home to Canada, and with this in mind always converted his furs into cash. But two weeks at rendezvous never failed to empty his pockets, and now, after twenty years, "he had not even sufficient credit to buy a pound of powder."

XII
Pilgrim's Progress

"A very mild man, and a Christian," one of Jedediah Smith's trappers said of him, "and there were very few of them in the mountains."

"No one who knew him well doubted the sincerity of his piety," observed a friend. It was a very personal kind of religion. He urged members of his family to have faith but had no reputation as a proselytist. Although in the mountains he sometimes quoted from the Bible, he more often cited ancient history. In the fur brigades he was noted for stamina, indifference to privation, and courage. Men who had seen his fearlessness, and his stoic endurance of hunger and thirst, admired and respected him. After he became a partisan there was never any doubt as to who was in command. Some of his men might call him "Old Jed" behind his back, but to his face he was always Captain or Mr. Smith.

Beyond a shrewd business sense and a talent for leadership, Jedediah Smith possessed scientific curiosity that stimulated a desire to explore unknown territory in the West and carefully record his findings and observations.

He first came to notice following a fight with the Arikaras on

June 2, 1823, when he gave a moving prayer for a dying comrade. Afterward, when William Ashley asked for volunteers to carry a request for reinforcements to Andrew Henry's post three hundred miles away, in country that was swarming with hostile tribes, Smith was the first to step forward. With a single companion he pushed through with remarkable speed, gave a succinct account of the battle, spoke of the urgent need for men, then turned back with Henry and the relief party.

Close to six feet two inches tall in his moccasins, Jedediah Strong Smith was lean and muscular, with keen blue eyes, a thatch of brown hair, and a clean-shaven, slender face. His mother, Sally Strong, was a Connecticut woman; his father, also Jedediah, came from New Hampshire and was among the first to follow the tide of emigration into New York State after the close of the American Revolution. There, in the newly founded village of Jericho, he opened a store, and there his son Jedediah was born on January 6, 1799, the sixth of fourteen children.

A family friend, Titus Gordon Vespasian Simons, a physician and scholar, undertook young Jedediah's education. When the doctor gave his pupil a book on the Lewis and Clark expedition, the boy admitted that his imagination was stirred by the descriptions of natural wonders, of Indians and wild animals, and that he was fired with the ambition to be the first to explore those parts of the Far West as yet unseen by white men.

The Smiths had little money, and there was a flock of younger sons to start in life. In order to help, Jedediah cut short his schooling and took a job as clerk on a Great Lakes freighter. Here he was soon meeting traders and trappers from the British fur companies, and since this was a calling that promised both profit and a chance to explore, he decided to join it. He left for St. Louis, the Western fur trade capital, early in 1822, taking his rifle, a few provisions, and his Bible. He could not have reached St. Louis at a better time, for William Ashley was just then recruiting men, and he hired Smith as a hunter.

Two years later he became Ashley's partner, and two years after that, at age twenty-seven, he became senior partner in the largest American company in the fur trade: Smith, Jackson and Sublette.

Under William Ashley the trapping frontier had been pushed

as far west as the Great Salt Lake. The area was still immensely rich in beaver, but Smith and his partners planned to send their hunting parties still farther west. The first step was exploration, and it was decided that while David Jackson and William Sublette stayed in the mountains and trapped with the main company, Smith with a small party would investigate that territory between Salt Lake and the Pacific, and determine not only California's fur potential but the practicability of shipping pelts from one of its ports.

As a result of this decision Smith and his little band became the first white men to cross Utah north to south and west to east; the first to reach California overland from the American frontier; the first to pass over its High Sierra, east, and traverse Nevada; and the first to explore the Pacific slope by land from Lower California to Fort Vancouver. In 1824 Smith opened South Pass to travel. The next year he and his party followed the Hoback River, crossed Jackson Hole, and then passed over the Tetons—the first white men to have done so since the Astorians.

Smith's geographical knowledge of the West soon exceeded that of all his contemporaries and was later incorporated in the Gallatin and Burr maps. As a result, thousands of his countrymen profited from his explorations, and in following the trails he blazed, they would change the course of Western history.

His range of interest is revealed in his report to William Clark, then Superintendent of Indian Affairs. In recounting his first trip to the Pacific Coast, Smith listed for Clark the names of the various Indian tribes, described their appearance and material culture, noted the terrain, the river systems, fertility of the soil, and indigenous plants and animals. He observed that Utah Lake marked the limit of the buffalo's western range. He named rivers and mountains, and sent Clark Indian artifacts and mineral samples.

He was more interested in describing his discoveries and observations than in recounting personal experiences. He therefore only briefly mentioned his long detainment in California by Mexican officials who suspected him of being a military spy. Little was said either about the hardships of the westward passage over the deserts where his entire party nearly perished from lack of water; or of the cold, hunger, and exhaustion endured during the first unsuccessful attempt to cross the Sierra Nevada east by way of the American River canyon. At that time Smith wrote in his journal:

"My horses freezing, my men discouraged . . . I then thought of the vanity of riches & of all those objects that lead men in the perilous paths of adventure. It seems that in times like those men return to reason & make the true estimate of things; they throw by the bauble of ambition, and embrace the solid comforts of domestic life. . . . But a few days of rest make the sailor forget the storm & embark again on the perilous Ocean, & I suppose that like him I would soon become weary of rest."

Regretfully he had then turned back to the valley where he decided to leave his men encamped along a river he called the Appelaminy (thought to be the Stanislaus) to trap and look after the horses and furs, while Smith himself searched for an easier passage over the Sierra and made his way east to the annual rendezvous. Two men, Silas Gobel and Robert Evans, volunteered to go with him.

It took them eight days to make the crossing by another pass, fighting their way through snowdrifts. But the cold was as nothing compared to the heat of the Nevada and Utah deserts where they went as long as two days without water, where all their animals but two died, and Smith and his men ate them to keep alive.

On the afternoon of July 3, 1827, they reached the rendezvous: "My arrival caused considerable bustle in camp, for myself and party had been given up as lost," he wrote. "A small Cannon brought up from St. Louis was loaded and fired for a salute."

Ten days later, his business finished, he was ready to return to California. In his journal he noted that the primary reason for this trip was the relief of the party he had left in California, but admitted that there was also a desire to explore "northwardly" the land lying between the mountains and the sea.

Agreeing to meet his partners two years hence at rendezvous in Teton country, he set out for California with a party of eighteen men, two Indian women (trappers' wives), and a string of pack animals. His plan was to follow the general course of his earlier trail, certain that his familiarity with it would make this trip easier. All went well until he came to cross the Colorado River, where the company was suddenly attacked by a war party of over a hundred Mojave Indians whose tribesmen had up to that moment been helping the mountain men ferry their baggage.

In the one-sided fight that followed, ten of Smith's men, including the faithful Silas Gobel, were killed, the two women were captured, and all the baggage and horses were stolen or destroyed. That was August 1827.

Once in California, there was another long detainment by the Mexican authorities. This time Smith was arrested and put first in what he described as "a dirty hovel which they called a guard house," then in "the Callibozo" at Monterey. After many conferences with the governor who debated whether or not to send Smith to Mexico City for further questioning, he was finally released and ordered to leave the province over the same route by which he had come.

For the sake of appearances, Smith traveled for two days along his old trail, but on the third day, when he was beyond all danger of apprehension, he turned around and went north.

By July 13 of the following year, Smith and his party, which had been enlarged by the addition of those men who were waiting for him at the Appelaminy, reached the Umpqua River (now the Smith) in Oregon. The next morning right after breakfast, Jedediah, as was his habit, set out to look for the day's trail. He took with him an Indian guide and two of his men, John Turner and Richard Leland. They went up the river by canoe, in search of a good place to ford with the horses.

As they were returning, a band of Indians suddenly fired on them. Smith and his party managed to scramble out of the canoe and escape into the thickets. Hearing shouts and gunfire downriver, Smith climbed to the top of a bluff and saw from there that his camp was in the hands of Indians. He made no attempt to go back but took the trail north with Leland and Turner.

"After severe hardships," he stated tersely, the three reached Fort Vancouver in August, surprised to find one of their party there. Arthur Black, who had come in just the night before, was the sole survivor of the raid. He had been cleaning and loading his rifle when the attack came, he said. Three Indians had jumped on him, but he shook them off. Seeing all his comrades struggling on the ground and the raiders stabbing them, he fired into the crowd and then rushed off into the woods, with several Indians in pursuit. Somehow, he succeeded in escaping, he would never know how. He then headed for the coast, so as not to lose his way in the dense forests, but had found nothing to eat there except a few berries. Within a week he was so weakened by starvation he gave himself up to some Indians he met, preferring death at their hands to his sufferings. They proved to be friendly Tillamooks who gave him food, treated him well, and after he had regained strength, guided him to Fort Vancouver.

Dr. John McLoughlin, chief factor at this Hudson's Bay post, "received the unlucky trader and his three surviving men with every mark and expression of kindness," reads an old chronicle. He also sent out a party to retrieve Smith's property. Horses, mules, furs—five hundred and eighty-eight beaver pelts among them—rifles, traps, books, papers, and most important, Smith's journals and those of his clerk, Harrison Rogers, were ultimately recovered. The British company bought the furs and horses for a little over two thousand dollars.

On March 12, 1829, after having spent the fall and winter as Dr. McLoughlin's guests, Smith and Black set off up the Columbia to go east for the rendezvous and to look for David Jackson, who was reported to be wintering in Flathead Indian country. The only clues to Smith's route are found in his brief, third-person report to William Clark, which states that he passed Kettle Falls and Flathead House, a Hudson's Bay post on Clark's Fork of the Columbia, then followed along the Flathead River and met up with Jackson in Kootenai country. From there "he proceeded and joined Mr. W. L. Sublette on the 5th August 1829, at the Tetons on Henry's Fork. . . ."

As soon as Smith reached his camp, Jackson sent off an express (Tom Fitzpatrick) to inform Sublette, then trapping in Jackson Hole, of Jedediah's arrival, and to ask him to cross the Tetons and join them in Pierre's Hole.

The partners met there on August 5, as Smith reported, and there the general rendezvous was held, more riotous than usual, one trapper remembered, because of Smith's safe return. Little was said about those who had not come back.

" 'Poor fellow! out of luck!' was the usual burial rite which the memory of a comrade received. . . . To have weak hearts would be the surest road to defeat in the next dangerous encounter. To keep hearts 'big,' they must be gay, they must not remember the miserable fate of their one-time comrades," Joe Meek explained.

From their encampment along the Wind River that winter Jedediah wrote his brother Ralph that it was in order to help those in need that he faced "every danger—it is for this, that I traverse Mountains covered with eternal Snow . . . that I pass over the Sandy Plains, in heat of Summer, thirsting for water, (and am well pleased if I can find a shade instead of water), where I may cool my overheated Body—it is for this that I go without eating . . . and, most of all, it is for this, that I deprive myself of the privilege of Society & the satisfaction of the Converse of My Friends! . . . "

He enclosed money which he asked Ralph to use first to help their parents; then if Dr. Simons needed anything, he was also to be helped. If any of their friends were "in a distrest Situation," Ralph was to be sure to let him know. "I Shall not forgive you, if you do not let me know you own Situation—be not too modest—," he added.

Ralph was also to find a good school in which to enroll three of their brothers. Here he was to consult Dr. Simons, "as it is my wish to carry them into some of the higher branches of Education."

At the 1830 rendezvous, Smith, Jackson, and Sublette sold their business to Jim Bridger and his partners. When the transfer was completed, Smith left for St. Louis with David Jackson and William Sublette, and a load of beaver fur worth over eighty-four thousand dollars.

As soon as he reached home, Jedediah began to give and loan money generously. He helped his father and gave a sizeable donation to his church. He gave Ralph's wife, who was Dr. Simons' daughter, a silver table service made to his order in New Orleans. He enrolled his brother Ira in Illinois College, and to get capital to launch brothers Peter and Austin in their business careers, he outfitted an expedition with trade goods for Santa Fe.

For himself he bought a farm in Ohio, near Ralph's, a town

house in St. Louis which was also to be a home for Peter and Austin, two servants, and an expensive gold watch with an engraving of George Washington on the case.

Jackson and Sublette, who had formed a new partnership, also decided on a venture to Santa Fe and agreed to look after Smith's interests. Then, late in February, he decided to go with his brothers, mainly to acquaint himself with the Southwest and include this information in the book and atlas he was preparing. He packed up his personal belongings—papers, books, specimens collected on his travels, pelts (the skin of the grizzly that had nearly killed him in 1823 was there), and put them in William Ashley's care. Then he made a will, naming Ashley, his "particular and confidential friend," the executor.

When the Santa Fe-bound party left Lexington that May, there were twenty-two wagons, ten of them belonging to Smith and his brothers, and one the joint property of Jedediah and his two former partners.

The year 1831 had been unusually dry. Between the Arkansas River and the forks of the Cimarron lay a level waste of some sixty-five miles where there were no landmarks to guide the traveler; where shifting sands wiped out the tracks of wagons that had gone before, and a network of buffalo trails led off in every direction. This was the most dreaded part of the route. *La Jornada,* Mexican traders called it, implying it might be the final journey. There were a few springs and water holes known to buffalo, Indian, and experienced traveler, but this was a first trip for the entire party.

Two days passed without water, and horses began dying. On the third day, when death faced them all, several men set off in different directions to hunt for springs while the main party waited. Smith turned south from their trail. With a spyglass Tom Fitzpatrick watched him urge on his staggering mount "until some three miles away he dropped behind a low eminence and disappeared from sight." Mile after mile Smith rode on in the face of "a hot burning wind," letting his horse go where it would. With unerring instinct the animal took him to the banks of the Cimarron. It was no flowing stream, Jed found, but here and there was a deep pool. From the largest of these he watered his horse, and then drank, himself.

In his preoccupation he neglected his usual caution. Just as he was about to mount and take the good news back to the party, he saw about twenty Indians watching him—Comanche hunters, lying in wait for buffalo to come and drink.

Fifteen miles, perhaps, lay between him and help. He knew his jaded horse could not outrun the Indian ponies. There was no recourse but to ride boldly up and parley, hoping to make peace. He told them by signs that there were presents for them if they would return with him to the caravan. But they did not seem to understand and began waving their blankets to frighten his horse.

The alarmed animal wheeled, and as soon as Smith's back was turned, the Indians rushed at him and hurled a spear that pierced his body. Facing them once more, he fired his gun and killed their chief. As he tumbled from his horse, the Comanches fell on him "like so many bloodhounds."

When he did not come back within a reasonable time, the party moved on and fortunately found its way to a water hole. Not until the men had reached Santa Fe did they learn his fate from a party of New Mexican traders who rode in at about the same time. They had with them Jedediah's rifle and brace of silver-mounted pistols, which they had bought from the Comanches. Unfamiliar with the workings of percussion locks, the Indians had readily sold them. The warriors told the traders about the solitary horseman who had come to the river, and how they had watched him water his horse and then drink, himself, before they decided to attack.

"Such my dear brother is the fate of our guardian and protector on this route," Austin Smith wrote Ralph, "but let us not grieve too much, for he is confided to a wise and . . . powerful being—."

XIII
The Battle of Pierre's Hole

July 18, 1832.

"Blackfeet! Blackfeet! a fight in the upper part of the valley!—to arms! to arms!" shouted the express as he came galloping over the fields.

The alarm spread quickly from camp to camp. "In a few minutes the plains were covered with whites and friendly Indians, rushing to the field of battle." As fast as a man could arm and mount, he was off.

The Blackfeet had been more than usually troublesome this year. William Sublette had a sharp encounter on his way to rendezvous and lost a number of horses. Fitzpatrick, who was ahead of the caravan, was ambushed and had to abandon his packhorse, and later the horse he was riding, and escape on foot into the mountains. He wandered five days without food and came into Pierre's Hole "more dead than alive."

Now the rendezvous was breaking up. On July 17 Milton Sublette and partner Henry Fraeb started off toward Pine Creek Pass with fourteen men and free trapper-partisan Alexander Sinclair and his brigade. With them was Oregon-bound colonist Nathaniel Wyeth with eleven New Englanders, novices all, who took this opportunity to secure an experienced escort through Blackfoot country.

The party encamped after covering only eight miles, "thinking that if we had neglected anything we should stand in need of, we would thus discover it." The next morning, "finding all things in order," they broke camp. But just as they were starting off someone noticed two parties of Indians coming out of a pass, about two hundred in number, Wyeth estimated. They had come over the hills from Moose Creek and were then filing out of Fox Creek pass. As the Indians drew nearer they were recognized as Blackfeet (actually kindred Gros Ventres), and it was seen that there were women and children along.

The Indians first saw the trappers as they looked down on the valley from today's Bald Hill, long an Indian observation point. Here stand the ruins of an ancient stone structure with doorway facing east, an Indian fort, mountain men called it, a lookout, although what its real purpose was no one knows.

Noting that the white men's party was small, some forty-two men, says Wyeth, they continued their march, and once they knew they had been discovered, came "yelling and whooping into the plain." One of the leaders was carrying a British flag.

Milton Sublette sent out two men to parley: a half-breed, Antoine Godin, and a Flathead Indian. If his purpose was peace, his choice of emissaries was poor for each man had a wrong to avenge: Godin's father had been murdered by Blackfeet along a river that for years bore his name; while the Flathead considered the Blackfeet responsible for all his people's troubles. As the two men rode across the open grasslands on the south side of present Darby Creek, Antoine asked:

"Is your piece charged?"

"It is."

"Then cock it, and follow me."

The Blackfeet had halted, and one of their chiefs advanced, alone and unarmed, carrying only the calumet of peace. As they met, he held out his hand in friendship, and Antoine took it.

"Fire!" Godin ordered. The Flathead leveled his piece and with its discharge the chief fell dead. Antoine snatched off the

Indian's scarlet robe, and he and his companion galloped back to camp, bullets and arrows whistling after them.

"The women and children were seen flying to the mountains," Wyeth observed. A few women, however, wives of chiefs and warriors, remained, and retired with their men to a thick grove of cottonwoods at the edge of a marshy meadow—a swamp, trappers called it—created by beaver damming Darby Creek. Here the undergrowth was heavy: bush willow, serviceberry, currant, snowberry, small tough aspen, and thorny wild roses. The floor of the wood was carpeted with clumps of violet and strawberry plants, thick grasses, and clover.

The women began at once to dig a trench in the soft earth and put up a breastwork or pen of logs and brush—about fifty feet square, as one trapper remembered, big enough to hold some of their horses—while the warriors kept the mountain men at bay with "a most destructive fire." Meanwhile, Milton Sublette sent off the express for reinforcements.

By the time the men from the rendezvous encampment began to arrive, the Blackfeet were already entrenched. Although the trappers immediately opened fire, it proved ineffective since the enclosure was so well concealed by underbrush in the depth of the grove. All they could do was shoot at random and hope each bullet would find a mark.

As soon as William Sublette came up he proposed that they push into the thicket and storm the fort. It was not a popular suggestion; even his Indian allies demurred, pointing out that the Blackfeet had the advantage of being able to sight their opponents as they broke through, and pick them off.

Sublette announced that he was going to lead the way, and expected the others to follow. His friend and partner Robert Campbell agreed to go with him. Before starting into the wood they made verbal wills, each appointing the other executor. Partisan Alexander Sinclair then decided to join them. The three pressed forward, crawling on hands and knees, single file, taking the lead by turns, and parting each bush slowly, cautiously, hoping to escape the vigilant eyes of hidden marksmen.

Those who had stood back began entering the swamp. It was then "every man for himself and God for us all!"—the mountain man's motto when he went into an Indian fight.

Still advancing slowly, some twenty yards at a time, the leaders at length reached a small clearing through which they could see the fort—a simple affair, screened with robes, blankets, and leather tipi covers.

All at once some slight movement betrayed them. A rifle cracked, and Alexander Sinclair, then in the lead, was shot through the body, a mortal wound.

"Take me to my brother," he said to Robert Campbell, as he fell. They carried him back to Pruett Sinclair who was in the rear.

William Sublette now took the lead, and while observing the breastwork carefully, noticed a Blackfoot peering at him through a crack. He took aim, and shot the Indian through the head. As he was reloading, he called Campbell's attention to the opening, telling him to watch it and he would soon "have a fair chance for a shot."

At that moment a ball struck Sublette in the shoulder and spun him partly around. His first thought was to test the arm to see whether it was broken. He found he could move it and was about to turn back to the work at hand when he became faint and slipped to the ground. Campbell lifted him up and carried him out of the wood.

The fire became brisker as more trappers penetrated swamp and thickets. But in hunting for the fort they became scattered, and a deadly crossfire took place. Nathaniel Wyeth and a party of Nez Percé—he ordered his greenhorns to stay in camp—entered from the northwest while Sublette's followers came in on the opposite side. Men began falling on both quarters, victims of their own fire.

The attack was continued all day with no perceptible results, and no offer of surrender on the part of the Blackfeet who were by then overwhelmingly outnumbered. It was at length decided to drive them out by setting fire to the wood, and brush and logs were gathered and stacked. But just before the torch was applied, the Blackfeet "commenced the most tremendous yells and shouts of triumph, and menaces of defiance," and one of their warriors spoke:

"You may burn us in our fort; but stay by our ashes, and you who are so hungry for fighting will soon have enough. There are four hundred lodges of our brethren at hand. They will soon be here—their arms are strong—their hearts are big—they will avenge us."

An Indian ally who understood Blackfoot translated it into his own tongue, and it was then rendered into English by a French interpreter. By the time the message spread from man to man it became so garbled the Blackfoot was reported as saying that the four hundred lodges were attacking the camps at the rendezvous site where some men had been left as guard.

All thoughts of setting the grove afire were abandoned. A party was quickly appointed to watch the fort, by this time silent, while the rest "galloped in hot haste to the rescue of the main camp." As darkness fell, the trappers at the battle site withdrew from the woods.

When it was found that the main camp was safe, "the rage of some was unbounded, and approached to madness" at what was considered a ruse on the part of the Blackfeet.

In the morning the trappers returned to the battleground and began advancing cautiously on the fort. They were unopposed, and when they reached it, found it occupied only by the dead. To Wyeth, the novice Indian fighter, "it was a sickening scene of confusion and Bloodshed."

The Blackfeet had withdrawn in the night, taking with them their wounded and some of their dead. The bodies of ten Indians lay inside the breastwork, and seven more in the brush close by; they later admitted to losing twenty-six.

"They must have left the fort in great haste for we found 42 head of horses, together with Fitzpatrick's which they had taken on the mountain." There was also a quantity of baggage that included hides and packs of furs.

The number of casualties among the mountaineers varies with each participant's account, but was probably not more than six killed and eight seriously wounded. Among the allied Indians sixteen were reported killed and six wounded, although these numbers differ, too.

One Indian ally among the dead was the venerable Horn Chief, a noted Shoshoni warrior. The moon was his supernatural guardian, and he received his instructions from her through dreams and visions. He had been told in one vision that he could not be killed by any object made of metal—only by horn.

A trapper who had observed the Horn Chief in many battles

wrote that, mounted on "an uncommonly fleet bay horse . . . he always rushed headlong upon his enemies without fear of death, and rendered himself so terrible to them by his prowess that his presence alone was often sufficient to put them to flight . . .

"He was a man of middle stature, of severe and dignified mien"; his face was "deeply marked by the wrinkles of age and thought," and his long hair was gray. He wore "a curious cap or crown, made of the stuffed skin of an antelope's head, with the ears and horn still attached, which gave him a bold, commanding, and somewhat ferocious appearance."

There are two versions of his death: One states that he was shot through the heart, not, his people said, by a bullet or arrow, but by some missile made of horn. The other account reports that he was hit by a spent ball, that he vomited blood, and died soon after, but that on examination of the body, his skin was found to be nowhere broken—proof that he was invulnerable to metal.

That day, the mountaineers and their red allies returned to the main camp near Teton Creek "to recruit the wounded and bury the dead," as Wyeth wrote. The wounded were attended by his brother, Dr. Jacob Wyeth, a Harvard graduate and physician; the dead were "buried in the Indian stile: which is by digging a hole in the ground, wrapping a blanket or skin round the body . . . placing it in the hole, and covering it with poles and earth."

By the twenty-fourth there was still no sign of the four hundred Blackfoot lodges, and Milton Sublette considered it safe to start on his way again. When the party came to the cottonwoods where the fighting had been, they stopped to look at the fort.

"The din of arms was now changed into the noise of the vulture and the howling of masterless dogs," reads Wyeth's journal. "The stench was extreme. . . . I soon retired from this scene of disgusting butchery."

William Sublette's wound was to keep him at Pierre's Hole several days more. Seven men who were going to St. Louis with him began chafing at the delay and decided to start off in advance under the leadership of Alfred K. Stephens, a partisan from St. Louis. In the group were young Joseph More of Boston and William Nudd, both of whom had been members of Wyeth's band, but having become disenchanted with the scheme for colonizing Oregon they had voted to return home. There were, in addition, John Foy, one of Sinclair's free trappers, and, it was said, two grandsons of Daniel Boone.

Passage of the Tetons was made safely, but while the party was riding through the lower part of Jackson Hole, they were attacked by some thirty Blackfeet "who lay in ambush about twenty yards from them, [and] suddenly sprang up and fired." More's horse wheeled in fright and threw him. He started to scramble up a bank but became panic-stricken and stood as if rooted to the ground. The Indians came up and shot him through the head.

His companions had galloped off at the first alarm, but Stephens and Nudd, halfway up the hill, stopped to look back, and seeing More's plight, turned around to help him.

On the night of July 27, a trapper in Pierre's Hole wrote in his diary: "This evening five of the seven men who departed for St. Louis, three days since, returned, and informed us that they were attacked yesterday by a party of Indians in Jackson's Hole, and that two of their number . . . were killed. The survivors saved themselves by flight, but one of them was wounded in the thigh." This was Alfred Stephens. John Foy was the second man killed.

Three days later Robert Campbell and William Sublette (his arm still in a sling) started for St. Louis with sixty men and the season's furs—eighty thousand dollars worth. During that day's march Stephens died "from mortification . . . in the wounded leg." He was buried "on the southeastern extremity of Pierre's Hole," in the shadow of the Tetons.

On August 4, after having crossed the Range and forded the Snake River in Jackson Hole, Sublette's party came on the four hundred lodges of Blackfeet of whose approach they had been warned. The Indians made no attempt to interfere with the caravan's passage.

That September Washington Irving met Sublette's company near Lexington, Missouri. The cavalcade, which stretched in single file for nearly a mile, was just moving through "a skirt of woodland."

"The mountaineers in their rude hunting dresses, armed

with rifles and roughly mounted . . . leading their pack-horses down a hill of the forest looked like banditti returning with plunder," he thought. He saw that "on top of some of the packs were perched several half-breed children, perfect little imps, with wild black eyes glaring from among elf locks" —trapper's children, "pledges of love from their squaw spouses in the wilderness."

One bright fall day some two years later, a band of Blackfeet appeared on the banks of the Portneuf River opposite Fort Hall, the trading post Nathaniel Wyeth had established. Their leader was a white man named Bird, "a tall strong man, with a brown complexion, and thick black hair"—a man of "good education." He was a former Hudson's Bay Company trapper who had been captured by the Blackfeet several years before and had elected to stay with the Indians. He had learned their language, married one of their women, and become an influential chief and leader of war parties.

Antoine Godin, whose act of vengeance had brought on the Battle of Pierre's Hole, was now working for Wyeth. Bird, seeing him at some task on the riverbank near the fort, called to him to come over: He had beaver to trade, he said. Godin crossed in a canoe.

The Blackfeet were seated in a circle on the shore, ready to smoke the calumet with him. Godin sat with them, and when it came his turn to take the pipe, Bird gave a sudden signal, and a volley was fired into Antoine's back. While he was yet alive Bird tore off his scalp and cut in large letters on his forehead N.J.W., Wyeth's initials.

He then "hallooed to the fort people, telling them to bury the carcass if they wished," and mounting his horse galloped off with his party.

The tragedy of revenge was complete.

XIV
Sacajawea's Son

Fort Mandan, February 11, 1805.

" . . . about five O'clock this evening one of the wives of Charbono was delivered of a fine boy. it is worthy of remark that this was the first child . . . and as is common in such cases her labour was tedious and the pain violent," reads Meriwether Lewis' journal.

René Jessaume, a trader and interpreter for the Mandans, told Lewis he had found that the rattle of a rattlesnake was helpful in hastening such a birth.

"Having the rattle of a snake by me, I gave it to him and he administered two rings . . . broken in small pieces . . . and added to a small quantity of water. Whether this medicine was truly the cause or not I shall not undertake to determine, but I was informed she had not taken it more than ten minutes before she brought forth."

The child was Jean Baptiste Charbonneau, son of the party's Shoshoni interpreter and guide, Sacajawea, that remarkable eighteen-year-old for whose valor and counsel during the long journey more statues, monuments, and landmarks have been dedicated and named than for any other American woman.

At the age of six weeks the little boy, usually called Pomp, a name customarily given by Shoshonis to a first-born son, began his travels with the expedition; he was carried in a cradleboard on his mother's back. Over the months the warmhearted William Clark fell in love with the beautiful child, saw great promise in him, and determined then to try and persuade the parents to allow him to bring up Pomp as his own son. On the homeward journey he named a two-hundred-foot rock column along the Yellowstone River, Pompy's Pillar, for his favorite.

In the journals of both captains there are frequent mentions of the child, indicating their interest and concern: He is nearly swept away during a squall; his face is red and swollen almost beyond recognition from mosquito bites; his clothing, cradleboard, and bedding are lost in a torrent and Clark, fearing he will take cold, sends the party on the run back to camp to get dry clothes.

"Charbono's Child is very ill this evening," Lewis wrote; "he is cuting teeth . . . has . . . a high fever and his neck and throat are much swolen . . . we gave him a doze of creem of tartar and flour of sulpher and applyed a poltice of boiled onions to his neck as warm as he would well bear it."

The sickness was a long one, and for weeks afterward there are entries by both leaders reporting Pomp's condition and their continuing care: "we still apply poltices of onions which we renew frequently in the course of the day and night."

On the expedition's return in 1806, Toussaint Charbonneau, the boy's father, was given his discharge at the Mandan villages, and his pay—five hundred dollars, and thirty-three and a third cents. Before going on to St. Louis, Clark talked to him about his future and that of his "butifull promising child." A few days later Clark wrote to him from aboard the pirogue on which he was headed downriver, to repeat his offers:

> . . . As to your little Son (my boy Pomp) you well know my fondness for him and my anxiety to take and raise him as my own child. I once more tell you if you will bring your son Baptiest to me I will educate him as my own child . . . Charbono, if you wish to live with the white people, and will come to me I will give you a piece of land and furnish you with horses cows & hogs . . . or if you wish to return to trade with the indians and will leave your little Son Pomp with me, I will assist you with merchandize . . .

Wishing you and your family great sukcess & with anxious expectations of seeing my little dancing boy Baptiest I shall remain your Friend

William Clark

Charbonneau came to St. Louis some time during the summer or fall of 1810 and tried farming a tract of land along the Missouri, not far from the city. But by the following March he was ready to give it up. Leaving the six-year-old Pomp in Clark's care, he and Sacajawea returned to Indian country to live.

The jurist-author Henry M. Brackenridge, traveling up the Missouri with Astorian Wilson Price Hunt, wrote in his journal on April 2, 1811:

"We had on board a Frenchman named Charbonneau, with his wife, an Indian woman . . . both of whom accompanied Lewis and Clark to the Pacific, and were of great service. The woman, a good creature, of a mild and gentle disposition, greatly attached to the whites, whose manners and dress she tries to imitate . . . had become sickly, and longed to revisit her native country; her husband, also, who had spent many years among the Indians, had become weary of a civilized life."

Less than two years later, Sacajawea was dead. John Luttig, a merchant who was working at Fort Manuel, noted in his diary on Sunday, December 20, 1812:

"This evening the wife of Charbonneau, a Snake squaw, died of a putrid fever. She was good and the best woman in the fort, aged about 25 years; she left a fine infant girl."

When the fort was abandoned the next March, Luttig took the little girl, named Lizette, to St. Louis, and applied to the court for guardianship. On Luttig's death in 1815, William Clark was appointed her guardian. What became of her is not known.

John Luttig's report of Sacajawea's death is confirmed by a list of expedition members compiled by William Clark before 1829, with notations as to what became of each one. After Sacajawea's name is written the word "Dead."

Clark's accounts show that in 1820 he was still paying for instruction, school supplies, and clothing for Pomp, now known as Baptiste. Reads one:

"J.E. Welch. For one quarter's tuition of J. B. Charbonneau, a half Indian boy, including fuel and ink. Amount, $8.37½."

Another:

"J. & G.H. Kennerly. For one Roman History for Charbonneau, a half Indian, $1.50; one pair of shoes for ditto, $2.25; two pair of socks for ditto, $1.50; two quires of paper and quils . . . $1.50 . . . one dictionary for ditto, $1.50; one hat for ditto, $4.00; four yards of cloth for ditto, $10 . . . one ciphering book, $1; one slate and pencils, 62 cents. . . ."

Three years later Baptiste was in Europe for further education. The twenty-six-year-old scientist Paul Wilhelm, Duke of Württemburg, on his way up the Missouri to make a tour of the West, met young Charbonneau and his father at Curtis and Woods' trading post. He recognized at once in the handsome, intelligent eighteen-year-old, the potentialities William Clark had observed in the small boy, and soon made arrangements to take him to Germany. They sailed from New Orleans that December and landed in France the following February.

At the duke's castle, Baptiste was installed as a member of the royal household, where he received training in court etiquette. At the "public obligatory school" that had been established at Stuttgart in 1599 he was given a classical education.

In German records he is mentioned as Paul's "daily companion" and his "huntsman in ordinary," who traveled with him in both capacities to England, France, Italy, and North Africa. Baptiste was present at the duke's wedding in 1827, and was with him two years later when Paul set out on his second expedition to the American West, a trip that would include the Tetons.

It is likely that on their arrival in St. Louis that December, William Clark, whom the duke visited, would have had a talk with Baptiste about his future. Clark was in a position to have started him in nearly any business or profession he might have chosen. Instead, for reasons that will never be known, young Charbonneau signed on as a hunter with Astor's American Fur Company which was sending brigades into the Rockies that year.

From this time on he appears briefly in recollections, reports, and journals of the day: at Taos; in St.Louis; at Bent's Fort, where it was noted that he "had been Educated in Europe to some extent . . . wore his hair long . . . down to his Shoulders," and "was the best man at the Fort on the 'Plains' or in the Rocky Mountains." There is mention of him being in the Green River valley, in Teton country, in Santa Fe, on the trail to California, and in the gold mines there.

In the fall of 1830, as a greenhorn, he was lost for eleven days in the Malade River wilderness, much of the time with nothing to eat. That winter Joe Meek met him at the mouth of the Platte, and together they rode on to the Rocky Mountain Fur Company's winter encampment on the Powder River.

The next summer he was present at the rendezvous in Pierre's Hole, and doubtless took part in the battle. The summer after, he was with Jim Bridger at the Green River gathering. Here Nathaniel Wyeth tells about him going off on foot, in the night, after some Indian horse thieves.

Since he disappears from the records after 1833 and there are no certain references to him again until 1842, it has been suggested that he may have returned to Germany.

In 1842 he was working for fur traders Bent and St. Vrain, and that July he entertained Lieutenant John C. Frémont who, on his way west with an exploring party, stopped by his camp.

Baptiste, in charge of a company of men who were boating the season's furs down the Platte, had been stranded when the river suddenly dropped to only a few inches in depth, and took up his "summer's residence," as Frémont wrote, on an island which he named St. Helena.

This island, the explorer continued, "had a fine grove of large cottonwoods, under whose broad shade the tents were pitched. There was a large drove of horses on the opposite prairie bottom; smoke was rising from the scattered fires, and the encampment had quite a patriarchal air. Mr. C. received us hospitably. One of the people was sent to gather mint, with the aid of which he concocted a very good mint julep; and some boiled buffalo tongue, and coffee with the luxury of sugar, were soon set before us . . ." The next morning "we parted with our hospitable host after breakfast."

Nothing was said about Charbonneau as a man of culture or education. But a month later Rufus B. Sage, a journalist-turned-trapper, who was gathering material for a book on the Rocky Mountains, also stopped at St. Helena. He wrote:

"The camp was under the direction of a half–breed, named Charbonard, who proved to be a gentleman of superior information. He had acquired a classic education and could converse quite fluently in German, Spanish, French, and English, as well as several Indian languages. His mind, also, was well stored with choice reading, and enriched by extensive travel and observation. Having visited most of the important places, both in England, France, and Germany, he knew how to turn his experience to good advantage.

"There was a quaint humor and shrewdness in his conversation, so garbed with intelligence and perspicuity, that he at once insinuated himself into the good graces of his listeners, and commanded their admiration and respect."

Sage was the only contemporary to have written at any length about Baptiste, to have pictured him as a gentleman of learning and keen discernment, and to have given some insight into his personality. Of the others who refer to him, only two mention his education. The gentleman and scholar, then, kept in the background and made only rare appearances. In the fur brigades he was known simply as Charbonneau the half–breed—hunter and partisan of the first rank.

As to his further relations with the duke, no record exists. In Paul's extant writings there is but one later mention of Baptiste. When in 1850 the duke was in California, visiting John Sutter at his Hok Farm, he wrote that he saw among the Indian workers there "a very intelligent youth who reminded me of B. Charbonneau. . . ."

At St. Louis in the summer of 1843, Baptiste signed on as a hunter and driver with a pleasure party that Sir William Drummond Stewart, Scottish adventurer and big game hunter, was taking into the Wind River wilderness and the Tetons. Going with them also was Jefferson Clark, a son of Charbonneau's former guardian, William Clark, and a nephew, William Clark Kennerly. Neither young man regarded him as an equal. When Kennerly was asked later whether Baptiste had talked about his famous mother, he replied loftily:

"I regret to say that he spoke more often of the mules he was driving and might have been heard early and late expatiating in not too complimentary a manner on their stubbornness."

Three years later, with the Mexican War under way, he was employed as a guide for the Army of the West, a regiment of dragoons under the command of Colonel Stephen W. Kearny.

Ten days out of Santa Fe, their starting point, Baptiste was sent back to serve as guide and hunter for Colonel Philip St. George Cooke and the Mormon Battalion, bound for California. Cooke noted in his journal, perhaps with some surprise, that his guide could read and sign his name. He also told of a time in the mountain country when Baptiste rode ahead of the train to hunt:

"I discovered Charbonneaux near the summit in pursuit of bears. I saw three of them up among the rocks, whilst the bold hunter was gradually nearing them. Soon he fired, and in ten seconds again; then there was confused action, one bear falling down, the others rushing about with loud fierce cries, amid which the hunter's too, could be distinguished; the mountain fairly echoed. I much feared he was lost, but soon, in his red shirt, he appeared on a rock; he had cried out in Spanish for more balls. The bear was rolled down, and butchered before the wagons passed."

When the battalion reached San Diego in January 1847, Baptiste received his discharge. He is not heard of again until nine months later with his appointment as alcalde for Mission San Luis Rey. His duties included the "care and protection of Indian servants and ex–neophytes," control of the non–Christian bands, and compilation of statistics and information on customs and manners.

But the following July he resigned. Being half Indian he was accused of favoring the Indians, and there were many complaints.

That January, James Marshall, an ingenious eccentric, had discovered gold in the tailrace of a sawmill he was building on the banks of the American River, for John Sutter. In the fall, when old mountain man Jim Beckwourth, who had also come to California as a guide, went gold hunting, he found Baptiste already "house-keeping," as he said, at Murderer's Bar, a mining camp on the American's Middle Fork.

Charbonneau probably spent a number of years prospecting along the river's various forks and tributaries, but by 1842 he had become a permanent resident of Placer County. In 1860 he was living in Secret Ravine, the scene of extensive placer mining during that decade; the next year he was working as a clerk in the Orleans Hotel in the nearby town of Auburn.

In the spring of 1866 he and two companions started for the goldfields of Montana. Before leaving Auburn he stopped by the office of *The Placer Herald* for a visit with the editor. Charbonneau told him he might not come back to California since he was "returning to familiar scenes. We felt . . . we had met him for the last time," the newspaper man commented.

Sometime during the first week in May, Baptiste took sick along the Owyhee River in southeastern Oregon and died a few days later at Inskip's Ranch on Cow Creek, at the age of sixty-one. His final illness had been either pneumonia or mountain fever, it was reported.

The editor of *The Placer Herald*, in writing about his death, mentioned that as a young man he had spent a number of years in Europe, "where he learned to speak as well as write, several languages. . . . Mr. Charbonneau was of pleasant manners, intelligent, well read in the topics of the day, and generally esteemed in the community in which he lived."

Baptiste Charbonneau was the most romantic and enigmatic figure in the lore of the Rocky Mountain fur trade. There are many puzzling aspects of his life which must remain unanswered. His contemporaries gave no insights into the man and if Charbonneau wrote anything revealing about himself, it has not been discovered.

The foremost question is whether he actually found fulfillment in the wilderness and on the frontier, which he may well have done; or if he chose that life only because, being half Indian—a man between two worlds—he feared failure in the prejudiced realm of the white man, and so chose the egalitarianism of the mountaineers.

XV
Peregrinating Peers

The American West held an irresistible fascination for many nineteenth-century noblemen, and they traveled far to see it for themselves. There was Maximilian, Prince of Wied-Neuwied; Lord Fitz-Williams; Bernhard, Duke of Saxe-Weimar; the Honorable Charles Augustus Murray; Sir William Drummond Stewart; Paul Wilhelm, Duke of Württemberg; and Edwin Richard Windham Wyndam-Quin, Earl of Dunraven.

Some went into the West solely for scientific investigations, some on king's business, others as avid big game hunters, and still others just to see its wonders. Most of them published books about their travels, and at least two of them went into Teton country.

Duke Paul of Württemberg and Sir William Drummond Stewart found themselves so well suited, physically and temperamentally, to the wilderness life that they went back to the Far West year after year. Its dangers and hardships, its constantly changing challenges, its beauty and solitude satisfied the love of adventure, the impetuosity, and romanticism that these two men shared. It also provided an escape from the demands and restraints of a homelife each found uncongenial.

Paul, who had close blood ties with many of the reigning houses of Europe (he was nephew to the King of Württemberg), was asked once how it felt to be always "so near to wearing the purple." He admitted that on returning from any of his extended trips into the wilderness, he opened his mail with "apprehension, even horror . . . lest something untoward had befallen my cousin or nephew. . . . My life is cast in ambitions of another kind. . . . "

Although of royal lineage and supposedly one of the richest men in Europe, Paul was also one of the most democratic and unpretentious. In the United States he made friends among all classes of people, and was an outspoken admirer of the American form of government. By the 1840s he was so well known and liked in this country that newspapers kept close watch over his doings and whereabouts. When in the fall of 1851 he made his appearance in St. Louis after being reported lost on a trip to Fort Laramie, papers all over the Union carried news of his safe return.

King Friedrich I of Württemberg recognized the potential abilities of his young nephew Paul and brought him to Stuttgart to supervise his education. He "secured for him the best teachers the . . . capital afforded" and encouraged the boy's interest in science and his aptitude for languages. Although the schooling was broad, it was the inspired teaching of the learned Dr. Johann Lebret that confirmed Paul's natural bent toward science, with specialization in botany and zoology.

In the traditions of family and station he also received military training, serving for a time in the army of his own kingdom, and later in that of Prussia. But high military rank did not interest him, and at twenty he resigned his commission to devote full time to scientific research and exploration.

By May 5, 1823, he had reached St. Louis, and on that day wrote to William Clark, asking for a passport which would enable him to travel through that "Country bordering the missouri and Columbia rivers for the improvement of botany and Natural history. . . . "

Permission was granted, and the twenty-six-year-old scientist was soon on his way up the Missouri, journeying sometimes by boat, sometimes by horse, and at other times on foot, bearing patiently the discomforts of frontier accommodations and the torments of mosquitoes, heat, thirst, and fever. He identified flowers, trees, grasses; birds, fish, reptiles, and mammals. He collected specimens and made detailed drawings. He examined the ancient tumuli and speculated on their past. He described those Indians, half-breeds, Negroes, Creoles, and white frontiersmen he met, including observations on their manners, customs, speech, and religion.

At a trading post upstream from the junction of the Kansas and the Missouri, he met Sacajawea's son and made those preparations for him to go to Europe.

At Fort Recovery, Paul learned that the Arikaras were on the warpath. This would keep him from traveling on to the Mandan villages where he hoped to make a study of those Indians whose cultured ways, peaceful disposition, and unusual customs would so fascinate painter George Catlin. Since three different tribes of Sioux were encamped near the fort, "I had at least the opportunity of seeing these people in their native environment, which . . . somewhat compensated me."

Paul's second trip to the United States, which took him at least as far west as the headwaters of the Missouri and included a visit to the Tetons, began in 1829, two years after his marriage to Princess Sophie von Turn und Taxis, and a year after the birth of their only child, the Duke Maximilian.

On December 23, 1829, General William Clark forwarded to the secretary of war Duke Paul's request for permission to travel in the Far West. In an accompanying letter Clark wrote that the duke had set off from St. Louis that morning for Council Bluffs, "accompanied by his servants (two), a clerk, and two hired men of the American fur company"—one of whom was probably Baptiste Charbonneau. "Please to signify to me your approval or disapproval of the extension of the Passport of this Prince to the Columbia and Pacific Ocean."

Again the duke traveled up the Missouri and this time was able to reach the Mandan villages, where old Charbonneau was then living. Paul spent more than a month there studying Mandan culture and customs, with the Frenchman acting as his interpreter.

This second trip took Paul into Wyoming's Medicine Bow, Sierra Madre, and Wind River Mountains, as well as the Tetons; to the Salt Lake desert, and into the homeland of the Kiowas and Utes. Since his journals, notes, and drawings for this journey have never been found, his trail can only be traced through references to it in his later writings, and by collateral sources. There is no mention of his having gone as far as the Pacific Coast this time.

The Fort Union records show that Paul had reached this trading post at the mouth of the Yellowstone by May 18, 1830, for on that day he bought "2 Madress Hkfs to Charbonneau—$5.00." As to whether these were for Baptiste or his father, there is no hint. Two months later the duke was by his own account "at the foot of the Rocky Mountains," and had either already seen "the Three Titans . . . the Triple Snow Peaks," as he called the Tetons, or would do so later. "These are covered with perpetual ice and snow, perhaps the loftiest mountains in all the scenery of the North American Alps."

Paul's arrival in the Rockies on July 18 was just two days after that of William Sublette's caravan from St. Louis, and the subsequent opening of the rendezvous in the Wind River Mountains. This coincidence of dates suggests strongly that the duke and Baptiste Charbonneau, by then a fur company employee, were both present at this gathering.

Since it is known that Paul went to the Missouri's Three Forks, it is logical that he accompanied one of the trapping parties there after rendezvous. The fact that in later writings he describes his delight at meeting again that "lovable old huntsman" Tom Fitzpatrick, makes it almost certain that he joined Fitzpatrick, Bridger, and Milton Sublette, who are known to have taken their men to the Three Forks that fall. Their trail ran north through the Bighorn Basin to the Yellowstone River (where Paul tells of finding coal deposits), and then turned west to the Missouri's headwaters. From there they followed the Jefferson, crossed the Divide, and worked south through Pierre's Hole where Paul would have seen the Tetons for either the first or second time. The company then trapped its way south to Ogden's Hole on the northeastern shore of the Great Salt Lake, which Paul mentions having seen.

He concluded this trip to the West by sailing alone down the Missouri in a small pirogue, a feat he afterward maintained was "successful in only ten out of a hundred cases." By October 30 he had reached St. Louis.

This time he was taking a Sioux chief to Württemberg. According to a contemporary German article, people were a part of his scientific collecting, for he had around him in his castle men from many different races, "not only Indians but also Nubians and Nigroes," brought back from his travels.

There is some evidence that he went to the Rockies in 1831 after a trip to Mexico. That he intended to return in 1851 is certain, for Father de Smet met him at Ash Hollow on September 23 of that year and wrote that Paul was then on his way "to enjoy a hunt in the Wind River Mountains. . . . His excellency must be indeed courageous, to undertake at his age so long a journey in such a wilderness, with but one man as suite, and in a wretched little open wagon, which carried the prince and his officer as well as their whole baggage and provisions."

But Paul, then fifty-four, and his companion, a twenty-four-year-old scientist and novelist, Balduin Möllhausen, had so many delays along the trail that it was already October by the time they reached Fort Laramie, too late in the season to go on to the Wind River or the Tetons, which Paul could see were already covered with snow. Reluctantly they turned back and encountered a series of incredible adventures that included near-drowning, capture by Indians, and a hairbreadth escape from death by freezing and starvation.

Although this was Paul's last expedition to that part of the West, he continued his explorations of other parts of this country until 1858, two years before his death.

Since he was the first trained scientist to go into Teton country it is unfortunate that his collections, descriptions, and drawings of what he may have seen there are missing. Of equal loss to the literature of the Far West is what he would have had to say about Tom Fitzpatrick, Jim Bridger, and the others, and his account of adventures among the mountain men.

William Drummond Stewart, the second son of George Stewart, seventeenth Lord of Grandtully and fifth Baronet of Murthly, was born in 1795 at Murthly Castle, where stands the Birnham Wood mentioned in *Macbeth*. Young Stewart was educated by tutors, and at age seventeen was started in a military career.

As a lieutenant in the Fifteenth (King's) Hussars, he took part in the Peninsular Campaign and at Waterloo, received the

Waterloo medal, and in 1820 was promoted to captain. A year later he was put on half pay when his battalion was mustered out. It is said that he then spent some time in the diplomatic corps in Italy. It is known that he traveled widely throughout Europe, Asia, and Africa, as a sightseer and avid sportsman.

On his father's death in 1827, the estates and titles were inherited by the oldest son, John; William received three thousand pounds in trust. An affair with a handsome laundress—a contemporary claimed that William "fell in love with her nether limbs when he saw her tromping blankets in a tub"— the birth of a son, and their subsequent marriage led to an irreparable breach with brother John, and prompted William to leave Scotland.

Early in 1833 Captain William Drummond Stewart arrived in St. Louis, having come overland by horseback from New York, armed with a fine Manton rifle ("costing 40 guineas") and introductory letters to William Clark, William Ashley, and William Sublette. When Sublette's caravan set out that May for the rendezvous at Horse Creek in the Green River valley, Stewart was riding with it.

Before reaching his first rendezvous he had experienced the exciting challenge of the buffalo hunt, had come to know the unexcelled savoriness of hump ribs spitted before the fire; had taken part in an antelope surround and shot elk, grizzly bear, and deer. He had shared the general uneasiness when hostile Indians lurked nearby, and had sat in a circle and smoked the calumet with peaceful ones. He came to appreciate the pageantry of braves on the warpath and villages on the move, as well as the charms of individual Indian girls who willingly shared his bower. He had listened to the mountaineers' tales, watched them dance around the night fire, and heard the French Creoles singing rondelets.

By the time he arrived at Horse Creek the spell was cast: He was to spend six consecutive summers in the Wyoming wilderness. After a three-year interval, he returned as Sir William, Lord of Grandtully and Baronet of Murthly, for his seventh and final trip to the Green River Mountains and the Tetons.

Unlike Duke Paul who took with him a minimum outfit and traveled on his own (narrowly missing death seven times), Stewart journeyed under the protection of the fur caravan, which enabled him to take along guests, fast horses with which to race the Indians at rendezvous, a cook, servants, dogs, and a wagon or two laden with luxuries. There was usually a tent, a carpet to roll out on the sward, a collection of Manton rifles, and that most contemptible of weapons in the mountain man's eyes, the "two-shoot gun." There was also fishing gear for his excursions to the New Fork lakes near the headwaters of the Green, where he took a party to spend several weeks away from the bedlam of rendezvous, hunting and catching quantities of "noble trout."

One mountaineer remembered that Stewart's stock of comestibles and supplies included boxes of sardines, condensed hotchpotch, hams, tongues, tins of preserved meats, bottles of pickles, porter, brandy, and port wine; coffee, sugar, flour, and such strangers to the trapper's mess as "pots and pans, knives, forks, spoons, plates, &c., &c."

He is described as being a man "of middle height and stoutly built," dressed in "a white shooting-jacket, of cut unknown in mountain tailoring, and a pair of trowsers of the well-known material called 'shepherd's plaid;' a broad-brimmed Panama shaded his face which was ruddy with health and exercise; a belt round his waist supported a handsome bowie-knife, and a double-barreled fowling-piece was *slung* across his shoulder." This was unusual attire, for early in his mountain career he adopted the practical buckskins of Indian make.

Although he clung somewhat to form in the wilds, and was at times known as a martinet, he won the mountain man's approbation by proving to be a crack shot, an experienced hunter, and an expert horseman. It did not take them long to discover that he was also unflinching in the face of danger. As one trapper observed, the "Capen" had a "ha'r of the grizzly in him."

His companions liked those stories he told around the campfire, of adventures in foreign lands, of "the curious cities, and the monuments of antiquity" he had visited, tales in which he never "put himself forward"; and they liked his bluff bounty for which he would accept no thanks. The Shoshonis were also his friends and usually honored him at rendezvous with an elaborate procession.

After rendezvous broke up, Stewart often went with one of the trapping parties on their fall hunt into Teton country, the Bighorn Basin, or to the Three Forks.

For the gathering of 1837 Stewart made special plans. Looking ahead to an inevitable return to Scotland, he invited the Baltimore artist Alfred Jacob Miller to go with him and paint life on the prairies and in the mountains, and scenes in his favorite lake country. These pictures he would hang on his walls in Perthshire to remind him of that country where he had found happiness.

Miller accepted, and posterity is indebted to both men. Through hundreds of vigorous field sketches made in black and sepia washes, in pencil, ink, and watercolor, and large studio versions in oil, the artist preserved a way of life that was soon to be gone forever.

To this rendezvous in the Green River valley Stewart took two wagons, three new "Joe Mantons," and a present for Jim Bridger. This turned out to be a "full suit of armor," complete with helmet and flowing horsehair plume. Bridger put it on, and Miller made two sketches of him wearing it. The artist noted that the armor "created a sensation." Other mountain men, including Joe Meek, were eager to try it on.

Since Stewart took the trouble to import the armor from England, his point may have been more serious than is generally supposed. Beyond the fun he anticipated at Bridger's expense, he doubtless also thought of the suit as an excellent defense for a man who had so often narrowly escaped death at the hands of the Blackfeet. It was certainly not levity that induced the haughty disciplinarian, trader Kenneth McKenzie, to order for himself a coat of mail from England.

There is no record of what became of Bridger's armor. However, one day in the summer of 1876, John Finerty, war correspondent for the *Chicago Times* who was attached to General George Crook's command, borrowed a field glass with which to take a close look at a party of Sioux who had been firing on them from a bluff. He could then see there were not as many as supposed—only about a dozen—and that they were "dressed in a variety of costumes"; and, although hard to believe, one fellow was "wearing a tin helmet with a horse-hair plume."

The rendezvous of 1838 was to be Stewart's last, for on his return to St. Louis that September he learned about the death of his brother, John. Not, however, until the end of the following May did he sail for Scotland to claim his titles. He was taking with him eighteen of Miller's paintings, two Indians—Shoshonis, most probably—and mountain-man Antoine Clement, a French-Canadian half-breed who had been his hunting companion for six seasons.

Some weeks before sailing, he wrote from New Orleans, where he wintered each year, asking his friend William Sublette to procure him "some tame deer," and to have Antoine, who was then in St. Louis, find "some gourds of the best form for dippers also some large ones for bottles . . . I wish him also to get some red-birds & keep them in cages as I wish to take them to England."

On November 26, 1839, Stewart wrote Sublette from London:

"I got your welcome letter at Murthly some time ago. I am now here on my way to Constantinople & Egypt & please God expect to be back in June when I hope you will be able to come over & see me." He was sending Sublette two pedigreed calves for his farm, and would follow this with a thoroughbred horse.

"I must now come to my own intention & inform you that I have not yet done with the United States. . . ." He was planning to be in New York "in the fall of 1840 with a view of going to the mountains in spring following if I can get a party to join me sufficiently strong. Pray let . . . my friends in the mountains know that if I am in life & health I shall be on the Susquadee [Green River] in July 1841 . . . Pray get me some young deer & Buffaloe & send them over . . . also any seeds you can get . . ."—the latter were of native flora. Stewart was recreating a bit of the American West in Scotland.

Starting in September 1840 Alfred Jacob Miller became artist in residence at Murthly Castle, in order to paint some of his large oil versions of Stewart's favorite subjects. He found Antoine Clement "metamorphosed into a Scotch valet"; the greasy buckskins had been laid aside for a "full suit of black." His only duties were to wait on table.

Stewart, Miller observed, was surrounded by "reminders of the Rocky Mountains," even going so far as to make his bed on some choice buffalo robes spread over a divan.

But it was August 1842 before Sir William, Antoine, and the two Indians were to sail for what Stewart termed "the land of the free, the friendly, and the brave."

He spent that winter again in New Orleans where he worked

on his novel, *Altowan*, based on his Rocky Mountain adventures, and on completing plans for the sentimental journey he would make into the Wyoming wilderness the next spring.

The party that assembled at St. Louis the following April numbered about eighty. Its leader was William Sublette, and its roster included members of the city's most prominent families—a Clark, a Kennerly, a Chouteau, a Radford, and a Graham. There was a physician, Dr. Steadman Tilghman; a priest, Father de Vos; a newspaper editor, Matthew C. Field, who covered the expedition for the *New Orleans Picayune*; a Scottish botanist, Alexander Gordon, who made "a large collection of flowers, plants, and herbs, important and new to the medical profession," and gathered seeds for Stewart to plant at Murthly. There were two young army lieutenants, Sidney Smith and Richard Graham; Sacajawea's son, Baptiste Charbonneau; a number of old mountain men and their Indian women; the hunter Antoine Clement, back in his element; two clerks, a cook, Sir William's valet, Corbie, who disapproved of the whole affair; and a collection of drivers and guides.

William Clark's nephew, William Clark Kennerly, recalled how it happened that he and Clark's son, Jefferson, were asked to go:

"It was a lovely evening in April, 1843, that the opportunity came for my first trip across the Great Plains. Among the guests at my mother's dinner table was Sir William Drummond Stewart. . . . After the ladies had left the dining room . . . Jeff and I listened with bated breath to tales of wonderful adventure in the far-away Rockies and . . . plans for another trip across the . . . prairies. Sir William probably noticed our intense interest . . . Anyway, he invited us to accompany him, and both being ready to go anywhere at any moment, we accepted with alacrity. My mother's consent was with some difficulty gained later."

The party started off up the Missouri aboard the *John Auld*. At Glasgow the steamboat *Omega* "came in behind us, and there was a stir of excitement when we heard that the artist, Mr. John James Audubon, was on that boat. A number of us went aboard . . . and listened to Mr. Audubon talk . . . and saw some of his specimens. In those days he liked to wear his gray hair rather long, which gave him a certain romantic wildness in appearance. . . . We found him an interesting talker. . . ."

The *Omega* happened this time to be carrying a contraband cargo of liquor destined for the Indian trade. Although the sale of spirits to Indians was forbidden by law, and inspectors were stationed along the river and the overland routes, smuggling had grown into a thriving business. On this voyage Audubon helped with an elaborate deception of the inspecting officer, to protect his personal supply.

At Westport the expedition started overland, heading for Stewart's favorite New Fork lakes. At Fort Laramie there were thirty or more lodges of Sioux who had come in to trade. Recognizing Jefferson Clark by his red hair and other strong resemblances to his father, the Indians honored him and his friends with a feast. The Clark boys had their first meal of "boiled young dog," mashed chokecherries, and dried roots. Afterward, they smoked the ceremonial pipe that was passed around the lodge, and then listened to the "oldest chief" give a long speech about the "Redheaded Father," as they called William Clark.

Fourth of July was celebrated on the banks of the Sweetwater by the consumption of a "monstrous plum pudding" which the cook had been industriously putting together each evening for several weeks past. After dinner there were speeches by Sir William and Matt Field and innumerable patriotic toasts. However, since they were in hostile Indian country, Stewart ordered one half the company to remain sober. The other half, given license, downed double their share, and the whole party's westward course had to be suspended until they recovered.

Going by way of South Pass and up the valley of the Green River they came to the first of the lakes, set like a gem in the midst of towering snowcapped peaks. They decided to name it, and since "it resembled a bit of Scottish scenery, we christened it 'Loch Drummond' in honor of Sir William and his native land."

To add authenticity to this replica rendezvous, they invited a village of Shoshonis, encamped nearby, to join them. After they came in "we . . . inaugurated horse races and different trials of skill. They were sportsmen of the first water and would bet with a right good will . . . We . . . lost many races, and especially were the red men our masters in foot races."

After several weeks spent hunting, fishing, and exploring the area, Stewart took the party north to see the Tetons and the curiosities of Yellowstone country. In Jackson Hole the anglers dropped their lines in the trout-filled streams and lakes, while the hunters rode over the meadows and sagebrush plains after deer and elk.

In Yellowstone several of the boys tried throttling a geyser. They packed its mouth with grass, covered it with a large, flat rock, then stood on the rock, hands clasped, and awaited results. These were the same every time: All were tossed high in the air, "like so many feathers."

Returning through Jackson Hole—to marvel again at the splendor of the peaks, they rode on to the waters of the Green. They made a final encampment on the New Fork before heading for South Pass and home.

At St. Louis the company disbanded "amidst much good fellowship." A farewell dinner party was given for Sir William at the Kennerly home, Persimmon Hill.

Although Stewart maintained a close connection with America through his friends there, he would never again take the long trail over the prairie to the Rocky Mountains or see his favorite haunts except in memory and through the romantic eyes of the painter Alfred Jacob Miller.

XVI
End of an Era

The 1832 rendezvous in Pierre's Hole marked the turning point in the Rocky Mountain fur trade. It was obvious by then that the field could no longer be monopolized by Ashley's successors. Captain Benjamin Bonneville, an army officer on leave, had entered the business that year with a large, well-equipped company, as had the shrewd and determined Nathaniel Wyeth. Bonneville had gone so far as to build a fortified post near the favorite rendezvous site in the upper valley of the Green. Trappers, seeing no reason for its existence, dubbed it Fort Nonsense.

But the Rocky Mountain Fur Company's most formidable competitor was Astor's American Fur Company, which had sent its first brigades into the mountains in 1829. Instead of despatching their own scouts to discover where the best beaver grounds lay, Astor's partisans—Andrew Drips, Lucien Fontenelle, William Vanderburgh, and their men—secretly trailed their rival's hunting parties. In 1832 they had turned up at rendezvous. Tom Fitzpatrick and Jim Bridger, the Rocky Mountain company's resident partners, who were well aware of the evils of competing on the same hunting grounds, proposed a division of territory; the offer was firmly refused.

After the Battle of Pierre's Hole, Bridger and Fitzpatrick made a point to be the first to set off on the fall hunt. They headed for the rugged Three Forks country in the hope of forestalling their rivals. It was not long, however, until they discovered they were being trailed. At first they "tried in every way to blind and baffle them; to steal a march upon them, or lead them on the wrong scent; but all in vain."

Exasperated by their perseverance, Fitzpatrick and Bridger decided to sacrifice their own hunt rather than share the profits with a competitor, and to take these rivals on a march that would cure them of dogging their footsteps. One of the Rocky Mountain Fur Company's men recalled that they no longer attempted to conceal their plans, but instead held them out as bait. With Astor's men close on their heels, they set off over the mountains for the headwaters of the Missouri. "Here, packing up their traps, they tarried not for beaver, nor even tried to avoid the Blackfeet, but pushed right . . . into the very heart of their country, keeping away from any part of it where beaver might be found . . . going away on beyond, to the elevated plains. . . ."

Suspecting at length that they were possibly being gulled, Astor's party divided forces. Taking no chances, a few men under Drips continued to follow Bridger and Fitzpatrick. The rest, under the leadership of the inexperienced Vanderburgh (a West Point graduate but a tyro in the mountains), turned back to look for beaver.

One morning Vanderburgh's scouts reported fresh Blackfoot sign—a partially butchered buffalo, obviously abandoned in haste. Taking seven men with him, he set off along the Madison River to look for the Indians' trail, and shortly came on another freshly killed buffalo and a briskly burning campfire. The nearby hills were covered with quietly grazing buffalo, which Vanderburgh interpreted to mean that the Blackfoot hunting party was small. Recklessly he pushed ahead toward a thick grove of cottonwoods where he suspected the Indians— no more, he was sure, than seven or eight—were hiding.

While crossing a ravine, "suddenly the lightning and thunder of at least twenty fusils burst upon our astonished senses," and there emerged from cover "more than one hundred warriors, erect in uncomprising enmity—both before and on either side of us, at the terrifying distance (since measured) of *thirty steps.*" There was a rapid exchange of fire, and Vanderburgh's horse was shot dead under him. "With unexampled firmness he stepped calmly from the lifeless animal, presented his gun at the advancing foe, and exclaimed, 'boys, don't run!'. . . ."

The chronicler was just then struck in the shoulder by a ball, the force nearly unhorsing him. "By desperate effort . . . I regained my upright position, and fled." Vanderburgh, "seeing himself surrounded, without the possibility of escape, levelled his gun and shot the foremost of his foes. The Indians immediately fired a volley upon him—he fell—they uttered a loud and shrill yell of exultation . . ."

One of his men, agonized at seeing the Indians attacking him with tomahawks and knives, cried out, "Our friend is killed! . . . let us go and die with him." His companions had difficulty keeping him from riding into the midst of the Blackfeet.

The next September the American Fur Company took revenge by inducing the Crows to rob Tom Fitzpatrick of his entire outfit and keep him from his fall hunt. While he was making a call of ceremony on the chief, a large band of braves rode into the trappers' camp where Captain William Drummond Stewart had been left in charge. They were friendly, and Stewart made them welcome. Once assured of the captain's goodwill and relaxed vigilance, they suddenly turned raider, drove off a hundred horses, and cleared the camp of traps, pelts, trade goods, guns, and ammunition.

As they were returning home with their plunder they met Fitzpatrick, and as one of his trappers observed, they "added insult to injury" by robbing him of horse, gun, capote, and watch. Fitzpatrick charged the American Fur Company with having instigated the attack. The Indians later confessed the fact, and the company agent as much as admitted it.

Each of the two big fur companies did everything in its power to harass and hamper the other: price-cutting, bribery, subsidizing small companies sure to annoy, selling goods to their rival's hired trappers, and luring away their best hunters, although, as one mountaineer recalled, it soon became "as much as a man's life was worth for a trapper . . . to be inveigled into the service of a rival," and many a murder was committed on this account.

A man's word could no longer be depended on. Not even written contracts were binding. Gone was the tradition of trust that had distinguished the traders' dealings with one another. The Indians were mystified by this strange conduct and lost all confidence in the whites.

At the rendezvous of 1834 the Rocky Mountain Fur Company, which William Henry Ashley had founded twelve years before, ended its notable career with a dissolution of the partnership. Henry Fraeb sold his interest for "forty head of horse beast, forty beaver traps, eight guns, and one thousand dollars' worth of merchandize," and Jean Baptiste Gervais followed suit. The remaining partners organized a new firm known as Fitzpatrick, Sublette and Bridger. The following year they merged with the American Fur Company, and in 1836, when partner Milton Sublette died, Fitzpatrick, Sublette & Bridger was dissolved.

The hard-fought battle for monopoly had been won by the company John Jacob Astor had founded, but it was a hollow victory. The Rocky Mountain fur trade's greatest days were over. An increasing number of rivals, a growing scarcity of beaver (the annual shipment to Europe was two-hundred thousand pelts), and depressed fur prices due to a decree of fashion made profits small. The once universal beaver hat was being replaced in popularity by the silk plush hat, and the demand for pelts dropped accordingly. The American beaver was saved from extinction only by this whim of the beau monde.

At the rendezvous of 1838, held in the Wind River valley, it was rumored that the Company was intending to close out its Rocky Mountain operations. "This caused a great deal of discontent among the Trappers, and numbers left the party," one of them noted.

However, the rumor was unfounded. There were to be two more Company-sponsored rendezvous, both held along Horse Creek in the upper Green River valley.

A young physician traveling with the 1839 fur caravan felt that the mountain man's days of glory "seem to be past, for constant hunting has very much reduced the number of beavers. This diminution in the . . . catch made itself noticeable at this year's rendezvous in the quieter behavior of the trappers. There was little drinking of spirits, and almost no gambling. Another decade perhaps and the original trapper will have disappeared from the mountains."

The 1840 gathering ended the rendezvous system. Thereafter the Company concentrated on its fixed posts, trading there with Indians and white trappers and hunters, shifting its business increasingly to buffalo robes. The Wyoming Rockies and the Teton Valleys were left to the British, and those Americans who in groups of six or eight, or with only a partner, continued to scour the old beaver grounds.

On the Company's withdrawal from the Rockies, many mountain men entered the Santa Fe trade, while others joined the Hudson's Bay Company forces. A few provident ones, like Warren Ferris, who had saved their wages, bought frontier farms. Some, like Joe Meek and Doc Newall, tiring after a few years of the small returns, gave up trapping. Taking their Indian wives and their children, they settled in Oregon where they became respected citizens.

Few chose to return home to the harness of conventionality and civilization. As one old trapper said: "Certain the old state come across my mind now and again, but who's thar to remember this old body?" There was the question too of the "diggins" being overcrowded: "It's hard to fetch breath amongst them big bands of corncrackers to Missoura." And of grub: "It goes against natur to leave bufler meat and feed on hog." The conclusion: "No; *darn* the settlements, I say."

Such men stayed on in the mountains. By working over the grounds carefully, they took enough beaver to supply their needs. They never abandoned hope that the price would return to six dollars a pelt, and their fortunes would be made.

With the start of overland migration and government exploration of the West in the early 1840s, some mountain men settled along the main trails, built supply posts, and served as pilots for emigrant trains and explorer's parties. Jim Bridger was one of them.

"I have established a small fort with a blacksmith shop & a supply of iron, on the road of the emigrant's on Black's Fork of Green river, which promises fairly. They, in coming out, are generally well supplied with money, but by the time they get here are in want of all kinds of supplies," Bridger told the St. Louis merchant Pierre Chouteau. "Horses, provisions, smith-work &c. bring ready cash from them . . . The same establishment trades with the Indians . . . who have mostly a good number of beaver with them."

On declaration of war with Mexico, many mountain men volunteered, and proved invaluable as guides across the south-western deserts and over the mountains into California, and as hunters for the troops. At the time of the Indian wars in the 1870s, their services were in demand as scouts, interpreters, and guides.

Although the trapper had never looked for gold in those wa-ters where he took beaver, he heard the siren call in 1849 and joined the rush to California. There some of them stayed to continue mining even after the cream was skimmed, or to hunt and trap in a small way, and open trading posts. Some aban-doned the role of mountaineer and became alcaldes, judges, teachers, school superintendents (Rube Herring was one), newspaper editors, and politicians on the new frontier.

With the establishment of the reservation system still other traders and trappers—Carson, Fitzpatrick, and Drips, for in-stance—became Indian Bureau officials.

After a few years, the men who had stubbornly clung to trap-ping abandoned the Wyoming mountains for those in Colo-rado. Over the next twenty years Teton country was deserted except for bands of hunting Indians and an occasional white trapper who returned to the old haunts.

The era of the mountain man had come to an end. In the Te-tons the uproar of the summer rendezvous was forever stilled; the big hunting and trapping parties were gone. The animals, unmolested, could regenerate their depleted numbers, the overgrazed herbage return to former abundance, and trampled meadows flower anew. Verdure masked the manmade scars. The wilderness briefly reclaimed its own.

XVII
Washakie

For almost sixty years Washakie, one of the great Indian personalities in history, was head chief of Wyoming's Eastern Shoshonis. He rose to command about 1843, a time when his people were faced with major problems and were under constant harassment from stronger and more aggressive neighboring tribes.

The year 1840 marked the end of the fur trade's best days and the beginning of the great western migration. The Shoshonis had been closely involved as hunters and trappers in the fur trade that had penetrated the heart of their country, and now the routes of overland travel were leading across their land.

Traders had taught the Shoshonis the importance of furs and how to trap. Contact with whites had introduced new concepts and values. With the depletion of the great buffalo herds, the Indians were losing their independence. Important economic and political decisions had to be made. The Shoshonis' only salvation lay in abandoning their old anarchy, suppressing their individualism, and uniting under a strong leader.

As early as 1830, Washakie had proved his personal bravery and prowess as a warrior and was noted in councils for sagacity and eloquence. Eight years later he was spoken of as one of three Shoshoni leaders at whose names the Blackfeet "quaked in fear."

Washakie gathered his scattered tribesmen, and by a form of benevolent despotism created his own nation, to be known as the Wind River Shoshonis. Conditions demanded firm rule and implicit obedience. "I am chief and whatever I do the others will agree to," he once said. Yet he was never accused of abusing his power. Whatever he gained, he shared equally with his people.

His standards were exacting. One inflexible law was that peace must be maintained with whites at all times. Any follower who harmed a white man or stole his property was promptly exiled.

By the 1850s Washakie had a thousand well-armed and well-disciplined mounted warriors, and horses enough to carry the women and children. Most important, he was able to hold his own against his enemies.

According to Indian tradition he was born in 1798 and given the birth name Pina Quanah, meaning Smell of Sugar. His mother was Shoshoni; his father belonged to a Flathead band, but was said to have been of Shoshoni, Umatilla, and Flathead blood.

When Pina Quanah was about five, his village was attacked by Blackfeet, and his father was among those killed. His mother escaped with her five young children to Salmon River country where they found a home among the Lemhi Shoshonis, possibly her own people. There they lived until Pina Quanah was a young man, "tall . . . easily six feet, of lighter skin than average and the most handsome Indian I have yet seen," observed a white man who met him early in his career. By this time he was known as Wa-sha-kie, The Rattle or Rattler, because of his habit of riding in among the enemy and frightening their horses with a buffalo hide rattle.

Around 1830 he crossed the mountains and went to live with those Shoshonis who made their home along the Green River. Family tradition makes him the hero of an encounter with the Blackfeet, around this time. Not only did he help defeat them, he followed the retreating warriors to the Missouri to recover stolen Shoshoni horses and to bring back every scalp that had been taken.

With the opening of the mountain fur trade Washakie had his first extensive contact with white men. He soon learned that by hunting for pelts and buffalo robes beyond his own needs he could trade them to the fur companies for those guns and ammunition needed for defense against raiding tribes. He brought his packs of furs into the annual rendezvous and encouraged his tribesmen to do the same. He came to know most of the mountain men and is said to have hunted and trapped with Jim Bridger and Kit Carson.

After the fur trade's decline, Washakie and his people made long excursions each year to Salt Lake City and other settlements to trade buckskin, buffalo robes, and pelts for ammunition, tools, calico, blankets, and beads. The blankets were used in trade with other Indians for buffalo robes, and the beads for tanned buckskin.

Washakie first came into official notice at a treaty council called at Fort Laramie in 1851. The government hoped to get the warring Plains tribes to make peace with each other and to recognize the right of emigrants, settlers, and goldseekers to cross their lands.

Several thousand Indians, mainly Sioux, Crow, Cheyenne, and Arapaho, all enemies of the Shoshonis, had already set up their tipis on the plains near the fort by the time Washakie came in. Corporal Percival Lowe, Second Dragoons, attached to the fort, described the Shoshonis' arrival.

About noon he saw a large cloud of dust in the west, and "soon a long line of Indians came moving down in battle array, arms ready for use and every man apparently expectant, the women and children and baggage bringing up the rear well guarded. . . . They were dressed in their best, riding fine war horses. . . ."

Just as soon as the Sioux sighted them they showed "great interest and some excitement at the approach of their hereditary enemies, and a few squaws howled in anguish for lost friends who had died in battle with these same cautiously moving warriors."

The Shoshonis advanced steadily. Washakie, riding his "big buckskin," was ahead of the rest, a figure of great dignity even at a distance. The post commander, Lieutenant Hastings, aware of the tension, ordered boots and saddles sounded.

Just as Washakie started down from the brow of the hill that overlooked the Laramie River, a Sioux, bow and arrows in hand, sprang on a pony and raced toward him to avenge the death of his father. An interpreter who had been watching this Sioux jumped on his horse and followed.

The Shoshoni column stopped and let out a shout of defiance. Washakie moved ahead, raised his gun, and took aim. But before he could fire, the interpreter had overtaken the Sioux, pulled him from his pony, disarmed him, and now stood over him. Lieutenant Hastings quickly mounted his troops and posted them.

Sioux chiefs then grabbed their horses and rode forward, and several more interpreters came up. There "then ensued a harangue between the interpreters and chiefs," Lowe wrote, the alerted soldiers looking on. Matters were settled peaceably and "the wild Sioux" was led back to camp, the Shoshonis meanwhile holding their ground.

The dragoons were impressed by Washakie's "cool, deliberate action . . . the staunch firmness of his warriors and the quiet demeanor of the women and children, who were perfectly self-possessed—not a single outcry from that vast parade save the one cry of defiance. . . ."

Jim Bridger, who was the Shoshonis' interpreter, told Lowe later that day: "These are the finest Indians on earth . . . Awful brave fellows, these Snakes; got the nerve; honest, too; can take their word for anything; trust 'em anywhere; they live all about me, and I know all of them."

Referring to the incident with the Sioux, Bridger went on, "My chief would 'er killed him quick, and then the fool Sioux would 'er got their backs up, and there wouldn't have been room to camp 'round here for dead Sioux. You dragoons acted nice, but you wouldn't have had no show if the fight had commenced—no making peace then. And I tell you another thing; the Sioux ain't goin' to try it again. They see how these Snakes are armed. I got them guns for 'um, and they are good ones."

Before the council met, the thousands of Indian ponies (ten thousand Indians had come in) had already grazed off the grass and herbage around the fort. The meeting place was therefore moved some thirty-four miles eastward where there was ample forage and water. Two companies of dragoons led the unusual cavalcade. They were followed by the carriages of the government officials and guests. Then came the long supply train, and finally the Indians in paint, feathers, and scarlet robes, their column extending for some two miles.

After the meeting convened, the Shoshonis were not included in the negotiations. The officials claimed they were not under the jurisdiction of the Central Superintendency which was being represented, but under the authority of the Utah district. Washakie was deeply disappointed. Beyond giving a short speech which reflected these feelings, he could take no other part. He was unable to analyze the treaty line by line, voice his opinions, raise objections, or refuse to sign, as he was to do at future councils where he was represented.

The entire meeting was disheartening for the Shoshonis who could only look on while the government turned over to their enemies the Crows land extending from the Big Horn Mountains south to the Wind River, land that had belonged to the Shoshonis when they ruled the Plains and was still their hunting ground. It was Wind River country that Washakie hoped to claim as a reservation for his people some day.

"The result of the Laramie treaty was that the Indians fought before they got home; war was carried on among them the same as before, and afterward war with the whites," wrote a participant in the council.

For the Shoshonis the treaty provoked years of bloody conflict with the Crows over hunting rights. The climax was reached in the Battle of Crowheart Butte.

Sometime between the fall of 1858 and the following spring, Washakie and his villagers set up a hunting camp in the Wind River valley, with their allies, Chief Taghee and his Bannocks, encamped a few miles south. A large party of Crows moved in and defiantly put up their tipis not far from the Shoshonis. Washakie sent a brave and his wife as peace envoys, but the Crows killed the man and scalped him. The woman escaped, got back to her own camp, and reported the murder to Washakie who immediately sent a runner to Taghee for reinforcements.

Big Robber, the Crow chief, had expected Washakie to rush into battle. When he did not, he taunted him with messages which called him a squaw and an old woman, afraid to fight.

When Taghee's warriors came, Washakie was then ready and sent Big Robber a message: "I am looking for you. When we meet I will cut out your heart and eat it in front of your braves."

This battle, fought mainly on Black Mountain, east and south of the Tetons, lasted four days. On the final day Washakie singled out the Crow chief and rode directly toward him. Big Robber, seeing him coming, shouted a challenge. They met with a shock that unhorsed them both, and drawing knives, they fought hand-to-hand. Although Washakie was considerably older, Big Robber was soon killed. It proved to be a decisive contest. Washakie won the respect of the Crows and gained rights to the disputed hunting grounds.

Whether he cut out the Crow's heart and ate it in sight of Big Robber's warriors will never be known. At the scalp dance held the next night Washakie was seen carrying a Crow heart on the end of his lance, but when asked about his challenge many years later, he said: "When a man is in battle and his blood runs hot, he sometimes does things he is sorry for afterwards. I cannot remember everything that happened so long ago."

The Shoshonis were to suffer more than any other tribe from the western migration. Washakie watched with alarm the constantly increasing travel on the trails that led across his people's land. Oxen, horses, mules, wagons, and men's feet were beating them into broad, hard roadways "as smooth as a barn-floor swept by the winds." On either side of these roads the grasses and other plant foods which supported buffalo, elk, deer, and antelope were grazed away by those animals belonging to Oregon and California-bound emigrants, Mormons, and goldseekers. Reckless men among them killed every Indian on sight. Many Shoshonis were without defense, while those belonging to Washakie's band were forbidden to retaliate. They were completely at the mercy of these trespassers and had to retire deeper into the mountain valleys to keep away from white men's trails.

Resentment mounted among all Indians along these travel routes. The warlike tribes favored uniting and driving the whites from their land. When they asked Washakie to join them, he refused, realizing that such warfare would mean the eventual annihilation of his people since the whites so far outnumbered them. Once when he looked over the plains he saw vast herds of game; now he saw only endless lines of white-topped wagons, and men on horseback.

He was aware, too, that the old nomadic life was doomed: "After a few more snows the buffalo will be gone, and if we do not learn some other way to get something to eat, we will starve to death." The only solution lay in keeping peace with the white man, and by so doing hope to gain some consideration. As early as 1858 he asked the federal government for a reservation and was doubtless the first Indian to do so.

But until Washakie's Shoshonis were given a reservation they continued to move from place to place east and west of the Rockies, hunting and fishing in the valleys that flanked the Tetons; summering beside Henry's Lake, northwest of those peaks; wintering along the Jefferson River, always keeping well away from the overland trails.

Although individuals, especially shamans, were admired for outstanding qualities, strong leadership or control was not tolerated by Shoshonis. There was some resentment, therefore, at Washakie's position as a ruler. A number of restless young men suggested that he was no longer the great warrior he had been and discussed a possible successor.

Giving no hint that he was aware of the discontent, Washakie mounted his horse one day and rode off. After "two moons" he returned, carrying seven scalps. He told his tribesmen he had gone alone on the warpath to test his prowess, that he had come on a band of his enemies, and had taken all the scalps himself. Holding them up, he said:

"Let him who can do a greater feat claim the chieftainship. Let him who would take my place count as many scalps." His leadership was never questioned again.

In the fall of 1868 the government finally set aside 2,774,400 acres for a Shoshoni reservation in the Wind River valley. After Washakie had studied the treaty, discussed it with the negotiator, and agreed to the terms, he spoke in council:

"I am laughing because I am happy. . . . The Wind River Country is the one for me. We may not for one, two or three years be able to till the ground. The Sioux may trouble us. But when the Sioux are taken care of, we can do well." He added: "I want . . . the privilege of going over the mountains to hunt where I please."

But he refused to move his people there until the area had been cleared of hostiles and an army post established. By 1872 adequate protection had still not been provided, and Washakie's reply to officials who urged him to settle on the reservation was:

"Tell the Great Father that I am desirous to settle down to farming and stock raising and to have schools as the government promised, but it would place my people in a defenseless attitude and subject them perhaps to a massacre. Please talk protection all the time."

He was right about the Sioux. The establishment of a small army post that allowed the Shoshonis to eventually move to the reservation discouraged full-scale attacks, but did not stop those frequent swift raids to steal horses, or the assaults on hunting parties.

In 1876 Sioux resentment over the building of the Bozeman Trail, with its string of military posts running over their lands, reached its climax. When Washakie learned that General George Crook was planning a campaign against the Sioux that summer, he sent word that he would join in a fight against his old enemy. Washakie was then seventy-eight.

On June 14, one hundred and twenty-five Shoshoni warriors, "resplendent in . . . feathers, beads, brass buttons, bells, scarlet cloth, and flashing lances," rode into Crook's camp in the Tongue River valley, "at whirlwind speed . . . in columns of two, like a company of regular cavalry." They had with them two large American flags and each warrior carried a pennon.

Two of Washakie's sons, Coo-coosh (Dick) and Conna-yah (Bishop), were there. Their father, however, was waiting for a band of Ute and Bannock warriors who had sent word they wanted to join him.

Some two hundred Crow fighting men with their chiefs had ridden in to Crook's camp, also intent on battling the Sioux. His red allies then assembled, the general was able to get his troops under way on June 16 right after breakfast.

"The Indians, with war bonnets nodding, and lances brilliant with steel and feathers, headed by their . . . chiefs, rode . . . in careless order on our flanks," wrote *Chicago Times* correspondent John Finerty. They soon moved into the lead, with their medicine men well in advance, for Crook had agreed, on the Shoshonis' advice, to let the red men arrange their own plan of march.

The company moved over rolling ground well watered by

many small, clear streams, and covered with rich grasses and "wild roses by the thousand." Staff officer John G. Bourke also noticed the abundance of blue phlox and the numbers of songbirds in every thicket.

Bourke, who would later make notable contributions to the understanding of Indian ceremonials and esoteric rites, now learned from the Indians with whom he was riding about a certain herb (he was unable to identify it) they carried to feed their ponies in the heat of battle, to keep them from losing their wind. He observed the importance of medicine men and saw how they could arbitrarily stop the march at any time. Although everyone was ordered to keep back during one such halt, Bourke was not too far away to watch the ceremonial smoking before a juniper in whose forks was a buffalo head.

Before dawn the following morning a large party of Crow and Shoshoni scouts rode out of camp to the north, rapidly disappearing from sight. A few hours later they came "flying" back, "shouting at the top of their voices, 'Heap Sioux! heap Sioux!' gesticulating wildly in the direction of the bluffs. . . .All looked . . . and there, sure enough, were the Sioux in goodly numbers, and . . . formidable array"—not less than twenty-five hundred, Crook estimated.

The general positioned his troops, and the Sioux and allied Cheyennes, under Chief Crazy Horse, swept down the bluff at full run. Finerty, who rode with the cavalry, wrote: "We went like a storm . . . too rapidly to use our carbines . . . our men broke into a mad cheer as the Sioux, unable to face that impetuous line . . . broke and fled."

The Shoshonis, stripped to breechclout, moccasins, and war bonnet, now took up their position at the head of a large hollow where some of the cavalry and a large part of the main command were concentrated. The Sioux, rallying, made a bold dash to sweep the hollow, but were met by a Shoshoni countercharge that took the Sioux and Cheyennes in flank and scattered them. "There was a headlong rush for about two hundred yards [that drove] the enemy back in confusion."

Collectively and individually the Shoshonis had been effective that day. Two scouts, observing General Crook's exposed position on a knoll, told him of his danger, and then "protected him in his withdrawal to safe quarters."

Tigee, one of Washakie's lieutenants, was commended for bravery when he stood over the body of Captain Guy Henry, who had been seriously wounded, and "held the hostiles at bay until both could be rescued."

Crook's forces were greatly outnumbered. Crazy Horse admitted later that he had sixty-five hundred fighting men on the field that day; Crook had only eleven hundred. That night the general decided to retire to his headquarters camp. The Shoshonis asked his permission to return home to hold a scalp dance. They assured him they would return directly after the ceremony. He allowed them to go.

On July 11, Washakie, that "grand old Chief," who reminded Lieutenant Bourke of Henry Ward Beecher, rode into Crook's camp with two hundred and thirteen braves. Beside him was a mounted warrior who carried the oriflamme of the tribe—a standard of eagle feathers attached to a lance twelve feet long. Each man was wearing in his headdress a piece of white drilling to distinguish him from the enemy.

"They were welcome," Finerty wrote, "as we had been seriously annoyed every night . . . by small parties of Sioux."

The Custer massacre had taken place just sixteen days before, and Crook now received orders to wait for reinforcements. While they waited, Washakie rode each morning to the bluff tops to scan the horizon through his field glass; then he would report his observations to Crook. Every forenoon and evening he drilled his men. They moved out "in columns of twos; first at a fast walk, almost a trot, afterwards increasing the gait. The young warriors sat like so many statues, horse and rider moving as one. Not a word was spoken until their leaders broke out in their war song. . . ." Then the whole column joined.

Down the valley they rode about three miles, but at a signal from Washakie they turned, and at another, "formed front into line and proceeded slowly for about fifty more yards. . . . He waved his hands; the line spread out as skirmishers." Then he yelled a command in a "shrill treble," and "the ponies broke into a frantic rush for camp, riding over sagebrush, rocks, stumps," the warriors all the while "yelling, chanting their war-songs, or howling like coyotes"—sounding, one officer thought, "not unlike the 'y-i-i-ip' of the rebels in '63."

Bourke, who was riding with them, thought what "fools" we

The wagon train of Smith, Jackson & Sublette, Rocky Mountain fur traders, leaving St. Louis, April 10, 1830, for the annual rendezvous, held that year near the Wind River Mountains in Wyoming. The train was carrying packs of trade goods for the Indians, supplies of coffee, tea, sugar, tobacco, liquor, guns, ammunition, blankets, and other wares for the trappers and hunters, as well as the long-awaited mail. Painting by William Henry Jackson.—Western History Research Center, University of Wyoming.

"The Trappers." Field sketch by Alfred Jacob Miller. Miller, a Baltimore artist, preserv
posterity a way of life that was soon to vanish. In 1837 he accompanied the fur trade
van across the Plains to the rendezvous held on the Green River, near Horse Creek,
east of the Teton Range, sketching Indian encampments and buffalo hunts; trappers
ers, voyageurs in their daily round.—Western History Research Center, Univers
Wyoming.

"Sunrise. Trappers and Voyageurs at their meal of Buffalo Hump Rib." Field sketch by Alfred Jacob Miller, made in 1837. Man in dark hat, seated back to the fire, appears to be the artist's patron, Captain William Drummond Stewart, Scottish nobleman.—Western History Research Center, University of Wyoming.

Codsiogo, a Shoshoni warrior. Denver Public Library, Western History Department.

Christopher (Kit) Carson, noted mountain man, guide, scout, and soldier. Photograph taken in 1868, two months before his death at age fifty-nine.— Western History Research Center, University of Wyoming.

Taboonggwesha, a young Shoshoni brave.—Denver Public Library, Western History Department.

Washakie, head chief of the Eastern Shoshonis for nearly sixty years. A noted warrior, leader, and orator, he was one of the great Indian personalities in history. In dignity and leadership his white contemporaries compared him with George Washington; in eloquence, with Daniel Webster. Photograph by C. S. Baker (wet-plate glass negative).—Western History Research Center, University of Wyoming.

Shoshoni encampment. Note designs painted on dark tipi in foreground. Photogra taken in 1870 by william Henry Jackson. —Western History Research Cent University of Wyoming.

Chief Washakie and two of his lieutenants, Tigee, left, and Pe-ri-go-shia, right. Tigee was commended for bravery when he stood over the body of Captain Guy Henry, who was seriously wounded during the Battle of the Rosebud, and kept the Sioux at bay until both he and Henry could be rescued.—Western History Research Center, University of Wyoming.

William Henry Jackson, pioneer photographer, artist, and author. This picture was taken early in 1872, before he left with the Hayden Survey party that was to explore the Teton Range and valleys. That summer Jackson made the first photographs of the Tetons.— Western History Research Center, University of Wyoming.

Dr. Ferdinand V. Hayden, physician, surgeon, geologist, paleontologist, mineralogist, and director of the U.S. Geological Surveys, who led his exploring parties into the field each summer. The 1872 survey of the Teton Range and valleys gave the public its first introduction to the wonders of that country through photographs by William Henry Jackson, drawings by W. H. Holmes, and reports by the eminent specialists on his staff.— Western History Research Center, University of Wyoming.

"Photographing in High Places." William Henry Jackson and assistant, eighteen-year-old Charles Campbell, readying equipment to make the first photographs of the Teton Range. The Grand Teton is seen looming above Campbell's hat. Jackson is kneeling beside his little dark tent. He was working with three cameras on this trip.—Western History Research Center, University of Wyoming.

The Grand Teton. Photographed from the west side by William Henry Jackson 1872. Jackson wrote that after a steep and dangerous climb through snow, he ar his assistant reached the top of a ridge. "Thousands of feet below us lay the i(gorge of Glacier Creek. . . . Above . . . towered the sharp cone of the Grar Teton. . . . I quickly set up my cameras and began one of the busiest pictu, making days of my whole career."—Western History Research Center, Univers of Wyoming.

The Teton Range, from the west. "One of the most stupendous panoramas in all America," William Henry Jackson said of this view, which he photographed in the summer of 1872. In all these photographs Jackson was using the wet-plate glass negative.—Library, The State Historical Society of Colorado.

John Merle Coulter, the twenty-
one-year-old botanist with the
Hayden Survey party of 1872.
That year he made the first reports on the flora of the Teton
Range and both west and east
valleys, and pressed an extensive collection. Two years later
he was made a professor at Han-
over College, at which time he
founded and edited the *Botanical
Gazette*. He had a distinguished
career as a botanist, educator
and author.—Western History
Research Center, University of
Wyoming.

Sidford Hamp, the seven-
teen-year-old topographical
assistant with the Hayden
Survey party of 1872. He
was a member of the climbing party that made the first
ascent of the Grand Teton by
white men. He did not, however, reach the summit. It
was, he wrote his mother,
"the hardest day of my life."
—Western History Research
Center, University of Wyoming.

Mount Moran seen across Jackson Lake. Falling Ice Glacier appears to be considerably larger than at present. Photograph taken by William Henry Jackson in 1878. —Library, The State Historical Society of Colorado.

Thomas Moran, etcher, illustrator, and landscape painter, after whom the Teton peak was named. He was a member of the Hayden Survey party of 1871 that explored Yellowstone country. His paintings of the area helped convince a hesitating Congress of the need for creating Yellowstone National Park. He did not see the Tetons until 1879. —Western History Research Center, University of Wyoming. Fritiof Fryxell Collection.

"Mount Moran," oil painting by Thomas Moran; dated 1903. The artist camped in Teton Canyon on the west side of the range in the summer of 1879. He climbed to the heights to make watercolor sketches of the peaks, from which studio versions were made later. He considered his paintings of the Tetons to be among his most significant works. —Western History Research Center, University of Wyoming. Friof Fryxell Collection.

Owen Wister, musician, composer, lawyer, and author of *The Virginian*. Part of the action of this novel takes place in Teton country which Wister first saw when on a camping trip in 1887. After six trips to the Far West he gave up the practice of law to become a writer of Western fiction. He was a grandson of famed Shakespearean actress Fanny Kemble. Undated photograph taken in Yellowstone Park. —Western History Research Center, University of Wyoming.

Fanny Kemble Wister, daughter of Owen Wister. This picture was taken at the JY Ranch in Jackson Hole in 1911, when Fanny was nine. She recalls spending her days riding bareback over the sagebrush plains and up the Teton slopes, through acres of wild flowers. "The Grand Teton was our mountain and the most wonderful mountain in the world." —Courtesy Mrs. Fanny Kemble Wister Stokes.

were not to incorporate this "finest light cavalry in the world, into our permanent military force."

Through his scouts, who were regarded by the army as "far the most serviceable of any to be found on the plains," Washakie kept well informed about the enemy and gave advice to the restive general.

"There is no more able man to manage an Indian Battle. He tells General Crook to hold on, make connection with General Terry and get all the outside troops he can before he risks another battle or he will be badly whipped, and the old man knows what he is talking about."

After Colonel Chambers came in with seven companies of infantry, Washakie warned Crook that he was still outnumbered three to one, and urged him to leave the Sioux alone for a few days. "They cannot subsist the great number of warriors and men in their camp, and will have to scatter for pasturage and meat," he told the general.

Washakie led a Shoshoni scouting party to the head of the Little Bighorn, found the hostiles on the move, and, noting the great numbers of horse and dog bones scattered about their abandoned camps, knew they were already short of food.

On August 3 Crook's command marched twenty miles northeast to Goose Creek where General Wesley Merritt had been ordered to wait, and on the fifth the combined forces moved on to make a junction with General Alfred Terry, coming from the east. They met him on the tenth.

Each had expected to find the enemy on his front, and when he did not, both realized that he had escaped. On a chance of catching up with the Sioux, the troops pushed along the Yellowstone to the Little Missouri, and went into camp at the head of Heart River.

"Ragged and almost starving, out of rations, out at elbows and every other exposed angle, out of everything but pluck and ammunition, General Crook gave up the pursuit of Sitting Bull at the head of Heart River," wrote staff officer Charles King. "The Indians had scattered in every direction. We had chased them a month, and were no nearer than when we started . . . They had burned off the grass from the Yellowstone to the mountains, and our horses were dropping by scores . . . There was no help for it, and only one thing left to do.

"At daybreak the next morning the orders came, 'Make for

the Black Hills—due south by the compass—seven days' march at least'—and we headed our dejected steeds accordingly and shambled off in search of supplies." The Shoshonis and Crows were permitted to return home.

Washakie was glad to leave for he had no patience with Terry's impedimenta: "a complete wagon train, tents and equipage of every description; artillery . . ." The chief felt the army's mobility was destroyed, and complained:

"With such mules nothing could be done; the infantry was all right, and so was part of the cavalry, but the pack train was no good and was simply impeding progress."

In recognition of Washakie's services, President Grant sent him a silver-mounted saddle. During the presentation, which was made in front of his warriors, soldiers at the reservation post, and Indian Service employees, the chief "stood straight and tall with arms folded, and tears running down his cheeks."

The Indian agent asked him: "What word shall I send to the Great Father?"

"Nothing. I cannot speak. My heart is so full my tongue will not work."

"Do say a few words so that President Grant may know how pleased you are."

Washakie replied: "When a favor is shown a Frenchman [white man] he feels it in his head and his tongue speaks. When a kindness is shown to an Indian he feels it in his heart, and the heart has no tongue."

Washakie's many white friends among army personnel and civilians always spoke of him with admiration, respect, and affection. They commended his wisdom, perception, foresight, ability for leadership, and his skills as a warrior. They remarked on his eloquence as an orator; on his forceful personality and commanding presence. They mentioned his graceful carriage and fine manners and were impressed with his "most gentle and intelligent face" and "kindly eyes." In repose his look was serious, "but when he smiled, his face would break into a charming expression delightful to look upon."

He spoke French and enjoyed using French words and phrases in conversation with white friends. Then he would refer to his hat as his *chapeau*; and his pony as his *cheval*; or he would thank someone with a gracious "*je vous remercie*," and a bow.

He was also a noted singer, and an artist and historian, painting on elkhide battle scenes and other important events in his people's history, as well as decorative depictions of buffalo hunts and antelope surrounds.

Over the years Washakie regularly enlisted in the army as a scout; the last time was 1898 when he was nearly one hundred. Records show that he took no part in active duty after 1889, but his enlistment was accepted each time as a means of remunerating him for past service.

Like all other tribes, the Shoshonis had their land troubles. The Wind River Reservation that was originally nearly as large as Connecticut was pared down after three treaties to one fifth that size. They also suffered from the government's unfulfilled obligations and broken promises. Although Washakie led in all the negotiations, he was often disappointed, troubled, and discouraged by the results.

In 1878 he had a meeting with Wyoming's governor, John Hoyt, who was impressed by Washakie's majesty. Hoyt wrote that the chief was seated on "what would have passed for a modest throne, covered with the skin of the panther [and] bear . . . his form as stately as that of Daniel Webster, and yet broader, his face wearing both the dignity and benignity of Washington, his grey locks hanging far down his shoulders. . . ."

He rose and addressed the governor:

> We are right glad, sir, that you have so bravely and so kindly come among us. I shall, indeed, speak to you freely of the many wrongs we have suffered at the hands of the white man . . . But I cannot hope to express to you the half that is in our hearts. They are too full for words.
>
> Disappointment; then a deep sadness; then a grief inexpressible; then at times, a bitterness . . . that kindles in our hearts the fires of desperation. . . .
>
> The white man, who possesses this whole vast country from sea to sea, who roams over it at pleasure, and lives where he likes, cannot know the cramp we feel in this little spot, with the undying remembrance of the fact, which you know as well as we, that every foot of what you proudly call America, not very long ago belonged to the red men. But the white man had, in ways we know not of, learned some things we had not learned; among them how to make superior tools and terrible weapons, better for war than bows and arrows. . . .

And so, at last, our fathers were steadily driven out, or killed, and we, their sons, but sorry remnants of tribes once mighty, are cornered in little spots of the earth all ours of right—cornered like guilty prisoners, and watched over by men with guns who are more than anxious to kill us off.

Nor is this all. The white man's government promised that if we, the Shoshonis, would be content with the little patch allowed us, it would keep us well supplied with everything necessary for comfortable living, and see that no white man should cross our borders for our game, or anything that is ours. *But it has not kept its word!* The white man kills our game, captures our furs, and sometimes feeds his herds upon our meadows. And your great and mighty government . . . does not protect us in our rights. It leaves us without the promised seed, without tools for cultivating the land . . . without food . . . without the schools we so much need for our children.

I say again, *the government does not keep its word!* And so . . . we are sometimes nearly starved, and go half naked as you see us!

Knowing all this, do you wonder, sir, that we have fits of depression and think to be avenged?

Hoyt admitted that he was do deeply moved "tears filled my eyes, and my response was for a moment tremulous." He promised Washakie he would report everything to Washington, and personally see that justice was done. Washakie came up, "took me warmly by the hand, and, with a steady look into my eyes . . . said, 'We believe you!'"

Hoyt mounted his horse, rode to the telegraph office, and wired the secretary of the interior, urging him to send assurances of goodwill, and follow them promptly with the needed supplies. Carloads of food, clothing, and tools were soon despatched, and a teacher ordered to the reservation.

On the morning of February 21, 1900, the post commander at Fort Washakie sent a telegram to the adjutant general, announcing the old chief's death the night before at eight-thirty. He asked for instructions. From Washington came the reply:

"Order full military burial for Chief Washakie of the Shoshones, rank of Captain. . . ." This was the first military funeral ever ordered for a native American.

The following afternoon Troop E, First Cavalry, rode over the snow to Washakie's cabin, formed in line, and presented sabers as the flag-draped coffin was carried to the waiting caisson. They then served as escort to the fort's military cemetery. Here they drew up at attention beside the open grave to wait until the last mourners in the mile-and-a-half-long procession came up.

At a signal, the Shoshoni women stopped their wailing, and the Episcopal graveside service was read by Washakie's friend of many years, the Reverend John Roberts.

The coffin was then lowered into the grave, and Troop E fired a three-volley salute. As the echoes of Taps died away among the snow-covered hills, the women commenced their keening again for the last chief of the Wind River Shoshonis.

XVIII
Continental Tea

The first party of American scientists to report on the Tetons went there through necessity rather than intent. Captain William F. Raynolds, a topographical engineer, who was leading an expedition to the sources of the Yellowstone River, found his entrance to that area blocked from the south and was forced to make a detour into Jackson Hole and across Teton Pass.

Raynolds, a thirty-nine-year-old West Pointer who was a complete stranger to the West, admitted his entire lack of "previous preparation" for an assignment that was to take him through a rugged wilderness "nearly one-fourth larger than all of France . . . and more than double the area of Great Britain." He had been ordered to explore the country drained by the Yellowstone and its principal tributaries, and the mountains in which they rise. While so doing he was to determine the number and disposition of the Indians living in that territory, its resources, climate, topographical features; the navigability of its streams, and the practicability of building rail or wagon roads either for military operations or for the use of emigrants and settlers. Further, he was to observe and report on a total eclipse of the sun, visible on July 18, 1860, north of latitude 52°. Two seasons (1859 and 1860) were thought sufficient to complete such a survey.

It was an assignment a hardy and experienced explorer might have found challenging. For Raynolds, who was neither physically nor philosophically ready to meet and overcome the hardships and obstacles, the expedition became a series of mishaps, frustrations, wrong turns, and major disappointments, while the exertion undermined his health.

With Jim Bridger as his guide, he set out on May 20, 1860, after seven months spent in winter quarters, to begin the second half of his assignment. His party included a dragoon escort, two topographers, a meteorologist, an artist and his assistant, and a geologist-naturalist-physician, Dr. Ferdinand V. Hayden. On this trip Hayden was to make the first analysis of the geological structure of the Tetons, Jackson Hole, Pierre's Hole, and the Snake River Basin and classify the fauna of that area. Later he would achieve renown through his own extensive surveys of the western territories and for his leading role in the creation of the world's first national park—Yellowstone.

Ten days later the Raynolds party was close to the sources of the Wind River. From there the captain had plotted his course for a crossing to the headwaters of the Yellowstone, keeping on the Atlantic side of the Divide. He would then cut almost diagonally across the future park and, by following the Gallatin River, reach the Three Forks of the Missouri.

Charted, it was simple, but Jim Bridger had said from the first that this was impossible, that they would have to "pass over to the headwaters of the Columbia, and back again to the Yellowstone." Consulting his map, Raynolds saw no necessity for crossing the Continental Divide twice. But that afternoon, as he was to discover, "directly across our route lies a basaltic ridge, rising not less than 5,000 feet above us, its walls apparently vertical and with no visible pass nor even cañon."

Bridger then turned to him and said, "I told you you could not go through. A bird can't fly over that without taking a supply of grub along."

Raynolds admitted: "I had no reply to offer, and mentally conceded the accuracy of the 'old man of the mountains.' " It was often hard for the trained topographer to accept the judgment and advice of the illiterate mountaineer whose school was experience and whose maps were mental.

He found some compensation for the wasted effort in views of the Wind River valley from the summit. Pen could not "adequately describe" the grandeur of the scene; "only the brush of a Bierstadt or a Stanley" could possibly do it justice.

In the morning he noted in his journal that he felt "elated" at the thought of making their next halt on the Pacific slope. That night's encampment, Bridger told him, would be on "the waters of the Columbia and within five miles of Green river, which could be easily reached. I therefore filled my canteen from Wind river, with the design of carrying the water to the other side, then procuring some from Green river, and with that of the Columbia, making tea from the mingled waters of the Gulf of Mexico, the Gulf of California, and the Pacific. . . ."

Their trail that day led up the point of a spur. Although steep, progress was good until they came to an extensive windfall that called for "much labor and a liberal use of the axe" to cut a passage through. Soon they were in snow, but making the horses take the lead by turn, they forced a way over and finally stood on the last ridge of the Atlantic slope. There a narrow valley, filled with snow, separated them from the summit. Turning aside to avoid it, they shortly found themselves floundering through still other deep drifts.

Then "Bridger for the first time, lost heart and declared that it would be impossible to go further. To return involved retracing our steps fully half way to the Popo-Agie, then turning north into the valley of the Big Horn . . . a course plainly inadmissable until every other hope failed."

Raynolds now decided to reconnoiter by himself, and "if possible find some escape from our dilemma. Dismounting, I pushed ahead through the snow, which was melting rapidly, and rendered travel both difficult and perilous. At times the crust would sustain my weight . . . at others it would break and let me sink, generally up to the middle, and sometimes . . . to my shoulders." In some places he was able to extricate himself "only by rolling and stamping, and in many places . . . was compelled to crawl upon my face over the treacherous . . . drifts. After great labor I found myself alone on the summit of the Rocky mountains with the train out of sight."

On surveying his surroundings he discovered a gap. If his men could be brought this far, he thought, their chief difficulties would be over. He turned back to lead them up.

Wet to the skin, and exhausted, Raynolds nevertheless managed to guide the party to the crest of the summit. Although the descent was gradual, it was not without problems, for the snow was deep in parts, and in others where it had melted the ground was "a perfect quagmire."

To their left towered "a bold conical peak" that Raynolds fixed as the topographical center of the continent, "the waters from its sides flowing into the Gulf of Mexico, the Gulf of California, and the Pacific Ocean." Because of this uniting of waters, "I named it Union Peak"; the gap through which he led them he called Union Pass.

"The day's march was by far the most difficult we have had . . . and wet and exhausted as I was, all the romance of my continental tea party had departed, and though the valley of Green river was in plain sight I had not the energy either to visit it or send to it."

Another day of hard travel followed. Again the ground was boggy; four horses who attempted to jump from a five-foot bank over a stream fell in and had to be lifted out. In one place the trail grew so narrow that the odometer wheels could not be kept upright, even with ropes, and finally overturned and rolled into the river, taking the mules with them. Nor was the weather obliging, as it snowed frequently throughout the march. Discouraged at the end of six miles, they decided to go into camp along Fish Creek, a tributary of the Gros Ventre River, where there was some pasturage, by no means good, "but better than at our previous camp."

Bridger, Raynolds observed, "seems more at a loss than I have ever seen him, and after reaching camp he rode in advance to reconnoitre." On his return he told the captain it would be necessary to make a short march the next day, news which Raynolds did not regret since their animals were exhausted.

By morning it was snowing hard. After advancing only three miles Bridger advised a halt in a clearing where there was some grass, since he knew of no other ground equal to it, which could be reached that day.

It was Raynolds' plan to keep as close to the dividing crest as possible, then recross to the headwaters of the Yellowstone by way of Two Ocean Pass which Bridger had first seen in 1825. He was anxious to verify Jim's account of the stream that separated in a marshy meadow at the summit, sending one portion of its waters to the Atlantic via the Gulf of Mexico, and the other to the Pacific. It was a never-failing source of wonder to mountain men, one of whom wrote:

"Here a trout of 12 inches . . . may cross the mountains in safety. Poets have sung of the 'meeting of waters' and fish climbing cataracts but the 'parting of waters and fish crossing mountains' . . . remains unsung as yet by all except the solitary Trapper who sits under . . . a spreading pine . . . beating time . . . with a whip on his trap sack. . . ."

Raynolds noticed that animal life here differed markedly from that on the Atlantic slope, and that Dr. Hayden and his assistants—one of whom was twenty-year-old James Stevenson—had been busily collecting specimens: "three or four squirrels previously unknown to us, double the number of birds, and a large and new species of rabbit." This was Baird's rabbit, *Lepus bairdii*, Hayden, known also as Rocky Mountain snowshoe hare.

Three days later they were still crossing ridges that separated the various forks of the Gros Ventre, their course heading nearly northwest. But the depth of the mud and the animals' exhausted condition made travel virtually impossible.

Adding to the captain's troubles, his men grew insubordinate and refused to bring on the odometer wheels: "It was with the greatest difficulty that I succeeded in enforcing discipline. . . ." Conditions dictated a short march, and a halt was called after eight miles.

Travel the next day was even worse: Mud in the valley of the North Fork forced them to the slopes where, among the pines, they found snow in "impassable banks." The open ground between was so sodden animals sank with every step: "I counted at one time 25 mules plunged deep in the mud, totally unable to extricate themselves."

To go on was clearly impossible. To remain was equally out

of the question. They therefore turned back on their trail for two miles and pitched their tents in a place where the animals could pick up a "scanty subsistence."

Bridger now climbed to the top of the ridge to survey the country and came back after dark to report. "Nothing but snow was visible. . . . Although he seems familiar with the locality, it is evident he is in doubt as to what is best to next attempt." After talking it over, he and Jim decide to make a thorough examination of the area the next day to try to pick out a feasible route to the upper valley of the Yellowstone.

In the morning they set off on their previous day's trail. Beyond the place where they had turned back they found a westerly fork that appeared to head in a low pass, and seemed promising. Again there was difficulty getting across snowfields and through mud. After leaving the stream the way grew steep, and the slopes were covered with scrub pines that tore the flesh as they pushed through. Under them were deep drifts that had to be tramped down before they could be crossed. For Raynolds "the labor was . . . excessive," but they at length reached the summit.

Here Bridger took one look around and announced that "we were on the wrong route and that our morning's labors had been wholly useless. . . . We had expended our efforts in climbing a spur."

Back to the valley they rode, deciding to stay with the main stream even though it headed east. There were more snow-drifts to push through, but after a mile the river valley suddenly widened, and its banks turned into tall, sheer cliffs.

"Bridger at once seemed to recognize the locality, saying, 'This is the pass!'" By this time Raynolds admitted to being exhausted, so they turned back to camp.

With a party of nine that included Dr. Hayden they went the next day to explore Bridger's pass. Soon after starting out, a mule tumbled into the river with its rider, both narrowly missing death. Once in the broad river valley they had seen the day before, Raynolds began finding obstacles which would hinder passage of the train. The most discouraging were the countless side gullies from two to four feet deep which crossed the trail and were completely hidden by snow. Into them the riders now pitched headlong without warning, and out of them they floundered "in a style at once ridiculous and exhausting." Still, he was determined to try to bring the party through if there was any hope of getting over the snow on the Yellowstone side.

But the view north from the dividing crest soon dashed the captain's "fondly cherished schemes," as he wrote. There was nothing in sight but pines and snow. He was convinced that an attempt to get through would result in the certain loss of the animals, if not of the entire party. Reluctantly he decided to abandon the plan to which he had "so steadily clung" and look for a route to the Three Forks. "After taking our fill of the disheartening view we returned to camp."

The following day (June 8), after hours of travel at a snail's pace through sticky mud, after miles of pushing through thick stands of pine and crossing numerous ravines, after an unnecessary climb up a steep ridge—"a mistake of Bridger's" —they came at last to the well-defined Indian trail leading from the Green River. There they set up camp in a meadow that offered some good pasturage.

In the morning, on setting out early, they had their first sight of the "snow-covered peaks of the Great Teton, dazzling in the clear atmosphere, with the reflected rays of the newly-risen sun." Their artist made a watercolor sketch, but admitted afterward that he had been unable to capture the "gorgeous coloring."

But this day that began so well was not without its usual reverses. Three pack mules ran away to the heights. One of them, slipping, rolled fifty feet into the river, injuring itself fatally. It struggled to the opposite shore before dying, necessitating a swim through the icy torrent to retrieve the pack. Next, one of the dragoon horses lost its footing and was snagged so badly they expected it would bleed to death. By stanching the blood with cotton, and sewing up the gash, they succeeded in saving it. That night when they came to count the herd, one packhorse was missing, "thus adding another to the mishaps of the day," Raynolds remarked.

June 11 found them following the Indian trail. During the morning they discovered a party of Blackfeet watching them from a ridgetop. Had Raynolds' usual pattern of misfortune persisted, the Indians would have attacked. Instead, when his scouts approached them, they fled. The captain nevertheless ordered the train closed up, and that night he doubled his guard.

The trail took them over a succession of ridges. "As we climbed the last we saw before us a wide, level valley, known as Jackson's Hole . . . its surface covered with luxuriant vegetation, the prevalent green . . . relieved by the bright yellow of a small variety of sun-flower that was . . . abundant. Through this valley we now rode rapidly . . . and pushed down the Snake in search of a ford, Bridger declaring that we could find none above."

But here there was no crossing either, for the river divided into "innumerable channels" and flowed with the "rapidity of a torrent," for the Teton snows were then melting.

A small party of Shoshonis, encamped on the west shore, swam their ponies over a few miles downstream and paid the captain a visit. They asked him for some tobacco, which he gave them; then, their curiosity about the party being satisfied, they returned to the other side. Thinking that this place where the Indians had crossed might offer a good ford for his train, Raynolds moved his camp there in the morning. He then sent two young soldiers, lance corporals Lovett and Bradley, to inspect the river and report. Within twenty minutes Lovett came rushing back with the news that Bradley had drowned.

"All hands started for the rescue, but the thickness of the underbrush and the swiftness of the current" rendered efforts useless. On learning that he had been swept away at the swiftest part, "all hope was abandoned. I sent men below to find the body and also offered the Indians a reward for his recovery, but thus far all has been in vain."

Every effort to find a fording failed, so a party was detailed to construct a raft. While they were at work, Raynolds started off to look for a crossing above the junction of the Gros Ventre even though Bridger had told him none existed. "After a ride of thirty miles, I returned to camp without accomplishing anything," he admitted.

The raft was tested the next day, but it "behaved so badly . . . it was promptly pronounced a complete failure." He then decided to try "Bridger's ingenuity," ordering him to construct the bull boat that the old mountain man had doubtless proposed at the start.

Raynolds then called on all hands to help. The biggest problem was to devise a covering for the simple willow-and-cottonwood-pole frame since no buffalo hides were at hand. It was decided to use the army-issue gutta-percha blankets even though in the captain's opinion they were "almost worthless." At Bridger's suggestion they waterproofed the blankets with a thick coating of pine resin, and then protected the whole with Jim's tipi cover.

"By night a very respectable boat was completed, rude in appearance, but promising to be serviceable," Raynolds wrote in a rare moment of optimism. He marveled that it was made "entirely without nails or spikes," the framework being bound together with leather thongs.

There was a long portage over sloughs and islands the next morning before a suitable point could be found to launch the bull boat. Then, manned by four of their strongest swimmers, and laden with a few packs, it got safely across the first channel. There a second portage was made to a place where both remaining channels could be crossed at once. The return trip was made in a single crossing by wisely launching the craft above the three channels. It was by then five o'clock in the afternoon, and work was suspended for that day. Raynolds noted gloomily that the river was rising rapidly, a fact he found "additionally discouraging."

Operations ran smoothly in the morning. The crew was reduced to three, and time for the round trip cut to three quarters of an hour. By the day's end seventeen trips had been made, but still much goods remained to be transported, as well as fifteen men and all the animals. Several attempts had been made to swim the herd across, but the moment they got into the rapids they turned back; no one wanted to try and lead them.

The following day Lance Corporal Lovett volunteered to take the animals to the west shore. They were divided into two bands and were finally induced to follow him. All reached the other side safely, although a good many were swept fully a mile downstream. This accomplished, the bull boat resumed her trips although the crew was, in Raynolds' opinion, "almost incapacitated" by sunburn and sore muscles. On this day however, there was no suffering from further exposure to the sun for it snowed heavily.

Ten more trips were made before all the men and baggage were across. Only the odometer wheels failed to reach the opposite shore. Raynolds' foreman, attempting to ferry them on the balky raft, was forced to abandon the wheels midstream.

Looking about the west shore the captain found the results of their two days' labor disheartening. Everything was so "greatly scattered and disordered," he complained, much precious time was going to be lost in repacking. They set up their camp right beside the Snake, on that beautiful plain just a few miles southeast of Taggart Lake. Views of the snowy Tetons, "the most noted landmarks in this region," were magnificent; nothing Raynolds had ever seen before could compare.

The delay enabled Dr. Hayden to investigate the geology of Jackson Hole. In the limestones along the flanks of the lower ridges he found "numerous fossils, mollusca, and corals," evidence of the ancient sea that had once drowned the area. He identified the many kinds of rocks deposited on the valley floor by the great glaciers. As the train moved up over Teton Pass on June 18, he was making notes on the "blue, cherty carboniferous limestone" seen in abundance "along the margins of the ridges . . . the siliceous rocks which lie above," the "many granitic masses, and . . . gray micaceous slates," that in part composed the range.

At the summit the captain noticed a pine tree into which was cut "J.M., July 7, 1832" and July 11, 1833." Bridger suggested it might have been Joe Meek's work, on his way to rendezvous.

While Hayden was observing animal life, flora, and geologic structure, Raynolds was discovering new troubles. On starting down the west slope, he found the Indian trail completely blocked by immense snowbanks. To avoid them the party had to climb a spur and break a new trail along the precipitous mountainside. Talus and boulders, loosened by the men and horses, began sliding and rolling on those who were in the lead, "seriously endangering" them and causing the captain additional worry.

The party marched nearly due north through Pierre's Hole which Raynolds felt "almost deserves the extravagant praise bestowed on it by Bridger, who declares it to be the finest valley in the world." He noticed that it was "carpeted with . . .

flowers," "brilliant" in color and rich in variety. On their right were the incomparable Tetons, changing in form and outline with every mile.

There was talk of climbing the Grand Teton, Hayden, for one, wanting to examine its structure closely. But Jim Bridger declared that this was impossible: many men had tried it over the years and all had failed. Besides, Raynolds was pressed for time. He had ahead of him a march of some seven hundred miles to reach the line of total eclipse. A little over a week and a half later he was to realize that observation of the eclipse would be another disappointment, for he then had five hundred miles to cover and only thirteen days in which to do it.

Now, as they traveled along the Teton Range, Hayden had to be content with observing it from a distance. He noted the westward tilt—"a little north of west," he found—and speculated on the cause. He examined the geological composition of the foothills and of the valley.

In his haste to reach the Missouri's headwaters and then turn homeward, Raynolds made no attempt to enter Yellowstone country from the west, although his failure to go there was for him the major disappointment of the expedition.

"We were compelled to content ourselves with listening to the marvelous tales of burning plains, immense lakes, and boiling springs, without being able to verify these wonders," he wrote.

Bridger told them stories about a mountain of glass that was there, and a prairie where rabbits, sage hens, antelope, elk, and bear had been turned to stone, "as natural as life"; where flowers bloom "in colors of crystal . . . birds soar with wings spread in motionless flight, while the air floats with music and perfume siliceous, and the sun and moon shine with petrified light." There, too, were bushes that bore "diamonds, rubies, saphires, and emeralds, as large as black walnuts."

Observed another mountain man with the party: "I tell you, sir, it is true, for I gathered a quart myself."

XIX
The Great Surveys

"Man-Who-Picks-Up-Stones-Running" the Sioux called Dr. Ferdinand Hayden after watching him hurry from gulch to slope to butte top, geologist's hammer in hand, filling a bag with rock samples.

A man of boundless energy and enthusiasm, his determination and drive had taken him from the teacher's desk in a one–room country schoolhouse through Oberlin College and on to a doctor's degree at Albany Medical School. But instead of settling down to a comfortable practice after his graduation in 1853, he chose to enter the field that interested him most, and accepted an assignment to collect fossils in the White River Bad Lands of Dakota Territory.

It was there that he earned his Indian name when a party of braves, puzzled by his actions, surrounded him, seized his sample bag, and dumped the contents on the ground. They concluded that he was perhaps insane, but that what he was doing in no way threatened their people, so they let him go.

Accompanying Hayden on this first expedition was another paleontologist-geologist who would later gain fame, Fielding Bradford Meek, and a thirteen-year-old runaway, James Stevenson, whom the doctor had met aboard the steamboat going up the Missouri. Keenly interested in natural history and exploration, and also in search of adventure, young Stevenson had slipped away from his home in Maysville, Kentucky, hoping to join a Hudson's Bay Company party. In talking with him during the voyage, Hayden noticed this interest. Explaining what he was about to do, he invited him to join the expedition, and Stevenson accepted. There followed a close relationship between the two that lasted over a quarter of a century and gave direction to Stevenson's life. He accompanied Hayden on all his subsequent expeditions up to the time of the Civil War, when the doctor entered the Union Army as a surgeon and Stevenson enlisted as a private. At the war's end, Hayden had risen to become Chief Medical Officer of the Army of the Shenandoah, and Stevenson had been promoted to captain. Their association was resumed, and in 1866 they made a tour of the Bad Lands under the auspices of Philadelphia's Academy of Sciences.

Soon after his discharge from the army Dr. Hayden joined the faculty of the University of Pennsylvania as professor of geology and mineralogy. With his summers free, he was able to lead government-sponsored parties to explore and survey those vast and little-known regions of the West, always maintaining, as one of his men observed, "a tenuous link with his professor's chair" by riding his horse "in a frayed but eminently respectable dress coat." In 1872, when he was appointed director of the Survey of the Territories, he resigned the professorship to devote full time to the new office.

Hayden had a distinct talent for discovering the most able and potentially able men in their fields, persuading them to join his expeditions, and then evoke from them their best efforts. As a result, the achievements of this small group of expert and enthusiastic scientists and artists were vast and lasting, and laid the foundation for our present knowledge of those areas they explored.

The photographer William Henry Jackson, who was just getting started in his profession, remembered well the July day in 1870 when Dr. Hayden, on his way to Wyoming, called at his photographic studio in Omaha. The doctor, "a dynamic, intense man," outlined his plans for giving the people of this country a true picture of the new West that miners, settlers, and explorers were opening. He had visions, he said, of establishing in certain choice areas, reserves that would be protected from "the cynical exploitation and exhaustion of a few," and "preserved in beauty for the worthy many." Words were of little use in trying to describe in Washington what might be seen in Wyoming. Drawings were always subject to charges of exaggeration and unreality. The new art of the camera might present Congress with a concept of the West that was indisputable. What did Jackson think? For an answer he took out a portfolio of photographs he had made the previous year.

The doctor spent some time studying the pictures of Indians and wilderness scenery. "Then, with a sigh, he remarked, 'This is what I need. I wish I could offer you enough to make it worth your while to spend the summer with me.'"

Jackson quickly asked what he could offer. Hayden smiled and shook his head. "Only a summer of hard work—and the satisfaction I think you would find in contributing your art to science. Of course, all your expenses would be paid, but—"

Hayden's enthusiasm was contagious. Jackson accepted, and after a month in the field the doctor asked him to become a permanent and salaried member of his staff. Jackson's career was launched.

It was recognized that what came to be known as the Hayden Surveys could accomplish more with less fuss and elaborate equipment than any previous and many later exploring parties. Before setting off across the plains Hayden would recruit from frontier army posts their surplus wagons, mules, and condemned cavalry horses. This solved his transportation problem. Jackson recalled that there were four heavy wagons to carry food, tents, blankets, and equipment, "and two army ambulances, light and fast, for side trips. All six were drawn by mules, while horses carried the men. And stylish horses they were . . . for superbly schooled mounts, I'll stick to army seconds." When the terrain became too rough for wagons, the baggage was shifted to pack mules.

The one exception to the rule of traveling light, was Jackson, who took along some three hundred pounds of equipment, and had an ambulance to himself. His outfit included a standard 8″ × 10″ camera, a stereo which, "with its pair of brass-barreled

Willard lenses . . . looked like a young cannon," and a 6½"×8½" also adaptable to stereoscopic work; a portable dark-room consisting of "a wooden box 30 × 16 × 15 inches, fitted with pans and trays, made so that it could be enlarged with a retractable canopy"; a full stock of chemicals, and glass enough for four hundred plates. "For its day it was a pretty flexible battery."

For those places where the ambulance could not go, there were over the years a succession of sure-footed mules—Hypo, Old Molly, and Gimlet were three well-remembered ones. Hypo was the first: "Carrying my cameras, tripod, dark box, chemicals, water keg, and a day's supply of plates, all loaded in big, brightly painted rawhide containers called parfleches, Hypo was good for as many miles as my horse was, and together we covered an enormous amount of ground off the road."

It was these independent excursions, or at least, "the spirit beneath them, that made this expedition and all the ensuing ones under Dr. Hayden so engrossing and satisfying," Jackson felt. "Every day we had an informal conference around the campfire and then we would set about our work individually or in groups of two or three. One little division might be assigned to calculate the flow volume of a stream; another would be given the task of sounding a lake; several other men might investigate the geology of the region or hunt fossils. . . . We all had work to do, and Dr. Hayden had the rare compound faculty that enabled him not only to select able assistants but to get all of them to pull together. On top of it, and with never a word, he made every man feel that each little individual side trip was vital to the whole—as indeed it was, the way Hayden apportioned the work."

The survey for 1872 had two main divisions. One field party, under the doctor, returned to continue its work in the newly established Yellowstone Park which he and his men had helped make a reality by means of thorough and highly readable reports, photographs by Jackson, and watercolors by landscape artist Thomas Moran.

The second party, the Snake River Division, was headed by James Stevenson, and its job was to explore, map, and report on the Grand Tetons and the country lying directly to the east and west of them. Although it was the smaller party, its roster was no less distinguished. There was Professor Frank H. Bradley, chief geologist, and his assistant W. T. Taggart; Gustavus R. Bechler and Rudolph Hering, topographers; William Nicholson, meteorologist; Dr. Josiah Curtis, surgeon and microscopist; and William Henry Jackson, photographer. Its two youngest members, C. Hart Merriam, the company's ornithologist-mammalogist, and John Merle Coulter, its botanist, were to be recognized internationally. Merriam, a prodigy, was only sixteen; Coulter had just turned twenty-one and was about to be honored with a professorship.

One of the party's three guests was Yellowstone Park's first superintendent, the enthusiastic Nathaniel Pitt Langford, who had lectured, written articles, and lobbied tirelessly to have the park established; he and James Stevenson would gain note this year as the first white men to climb the Grand Teton.

To take pictures of the Tetons, never before photographed, Jackson added an 11" × 14" camera. "The . . . need for big pictures compelled that course, since satisfactory enlargements from small negatives could not be made. . . ."

Because it was "impossible to prepare and develop the bigger plates in my portable dark box, I now had to set up a dark tent every time I wanted to make a picture. This little tent had a conventional cover of grayish-white canvas; but inside it was lined with orange calico to cut the actinic rays."

The mountains were approached from the west by way of Fort Hall—not the old fur trading post built by Nathaniel Wyeth, but a military post established some forty miles from its ruins. There horses and mules were recruited, and on July 12 the party, numbering thirty-seven mounted men and twenty-five pack animals, set off in the morning. At Market Lake Station they left the stage road and turned east, directly toward the Tetons whose highest peak had been visible for many miles, towering on the horizon.

Their guide was Richard (Beaver Dick) Leigh, an English adventurer, whose father had been a member of the British navy, and his grandfather, a colonel in the Sixteenth Lancers. At the age of seven Dick had gone with a grown sister to Philadelphia. At fifteen he saw service in the Mexican War, and afterward turned Rocky Mountain trapper. With his Shoshoni wife, Jenny, and their four children, he became the first settler in

Pierre's Hole. To the Indians he was known as The Beaver, because of "two abnormally large front teeth in his upper jaw"; to white men he was Beaver Dick.

"We must depend on his guidance in fording streams, crossing mountain passes, and avoiding collision with unfriendly tribes," Langford wrote. "Dick seems truly to be a genuine mountain monarch, for there is not a stream, lake or range in any direction from us, for hundreds of miles, with which he is not familiar. He has the entire mountain region in his mind's eye, like a map, and his intelligence on all subjects connected with our march through the country, is the very thing we need. . . ."

By July 23 they had reached Pierre's Hole, "carpeted with the heaviest and largest bunch-grass I have ever seen," Langford remarked. He observed meadows full of camas, its bulb "sweet to the taste, full of gluten, and very satisfying to a hungry man"; and an abundance of yampa, also sweet, and suggestive of parsnip. In the woods, in open meadows, and along the streams he found "large patches of strawberries of the finest flavor."

Jackson noted that this valley was "a game paradise. Our various parties were kept supplied with fresh meat without having to hunt for it, deer, moose, or mountain sheep being nearly always in sight when needed. It was equally easy to get a mess of trout near by. Bears were abundant also. . . . One of the topographers, working on the plateau above timber line, counted eleven . . . during a day's observations."

Camp was made in a grassy meadow in Teton Canyon, where two prospectors already had a tent. One of them, also a hunter of some note, was Phelps, after whom the lake in Jackson Hole was named. Beaver Dick set up his tipi nearby, and his little boys, Richard, Billy, and John were soon on intimate terms with the explorers, running in and out of their camp at will and playing games with the younger ones. It was noticed that Dick, unlike many mountain men, was deeply attached to Jenny and their children. He was, in the opinion of several, "an exemplary family man."

One night he invited some of the party to taste beaver cooked mountain style. "I confess," Langford wrote, "that my appetite was not much sharpened on being told that the animal had been boiled entire, and . . . the dressing done after the cooking was completed." But its "superior flavor, succulence and tenderness" convinced him that "the civilized method of cooking pigeons" applied equally well to beaver.

In the canyon's stands of spruce, fir, and pine, on the wooded foothills and the rocky slopes of the Tetons up to and above timberline, and in Pierre's Hole itself, there was an abundance of plant and animal life for Coulter and Merriam to collect and identify. Birds were more numerous than mammals, and among the many—pink-sided juncos, horned larks, western warbling greenlets, olive-sided and little flycatchers, ruby-crowned kinglets, black-headed grosbeaks, olive-backed thrushes; titmice, robins, bluebirds, and finches (Cassin's purple, grass, green-tailed, and pine)—there were two which Merriam singled out for special mention. One was the western tanager, found in numbers in Teton Canyon. Perched in the pines, its vivid colors contrasted sharply with the dark-green needles. The other was the lazuli bunting, abundant in streamside thickets where he listened to them sing in chorus.

Flora was even more plentiful than birds, and Coulter listed some hundred and twenty-three flowering plants found up to the twelve-thousand-foot level. In addition, he catalogued trees, shrubs, grasses, ferns, mosses, lichens, and fungi. The Tetons were so much higher than any other mountains they had explored, "and are exposed to such severe cold from snow and winds, that, above 10,000 feet, I gathered a flora such as I saw nowhere else in the trip. . . . A fine field was presented here for the collection of truly alpine plants, and no opportunity was lost for observing anything peculiar to this elevation, unusually exposed, as it is, to tempests." At eleven thousand five hundred feet and above, he found columbine, heather, phlox, sky pilot, hawksbeard, whitlow grass, alpine avens, and the unique purple saxifrage.

The geologists were meanwhile examining the valley floor, noting the many erratics—"huge blocks of limestone and granite bowlders . . . strewn over the prairie surface," transported there by glaciers; studying the structure of the foothills, discovering fossils, and searching the streambed gravel for further clues to the range's components.

Following Teton Creek up through its canyon, they passed thirty or forty beautiful cascades within three miles. Bradley noted that many of them were formed "by the descent of lateral streams into the main Teton, and followed each other in almost continuous succession down the rocks. . . . On every hand we saw them through the pines, at a height of thousands of feet, veiling the rocks and leaping into pools of foamy whiteness." Their thundering echoed through the gorge.

Coming at length to the Grand Teton, where Teton Creek rises, they were soon able to disprove the early theory that the range was composed entirely of eruptive rocks. They found the mountain's central nucleus to be made up of "granites, gneisses, and schists"—granites that are known to be two and a half billion years old, and gneisses that are among the oldest rocks in North America, recording some of the earliest events in its geologic history. They discovered the dike that crosses the saddle just south of the Grand Teton, and traced it over the canyon and up the western wall.

William Henry Jackson was spending "every daylight hour exploring canyons and traversing snowfields above timber line in search of views of the higher peaks." John Coulter and his assistant, Philo P. Beveridge (who pressed the collection), were attached to the "photographic corps," which included Jackson's assistant, 18-year-old Charles Campbell, and a packer named Aleck.

Between the two forks of Teton Creek "is a high tableland well above timber line and covered with fields of perpetual snow. This plateau leads directly up to the Grand Teton but is cut off from it by the deep gorge of Glacier Creek.

"With two pack mules, one to carry the blankets and food, the other, Old Molly, taking the photographic outfit as her regular job, we camped three days at the verge of timber line on this plateau. From this point we extended our explorations for effective viewpoints.

"At one place we had to pass around a narrow high ledge, an extremely dangerous undertaking through the deep, sloping snow. But we made it, and almost immediately were rewarded with one of the most stupendous panoramas in all America. Thousands of feet below us lay the icy gorge of Glacier Creek, while on the eastern horizon the main ridge shimmered in the mid-morning sun. Above all this towered the sharp cone of the Grand Teton, nearly 14,000 feet above sea level.

"I quickly set up my cameras and began one of the busiest picture-making days of my whole career." He was using the 11"×14", the 8"×10", and the stereoscopic.

"It was one of those rare days when everything I wanted could be had with hardly a shift of the dark tent. Everything, that is, except water. While Charley and Aleck went off to fill their rubber water bags from a trickling snow bank, I crept under the small tent and started to coat a plate."

The next day they crossed the canyon of the left fork of Teton Creek "to another plateau for more comprehensive views of the entire range beyond. The way was difficult and there was more snow to fight through to reach the vantage points for pictures, but these troubles were soon forgotten as the glorious panorama opened before us."

During the ten days they were out, they had no contact with the main camp except through a messenger who was sent to renew their food supplies. "We made our camps wherever night overtook us, or wherever it was most convenient for the work in hand. . . . We lived in the open, without tents. . . ."

James Stevenson and Nathaniel Langford had not been idle. Their days had been spent in exploring the canyons and ridges for the best approach to the Grand Teton, preparatory to climbing it. They were not encouraged by these reconnaissances, but on returning from the final one felt "more determined than ever that the enterprise should not fail for want of effort." That afternoon they picked out a site for a temporary base camp along the right fork of Teton Creek, "intending from that point to accomplish the ascent and return in a single day."

XX
Conquering the Giant

For many days the chief topic of conversation around the campfire was the proposed ascent of the Grand Teton, Nathaniel Langford recalled. Beaver Dick gave them no encouragement. In 1843, he said, a trapper-explorer named Michaud had made the attempt. He had taken along "ropes, rope-ladders, and other aides," but had met with so many formidable obstacles he had to give up. "You can try," Dick added, "but you'll wind up the same way."

On July 28, the climbing party of twelve, plus a cook, moved nine miles up Teton Canyon to the base camp. At four-thirty the next morning they turned out of their blankets (the thermometer read eleven degrees above zero), ate a hearty breakfast, and half an hour later started off, determined to reach the "topmost summit of the loftiest Teton." Each man was carrying an alpenstock and a bacon sandwich. For seventeen-year-old Sidford Hamp, fresh from England, began the hardest day of his life.

Straight up the canyon they went for the first two miles, over an area covered thickly with fallen burned trees. This was followed by a climb through a talus-choked ravine so steep they had to pull themselves up by "clinging to the points and angles of projecting rocks." On the summit of the first ridge their aneroids registered nine thousand feet elevation. Pausing here for breath, the party observed that as far as they could see, looking northward, "peak rose upon peak, and range stretched beyond range, all glistening in the sun like solid crystal." Immediately around them were vast snowfields, rough and hummocky, like an ocean frozen in the midst of a storm. Here were groups of windswept, gnarled trees, and gorges sheeny with ice. From the heights tumbled numerous falls and cascades. One of the party who had explored the Alps assured them that he had seen no views which could compare in extent and immensity with those of the Teton Range.

Along the edges of these snowfields geologist Bradley found the large, shiny blossoms of the alpine buttercup, *Ranunculus adoneus*. Some of the bright yellow flowers had pushed through their covering of snow; vegetative growth had evolved enough heat to melt a passage for the plant. Moving on ahead he soon came on a variety of alpine blooms—"white, blue, purple, crimson, and yellow stars in their carpets of moss-like leaves."

The party now headed for the next ridge. "Our route was over huge bowlders alternated with snow." The sun had not yet struck this slope, and the surface was so icy that young Hamp was forced to crawl on his hands and knees most of the way.

"Two miles of this kind of exercise brought us to the second ridge . . . composed of crumbling rock. . . . The view from this point was magnificent, but almost disheartening. . . . Another stretch of snow, rising to a sharp ridge, lay in front of us, at least five miles in length, across which, in our line of travel, was another upheaval of crumbling rock."

Some of the men, preferring to cross the snowy ridge rather than descend the talus below them, crawled around the side of the gorge. In taking this route, topographer Bechler became the first and only casualty. Jumping aside to avoid being hit by a large rock that "whistled by him like an avalanche," he fell and rolled down against an outcropping boulder. Although he received a bad sprain that was to trouble him for several days, he insisted upon continuing with the party.

Those who went the other way crossed a lake "about 600 yards long by 200 wide, covered with ice from twelve to fifteen feet thick." There was nothing to indicate that it had ever been open; "the ice which bound it, as well as the snow surrounding, seemed eternal. So pure and clear was this frozen surface, that one could see, even at its greatest thickness, the water gurgling beneath." Here in the snow Sidford Hamp discovered the tracks of a large grizzly bear.

From a distance this lake had seemed to lie at the very base of the Tetons, but after passing over it they found that at least two miles of corrugated snow stretched between them and the range. "There is no greater wonder in mountain scenery," Langford reflected, "than the tendency it has to shorten the distance to the eye, and lengthen it to the feet."

Beyond the lake they climbed the last of the rocky ridges, the steepest one yet, and from the crest looked around them. They seemed to be in the very heart of an arctic region. All about was snow and rock and ice. "Forward or backward everything was alike bleak, barren and inhospitable."

The party now pushed on to the base of the saddle between the Middle and Grand Tetons. At this point several men, discouraged by the sight of the highest peak still towering several thousand feet above them, decided to turn back. The injured Gustavus Bechler was one of them. The rest lost no time in selecting from among the numerous ravines they found running up the slope one they hoped would be free from lateral obstructions. Only five succeeded in getting through to the saddle: Stevenson, Bradley, Langford, Hamp, and Charlie Spencer, Langford's 17-year-old nephew. Stevenson, who was a rapid climber was already out of sight by the time the others got there.

Hamp wrote his mother that in reaching the saddle there had been one final snowfield to pass over. As he was crossing, it occurred to him that if he should slip he would be surely "smashed" on the rocks just below. He did slip, and to Langford his "destruction seemed inevitable. . . . I saw him fall and supposed he would be smashed to pieces," for he slid "with fearful rapidity." He fortunately had the presence of mind to quickly turn over on his stomach and stretch out his legs, landing feet first among the rocks. He assured his mother that he had been unhurt and urged her not to worry about him. He did admit that after this experience he was "jolly glad" to get to the saddle. Here the wind was so strong it threatened to blow away the bacon sandwiches they were eating. It was "a fierce west wind," Bradley reported, "forty to fifty miles per hour— sweeping across the saddle with such force that the loudest shouts were inaudible fifty yards to windward."

After resting half an hour, Langford, Hamp, and Spencer went on. Bradley watched them push "directly up the long slope of *debris* leading from the saddle into the gorge on the west side of the peak." He was waiting for an assistant to bring up the mercurial barometer with which he would measure the altitude on the summit of the Grand Teton.

While waiting, he examined the rocks on the saddle and to the east of it, and observed that here, climbing was greatly "hindered by steep slopes of snow, some of which consist wholly of hail-stones from a third to a half inch in diameter. . . .

"My highest point was about 12,000 feet, about half a mile east of the main saddle." From here, looking toward Jackson Hole, he noticed that the mountain descended in bare rock slopes for over four thousand feet, where it merged with a belt of spruce and pine. "In the upper edge of this belt, a small lake, partly iced over, occupied a notch in the base of the mountain immediately beneath me"—probably Amphitheater Lake. He could see the valley of the Gros Ventre River with its bright red cliffs, and follow the meanderings of the Snake through the sage-covered plains.

But the barometer never arrived, for the messenger had long since turned back. By the time Bradley realized something had gone wrong, it was too late for him to go on to the summit.

Langford, Spencer, and Hamp soon met Stevenson who told them he had been stopped about two hundred feet beyond by a sheer rock face. He had made several attempts to scale it, and had once "lost his foothold, his entire weight coming from his hands, while he hung with his face to the wall. It was impossible without a leap to reach a standing place, but by loosening his hold without one, he would drop several hundred feet down the mountain." Fortunately, there was a coating of ice and snow on the rock, and by kicking at it repeatedly with the toe of his boot he was able to make an indentation deep enough to support one foot. He then managed to jump safely to a narrow rock bench.

They were too near their goal now to give up. They decided to try the rock face again. "In about an hour " or so it seemed to Hamp, they came to a crevasse down which they could see "40, 50 or sometimes 100 feet." Thoughts of slipping recurred to him. By this time both boys admitted to being tired; Langford concluded it was best for them to wait there. They sat down on a rock ledge and rested "while the other two got to the top."

Reaching the summit was not that simple, according to Langford. First there was that rock face to scale:

"A rope which I had brought with me, cast over a slight projection above our heads, enabled me to draw myself up so as to fix my hands in a crevice . . . and then, with my feet resting on the shoulders of Captain Stevenson, I easily clambered to the top." He then let the rope down to Stevenson who took a firm hold, and with the aid of his staff soon worked his way to Langford's side. Above them was an expanse of ice "overlying the rocky surface at an angle of 70°, and fastened to it by slight arms of the same brittle material." This seemed insurmountable at first. "Beside the danger of incurring a slide which would insure a rapid descent to the base of the mountain, there was the other risk, that the frail fastenings which held the ice-sheet . . . might give way while we were crawling over it, and the whole field be carried with us down . . . the precipice. But the top was just before us, and we preferred the risk to an abandonment of the task. Laying hold of the rocky points at the side of the ice-sheet, we broke with our feet in its surface a series of steps, up which we ascended, at an angle deflecting not more than twenty degrees from a vertical line. . . ."

Once over this obstacle, only "fragments and piles of granite . . . lay between us and the summit." Stevenson saw that there was no wildlife here except swallows skimming the snowbanks for insects, and that all vegetation except lichen stopped at about three hundred feet below the Teton summit.

At three o'clock, after ten hours on the trail, they stood on "the highest point of the Grand Teton. . . . We felt that we had achieved a victory, and that it was something for ourselves to know—a solitary satisfaction—that we were the first white men who had ever stood upon the spot we now occupied."

In his report, Dr. Hayden wrote that in these mountain regions during certain months, usually August and September, the air is filled with clouds of grasshoppers. They often rise to the height of many thousands of feet. This year, in passing over the Tetons, they became chilled and dropped onto the snow and ice in vast numbers. Gradually they melted the surface, creating hundreds of little pockets. The roughness imparted by the countless tiny holes enabled Stevenson and Langford "to cling to the almost vertical sides of the peaks, and complete the ascent."

Young Hamp wrote his mother that at three-thirty they began the descent. "Mr. Stevenson got a long way ahead (for he is very active) and left us three to ourselves again. At one place we had to be let down by a rope & in another there was a . . . waterfall . . . we had to cross with about 2 inches foot-hold and no hand hold. . . ." They then came to a high ridge of snow that was in some places "less than a foot wide, but we got over all right & then got into the pine woods near camp at last." After walking half a mile more, the party saw the welcome blaze of the fire and "we were just going to hurry forward rejoicing when we found before us a great precipice which we dare not descend for it was quite dark as the sun had set before we ascended the great snow ridge. Well we had to go back and jump streams & climb over fallen trees all in the dark with pine trees all around us, but after wandering for 1½ hours we struck the camp weren't we rejoiced it was just 10 o'clock when we got in & we had been walking just 17 hours. I was so *awfully* tired that I could eat nothing but went to bed directly & didn't I sleep so ended my most adventurous day."

Langford wrote that their welcome the next morning at the main camp in Teton Canyon was boisterous and noisy. Their success put everyone in good humor: "We woke the echoes of the canõn with songs and shouts."

Twenty-one years were to go by before white men again succeeded in climbing the Grand Teton. In September 1893, Dr. Charles H. Kieffer, an army surgeon stationed at Yellowstone Park, made the ascent with two companions. In 1898, W. O.

Owen, having tried seven times and failed, got to the top with a small party led by Reverend Franklin Spalding. Refusing to believe that Stevenson and Langford ever reached the summit, ignoring Dr. Kieffer's climb, and giving no credit to Spalding, he had himself officially declared the first white man to climb to the summit.

After 1898, over a quarter of a century was to pass before anyone conquered the Grand Teton again.

XXI
Mystery of the Grand Teton

"Here lives a man who dreamed a dream, and the mysterious strength of his vision is in him."

— Frances Densmore

From the summit of the Grand Teton, Stevenson and Langford discovered "on top of an adjacent buttress, but little lower than the one we occupied . . . a circular enclosure, six feet in diameter, composed of granite slabs, set up endwise, about five feet in height ," and of irregular shape.

Climbing down to it, they stepped inside and found themselves a foot deep in detritus—"minute particles of granite, not larger than common grains of sand . . . worn off by the elements from the vertical blocks."

"A period of time which human experience cannot calculate, was required to produce this wonderful disintegration of solid granite," Langford felt.

As the two men sat within the enclosure, well protected from the wind, and finished their lunch, they speculated about those who had preceded them here, and doubtless to the summit. The builders could not have been any of the Northern

Plains Indians of recorded history, they concluded. Ancestors perhaps, or a different people entirely.

Had curiosity prompted these people to scale the mountain, or had it been a test of skill and endurance, they wondered.

The enclosure had obviously entailed considerable work in the selection of slabs of more or less uniform height; in conveying them to the site, setting them on end, and embedding them so as to withstand the strong prevailing west winds and the violent storms that buffet the Tetons. They must have come often and stayed long enough to have required a shelter.

There then arose the question of what these ancient people were doing there. The enclosure's position was too high for a lookout, nor would it have been used as a covert for hunters, for although grizzly and bighorn sheep frequent the loftiest crags, these animals could be found in greater number at more accessible locations.

Langford admitted that they had never before seen an Indian relic that so excited their curiosity and prompted so many questions.

"It was," he wrote, "the great wonder of our day's work."

As Hayden's men were to discover when they came to climb more Rocky Mountain peaks, there were similar stone enclosures on many of them. On butte tops and prominent bluffs they would find stone circles, ovals, triangles, cairns, and wheels.

Captain William A. Jones, a topographical engineer whose 1873 reconnaissance of northwestern Wyoming completed Captain Raynolds' assignment, made a study of those stone works he found, taking measurements and rendering scale drawings. Many could "readily be dismissed from consideration by regarding them as mere coverts for hunters . . . but there are some which will scarcely admit of so simple an explanation," he wrote. These were the ones that had been placed "in such situations that they could never serve as landmarks for travelers or topographers, nor yet as a means of concealment from animals." These circles and triangles of well-embedded stone were invariably located on the tops of bluffs or other elevated positions, unprotected from the elements, and with unobstructed views toward the east. The areas were not suitable for habitation.

On one moundlike hill in the Wind River valley he found what seemed at first to be three individual cairns. On close inspection the three points were found to be related and to form a triangle with a base of thirty feet and sides of fifty feet; the base opened east. He felt there was some unexplained but definite connection between this form and several nearby open circles.

Counting the stones in one circlet (inside dimensions three by six feet), he found the number to be nineteen although the ring would have been complete with less. He wondered if the number of stones might not have some mystic significance, since "four circles at Boscawen and adjacent places in Cornwall have been each formed of nineteen stones." Was this pure coincidence that a circle in Wyoming held the same number? Since the time of Jones' investigation, other circles of nineteen stones have been reported in Gros Ventre and Jackson Hole country.

The captain could find no explanation for these enclosures except a ceremonial one. "They are certainly not very recent, and the Shoshones are unable to account for them, except by referring them, as usual in such cases of doubt, to the agency of the Great Spirit or *'Tam Apa.'* " Jones had for a guide the noted Sheep Eater medicine man, Togwotee, whom he doubtless questioned concerning the stone forms.

On an exposed shoulder of Medicine Mountain, in the Bighorn Range, there is a large circle or wheel of individual stones that measures eighty feet across its face. It has a central cairn or hub some fourteen feet in diameter, from which radiate twenty-eight spokes that connect the rim. The central cairn is older than the spokes. Five smaller cairns, each an open circle four feet in diameter, are found at irregular intervals along the periphery of the wheel, while a sixth cairn lies about fourteen feet beyond the rim on an extended southwestern spoke.

The Shoshonis say they have no knowledge of the wheel's origin or purpose. The Crows, when asked about it soon after its discovery in the last century, were aware of its existence but not its exact location. It had been put there, they said, as a pattern for their tipis.

Recent studies of this wheel, and others in Canada, have revealed alignment of the cairns to mark the summer solstice sunrise and sunset, as well as the rising points for the stars Aldebaran, Rigel, and Sirius, brightest in the summer skies. It is believed these celestial observations were used by early Plains dwellers for setting the dates of important ceremonials. It has also been found that in some of the more simple wheels (they vary in complexity and size) certain spokes point to other wheels and cairns. This relationship between stone works was recognized by Captain Jones.

Stone enclosures like the one Stevenson and Langford discovered are now thought to have been used for vision quests. It is believed that those first people who came into the Teton valleys sought their spiritual guardians in the enclosure on the west face of the Grand Teton. Here they would have fasted, thirsted, perhaps torn their flesh with thorns, as was the practice with some tribes, and prayed for a supernatural visitor.

To most North American Indians, power and success in life came through dreams and visions. These so profoundly affected daily life a person could hardly function without them. A war party might be called together or disbanded because of a dream or vision. Arapahoes received new decorative design ideas through spirit revelation. Some men had sacred songs and dances, new rites and prayers revealed to them.

Very strong visions led men to become shamans. Others, inspired by dreams, became healers or were endowed with the power to insure a successful hunt. In some tribes women were born with certain powers and could also seek visions that benefited the entire tribe.

Some parents instructed their boys when they reached seven or eight years to fast and seek the blessing of a spirit. Others did not encourage them to embark on quests until they were in their late teens. What is sometimes called the Youth Vigil marked the second period in an Indian's life. The essence of the rite was a solitary fast and prayer undertaken in the wilderness, and the purpose was the quest of a revelation that would disclose the presence and character of that supernatural being who was to become the young person's spiritual guardian.

From early childhood the god-seeker had been well prepared for the experience. He had been told stories about sacred beings, and given countless descriptions of visions and supernatural experiences. These helped to shape those sense impressions that came to him during his four or more days of seclusion on a mountain top or other remote area. Hunger, thirst, loneliness, and fervor usually induced a revelation that fitted into the visionary pattern of his people and inspired an interpretation of things seen and heard. For those who made the ascent to the Teton enclosure, the physical exertion and elevation would have intensified the seeker's highly emotional state.

Guardian spirits varied greatly. Animals—buffalo, bear, deer, elk, eagles, and sparrow hawks—were frequent visitants. They appeared at times in human guise, but on vanishing usually assumed their true form or gave some clue to their identity. There were also fanciful patrons like dwarfs, and celestial ones like the moon or stars.

The relationship between supernatural guardian and protégé was usually like that of father and son. Some accounts of visions even quote the patron as saying: "I will have you for my child." From him the young man learned prayers, a sacred song, and certain taboos. On the strength of successive visions, the youth might assemble a medicine bundle—a wrapper containing sacred objects indicated by the spirit.

After the seeker had attained his vision he returned to his village. To indicate his success, he would usually enter singing his newly learned sacred song. He was not questioned about his revelation, nor did he speak of it until after purification and a specified time lapse. Once he had related his experience it became a part of tribal folklore.

For some the vision quest was not successful. In such cases, rather then be doomed to failure throughout life, many tribes allowed a successful visionary to sell a part of his power to the less fortunate, "adopting them as his supernatural patron adopted *him,* making for each of his disciples a replica of his sacred paraphernalia, teaching him the sacred songs, and warning against the breach of any taboo associated with his medicine."

The vision quest was not limited to youth nor was it always personal. Indian tradition is filled with tales of leaders and shamans who undertook the solitary fast and vigil in the wilderness solely for the welfare of their people.

In the central cairn of a wheel in Alberta, artifacts have been found which indicate that its construction was begun when the pyramids of Egypt were being built, four to five thousand years ago. Other wheels, including the one on Medicine Mountain, appear to be of much more recent date, probably eighteenth century.

The earliest inhabitants of the northern Plains of whom we are aware are supposed to have had no astronomical knowledge, nor to have been builders in stone.

Who, then, were these people who apparently made observations of the summer solstices and stars, and whose young men sought supernatural experiences in such enclosures as the one near the summit of the Grand Teton?

XXII
The Other Side of the Mountains

James Stevenson had planned to take his train over Teton Pass into Jackson Hole, follow the Snake north to its sources, and then cross into Yellowstone Park for a meeting with Dr. Hayden's party in the Lower Fire Hole Basin. But Beaver Dick "threatened us with impassable fords on that route, owing to high water from the melting snows." It was then proposed to go over the mountains at the head of Falls River. Dick objected to this course too because of the extensive tracts of fallen timber. He could find no fault with the suggestion that they follow the valley of Henry's Fork.

The party was reluctant to leave Teton Canyon's fine forests of spruce and pine, its foaming cascades, and its constantly changing views of the Grand Teton, ringed by clouds, veiled by falling snow, rosy in the flood of setting sun, or gray and awesome in early morning light. Although they did not know it then, they were not seeing this country for the last time. They were to return twice more for further studies.

Riding through Pierre's Hole they saw again the many antelope grazing on the plain; watched grouse scurry for cover as they passed; observed the flocks of ducks and geese swimming in the swamp ponds; and around their boggy edges noticed the deep, watery footprints of elk and moose.

Traveling northward geologist Bradley remarked on the simultaneous presence of spring and fall flowers, which is characteristic of regions where summers are short. "In the same field we often found violets, strawberry blossoms and fruit, monk's hood, geranium, everlastings, and fringed gentian. . . . "

On reaching Henry's Lake they were surprised to find a ranch at its head. "No one was at home, nevertheless we entered the house & ate some meat, bread, butter & treacle," Sidford Hamp wrote his mother; "it may seem strange to you civilized people at home to hear of anyone entering another man's house in that style but out here in the mountains it is quite customary." Shortly after leaving the house they met the owner, Gilbert Sawtelle, and told him what they had done; "he said we were quite welcome to come again any time we liked."

During the several days the party stayed at Henry's Lake, surveying and photographing, the spacious log ranch house, which was home for a group of commercial hunters and fishermen, became a rendezvous for the explorers. "Sawtelle is a man of mark," Langford observed. "He exhibits in his life, and conduct, the signs of a careful early training, and carries beneath a rough exterior the manners and feelings of a gentleman."

Sawtelle told them they were fortunate to have escaped a raid by horse thieves, who were caught near his ranch just a few days before. Three of them were killed by a sheriff and his posse, but the others surrendered. The captives said that there was still another gang at large which had planned to follow Dr. Hayden's party up the Yellowstone, steal their horses and pack mules, then cross over to the Snake and lie in wait for Stevenson.

After going over the divide by way of Targhee Pass, Jackson struck off independently with a small party, in the hope of finding some good scenes to photograph. Langford joined them, and they relied on his knowledge of the area to pilot them through to the Lower Fire Hole. "Trails were obscure and landmarks indefinite, so it is not altogether surprising that we went up the Gibbon Fork instead of the Fire Hole. . . . We were hopelessly at sea . . . until we finally ran up against a water-fall—known later as Virginia Cascade—which definitely proved, according to Langford, that we were not on the Fire Hole River."

Since night was coming on, they camped where they were on a little flat among the trees. Hamp, who was one of the party, wrote that they had not "a scrap of food, or a drop of water . . . we built a shed with young pine treees, & made a big fire for . . . we had only our saddle blankets; we fired our pistols a few times . . . but saw or heard nothing of the others . . . " In the morning Jackson climbed a tall pine on the hill above them, and from there saw the columns of steam rising from the hot springs along the Fire Hole River. With the general direction in mind, they struck for the river, finally found the trail, and reached Stevenson's camp around noon, where they ate for the first time in twenty hours.

They then decided to examine the various hot springs, pools, and geysers here. As they were walking from one group to another, they came suddenly on letters a yard high, drawn in the scaly crust of silica. They spelled out BILL HAMILTON, the name of a well- known mountain man, now turned guide. They suspected he was leading Hayden's party and looked around for further clues. Not far off they found more scratching in the crust which read: August 13, 1872.

"That's today!" someone shouted. Cutting short their inspection of the geysers, the whole party mounted their horses and pushed on in search of Hayden.

Although traveling widely divergent routes, the various divisions arrived at the appointed rendezvous almost simultaneously the following day. When assembled, there were about sixty men and more than a hundred horses and mules.

"A spirit of jovial good-fellowship dominated the gathering. It had, in a way, something of the nature of a trappers' rendezvous of half a century earlier," Jackson felt.

This meeting was mainly for the purpose of comparing notes as to what had been done, and for mapping out a program for the continuation of the work. Another object was to despatch by the pack train that brought in supplies all of the accumulated specimens as well as the negatives Jackson had made so far.

The next morning, at a gathering of the entire company, Dr.

Hayden gave one of those inspiring talks that made each man aware of his contribution to the whole. In closing, he suggested three names for honorary membership in the survey: Thomas Moran, Nathaniel Langford, and William Blackmore, a London lawyer, financier, and museum founder, who was one of the doctor's guests (he was also Sidford Hamp's uncle.) Blackmore's financial contribution to this survey had made possible its extended work. All three names were approved.

Langford then proposed that the Grand Teton be named for Hayden. This motion was received with such enthusiasm that the doctor had to get to his feet again to acknowledge it. For a number of years the peak was known as Mount Hayden, and so designated on maps, but as is often the case with such changes, acceptance of the new name was not universal. Many people continued to call the peak the Grand Teton, and as remembrance of Hayden's achievements began to fade, the original name was adopted again for general use.

Within a few days all the parties had separated, each on its special mission. While the Snake River Division waited for Stevenson to return from Virginia City, Montana, with the supplies, seven of his men joined Jackson's photographic corps for an exploration of Yellowstone Falls and Lake. The rest made specialized studies in the geyser basins.

On the last day of August Stevenson returned, and on September 3, the party started south to look for the sources of the Snake and to explore and map the Tetons from the east side. Only Jackson stayed behind to continue his work in Yellowstone Park.

They discovered the headwaters of the Snake in a mountainous area southeast of Elk Ridge. There in a flat valley divide are two small ponds, close together, covering from eight to ten acres each. One "is the ultimate source of Snake River, while the flow from the other joins Buffalo Fork, and so reaches the Snake just below Jackson's Lake," Bradley reported. Looking south and west from these heights they could see the Tetons looming up "grandly" from behind the mountain mass that separated the party from Jackson Hole .

Following the Snake's course they explored and surveyed its forks and tributaries in all directions, until they came to where it enters the lake. "The Teton Range had been before us for many days as a prominent feature of the landscape, but now its peaks stood up as the features of main interest, bounding the valley on the west with a series of roof-like ridges and pointed peaks, well besprinkled with patches of snow." Beaver Dick, who met them here after having crossed from the valley of Henry's Fork (where he left Jenny and the children), reported successive storms in that region which had left snow on all the heights.

All about them were signs of fall—cottonwood and aspen turned gold and pale red, mountain ash a deep crimson; sumac leaves were scarlet, and willow, a rich yellow. The days were crisp and clear, and "the peaks stood out sharply, while the gaps and cañons were full of a deep-blue, smoky light."

As they rode along the east shore, and more of the range opened before them, the intricacies of the higher peaks came into sight, and they stopped often to admire their varied shapes and finely cut facets. They gave "the beholder a strong sense of sublimity," Bradley wrote.

They regretted that Jackson was not there with his cameras; but in his place was the artist William Henry Holmes who made some skillful line drawings of the range. Like so many of Hayden's men, he had a number of talents: anthropologist, archaeologist, ethnologist, geologist, and painter. He later became professor of archaeologic geology at the University of Chicago, had charge of the archaeological explorations of the Bureau of Ethnology, was appointed curator of the National Gallery of Art, and had his paintings hung in the Corcoran Gallery.

On reaching the southeastern angle of Jackson Lake, they saw that the Snake River left it at this point and ran eastward to the valley of Buffalo Fork, instead of following what was obviously its natural channel at the south end of the lake. In looking for the answer, they discovered four old terraces plainly marked along the river. The third terrace, lying above the Snake's present level, formed wide plains to either side of it below the mouth of the Buffalo.

Crossing these plains westward, directly toward the mountains, they came to a series of high, steep, narrow ridges covered with immense masses of granite and heavily timbered. Within the last of these concentric ridges they found a lake lying at the mouth of a deep canyon running far back into the range. "Here at last we have the clue to the mystery," wrote one of the party. This cañon, like all the other large ones of this range, was occupied by a glacier, whose terminal moraines now hem in this lake. . . ."

Although the old river valley had apparently not been fully blocked by the flow of silt which passed beyond the moraines, the obstruction had been sufficient to force the river to find another outlet and channel.

The party named the lake they found there "Leigh's Lake, after our guide, Richard Leigh (Beaver Dick)." About a mile south they discovered a second lake in a canyon mouth and called it "Jennie's Lake, after Mrs. Leigh."

Pushing up the gorge at the head of this lake (present Cascade Canyon), geologist Taggart found "a cluster of falls and rapids about 250 feet high, with lofty, precipitous walls on either hand," today's Hidden Falls.

Three more lakes were discovered, all glacial, and they, in turn, were named Bradley, Taggart, and Phelps.

In Jackson Hole they found constant sources of wonder and delight. Near Blacktail Butte the sagebrush was burned off, and grass had grown up thickly. Here they saw large herds of antelope grazing, the first they had seen since leaving the upper Madison Canyon. In those places where the sage had not burned, countless chipmunks were busy gathering the seeds, "biting off the long spikes and stripping them from end to end, passing them back and forth through the mouth, as one would an ear of corn."

In the Snake River, near Jackson Lake, they found for the first time "large and beautiful" trumpeter swans. There were also wheeling flocks of juncos and titlarks. Brewer's blackbirds darted in and out among the rushes; Swainson's hawks circled above the valley, and white-crowned sparrows whistled plaintively in the thickets.

One morning near the end of September, when snow was an inch deep on the ground and still falling, Merriam made his way up a little canyon a few miles north of Jackson Lake "in the hope of meeting some rare birds. I had not gone far when to my great delight, I saw a pair of water-ouzels on a rock in the middle of a rapid stream which flowed out of the cañon. To my surprise one of these birds dove directly into the rapids, and in a few moments returned with a worm in its mouth." This was his introduction to the ouzel.

Although the flowering season was past, Coulter found a few late blooms. There were pinedrops at Jackson Lake, and on the plains, globemallow and penstemon. In the crevices of shaded rock ledges there were several kinds of fern. Coulter now observed the marked difference between the west and east slopes of the Tetons, the Jackson Hole side being much more densely timbered, and the trees much larger and less gnarled.

Frank Bradley had hoped to climb the Grand Teton from the east "and so retrieve my lost honors"; but the early snows, which had covered the upper slopes, made "the attempt too hazardous to be justifiable."

After exploring the valley on both sides of the Snake, and naming two more peaks—Mount Moran, and Mount Leidy, after Professor Joseph Leidy the eminent comparative anatomist who was a member of the survey—the party divided. The main company, headed by Taggart, crossed Teton Pass to define its geology and map the area, while the others continued south along the river into Jackson's Little Hole and on through the Snake's Grand Canyon.

On the evening of October 8 the two parties met beyond Swan Valley and went on together to Fort Hall. The return to Ogden was made by stagecoach. "With so many of us . . . in addition to the regular travel, the capacity of the two six-horse Concord coaches was rather overtaxed. I was on the lead coach carrying twenty-two passengers, making a crowded interior with ten on top or outside," Jackson remembered. "Five or six men sat on the seats with the driver, but the rest of us had to roost on the deck behind. I took the latter place by choice, as there was an opportunity to spread blankets and lie down."

The coach following theirs was held up by road agents who broke open the strongboxes and relieved the passengers of money, watches, and jewelry. "Fortunately our boys had not been paid off, most of them having only enough cash in pocket to take them to Ogden."

At Ogden they met Dr. Hayden who gave them their pay and their discharges. The season's work was done; the survey had made initial explorations of a territory that was unknown to all but a few remaining mountain men.

In 1877 and 1878 they returned to the Tetons, "the summit of the world," as Hayden called them, to make more comprehensive studies on both sides of the range. The 1877 expedition had the distinction of having as its botanists Sir Joseph Dalton Hooker, director of Kew Gardens and president of the Royal Society, and Professor Asa Gray of Harvard. Twenty-nine thousand miles were explored and mapped that season, making, Hayden felt, "a very considerable addition to our knowledge of the Western country."

The next year (1878) Jackson took his cameras to the east side of the Tetons, approaching them from the south by way of Green River, following the old Indian and trapper trail. With this party was yet another brilliant young man, Albert Charles Peale, a twenty-three-year-old doctor of medicine whose specialty was mineralogy. He was the great-grandson of Charles Willson Peale, painter, scientist, man of letters, and friend of George Washington.

There was every evidence of an early winter that year. By the first week in September, Jackson recalled, "ice in the mornings was the rule," and some snow fell almost daily. In order to complete his work before the season closed, he could only allow himself a few days in Jackson Hole. He climbed Signal Mountain for some striking panoramas and took other exceptional views of the range from across Jackson Lake.

The geologists and topographers were in Jackson Hole and Pierre's Hole for still further study, and for another ascent of the Grand Teton, this time to set up a triangulation station on the summit.

Chief topographer A. D. Wilson, his assistant, A. C. Ladd, and the packer-hunter Harry Yount made up the climbing party that set off up Teton Canyon. But they never did get to the top. On reaching the final saddle, they stopped to examine the peak from that side and found that a narrow hallway, with nearly vertical walls of granite, led almost to the summit. They started up and were soon at the notch formed by the two walls as they cross the peak; "but much to our chagrin, we could find no means of getting up the [wall] to our right, which we must do to reach the high point." At its lowest point this wall was about forty feet high, and "without a break anywhere that a man could possibly crawl up.

"Thus we found ourselves completely blocked within a few feet of the top. . . . Now for the first time, after climbing hundreds of peaks during my twelve years experience, I was compelled to give up reaching the summit, at least from that side." Had there been time Wilson would have tried it from the east side.

Turning to their left, they climbed to the summit of the western point. From there they saw the circular enclosure of rocks, of Indian origin, "such as are found on many of our Western mountains, [and] are very ancient." On this spur the topographers set up their instruments and took observations.

The next day Wilson and his party moved north through Pierre's Hole toward Henry's Lake, to make primary triangulations from Sawtelle's Peak.

One night as they lay about the campfire, smoking and talking after an excellent dinner of roasted mountain sheep, they were startled by the sound of shots directly behind them. "As quick as a flash we dropped to our hands and knees and crawled for our rifles. . . ." Just as Wilson picked up his gun he heard their animals start off on the run. "I knew at once that we were left on foot beyond all redemption, as the Indians were on horseback and already had the start of us." The topographers stayed where they were for a while, but finding that some Indians still lurked about, concluded they were going to rob the camp at daylight. Since Wilson and his men were in an exposed position, they decided to crawl out to a nearby wood "where my little party of five, with our four guns, might stand a better chance if they should find us."

Picking up blankets and enough provisions to last three or four days, they cached the instruments and then set out. Fording the river, they felt their way along to a heavy stand of pines, where they rolled up in their blankets and went to sleep. At dawn they were wakened by a volley being fired into their old camp. Hastily they packed up and started off in the direction of the Lower Geyser Basin, where they hoped to find one of Dr. Hayden's parties. If they failed, they had ahead of them a walk of a hundred and fifty miles to Mammoth Hot Springs where they knew some of their men would be at work.

Coming to a bluff that had a view of their first camp, Wilson's party climbed to the top. Through a field glass they could see that everything had been torn apart, and that several Indians on horseback seemed to be hunting for their trail. They did not linger.

After three days' hard walking they arrived at the geyser basins where they found the doctor and several other parties. Borrowing three mules from Jackson, Wilson and Harry Yount rode back to try to rescue the instruments. Reaching the old camp at about noon the second day, they found it in shambles; the cache had fortunately not been discovered.

Storm followed storm, and by September 24, six inches to a foot of snow lay throughout Yellowstone Park. They decided to leave before it was too late to cross the mountains.

Going by way of Two Ocean Pass, the explorers kept the Tetons on their right until they crossed Buffalo Fork. Then, turning east, they rode over Togwotee Pass, named by Captain Jones for his Indian guide. They reached the Wind River valley after five days of "hard struggle through snow, timber, and rocks." Their destination was Rawlins, Wyoming, and the Union Pacific Railroad.

Jackson, who was riding with Hayden, remembered that when they reached Two Ocean Pass, everything was frozen solid, "and we had to break a lot of ice before the doctor had proved that the small spring beneath actually emptied, as the trustworthy Bridger had reported, into both the Atlantic and the Pacific. With this last small investigation the labors of the old Survey may be said to have ended."

Before the spring of 1879, the various rival geological and geographical surveys which had been exploring the West simultaneously—some under the aegis of the General Land Office, some under the Department of the Interior, and others under the War Department—were consolidated into the present United States Geological Survey, under one authority.

Dr. Hayden stayed on, but no longer as director. The fruitful collaboration with James Stevenson also came to an end . The younger man, finding that his interest lay in the culture and language of the Indians, transferred to the Bureau of Ethnology. The remainder of his brief life (he died suddenly at forty-eight while traveling from New York to Washington) was devoted to studies of the native races of Arizona and New Mexico. After his death this work was carried on ably by his wife, Matilda Coxe Stevenson.

In the new survey there was no provision made for photography, so William Henry Jackson had to start anew. Most of the other talented young men also went their separate ways, each to achieve distinction in his particular field. The great Hayden Surveys were over.

XXIII
Immortalizing the Tetons

In 1871 *Scribner's Magazine* asked the thirty-four-year-old, British-born artist Thomas Moran, who had exhibited in the Paris Salon, to illustrate an article, "The Wonders of Yellowstone," written by Nathaniel Langford.

The article aroused a storm of protest from readers who refused to believe Langford and accused him of writing fiction. Dr. Hayden, who had heard him lecture that January, was convinced he was not drawing on his imagination and decided to make his survey for 1871 in the Yellowstone country. He was aware that the colors found in Western landscapes often defied description, and he had seen enough of Moran's color work to believe he could capture them faithfully. His pictures, with Jackson's photographs, should satisfy all doubters. He invited him to join the survey, and the artist accepted.

With infallible judgment, Hayden had chosen the best man. Moran, fascinated by color and the dramatic in nature, had found inspiration in Turner, and in 1861 he had made a trip to England to study and copy some of Turner's originals.

Moran, who had not yet met with any financial success, had to borrow the money to pay for his trip west. In June 1871 he set off by rail for Corrine, Utah. There he boarded a stagecoach for the four-day, nonstop ride (except for hasty meals and a change of horses) to Virginia City, Montana, where he was to meet the Hayden party. Ignorant of Western ways, he was curious to know why the driver was so heavily armed, and finally asked. "Road agents," a fellow passenger replied brusquely, which left him no wiser since he interpreted this to mean station agents along the route, or men who kept the road in repair. Why, he wondered, must one have to guard against *them*?

"Prior to 1871 Moran had never known a true wilderness, and he was as poorly equipped for a rough life as anyone I have known," wrote William Henry Jackson. An attack of rheumatic fever in his teens had left him "frail, almost cadaverous" in appearance; "he seemed incapable of surviving the rigors of camp life and camp food. Yet within forty-eight hours he was writing to a friend: 'You should see me bolt the bacon.' "

From Virginia City the survey party moved on to enter Yellowstone by way of Mammoth Hot Springs, then the easiest approach. Thomas Moran had never ridden a horse before, but undaunted, he simply tucked a pillow over the cantle of the saddle to cushion his bony frame. Once he was mounted, his appearance was picturesque, Jackson thought: "The jaunty tilt of his sombrero, long yellowish beard, and portfolio under his arm marked the artistic type, with something of local color imparted by a rifle hung over the saddle horn." He adapted quickly to wilderness living, and was soon distinguishing himself as an expert fisherman and camp cook. Once, when a string of trout had been brought in, he "modestly showed us a way of cooking that was new even to the experienced woodsmen among us. He dug a shallow hole . . . beneath the fire, wrapped several fish in wet paper, placed the package in the hole, covered it with dirt, and raked some coals over the spot. Half an hour later we were dining on delicious baked trout."

Although by nature a shy man, he made friends easily . This ability to make people like him instantly was, Jackson felt, one key to his genius. "He had so much to give and gave so unstintingly that even a mountain or a waterfall must have responded to his charm." Self-taught in art, he was also self-educated and "astonished every member of the party, including Dr. Hayden, with the extent of his knowledge. It reached into every field."

He became greatly interested in Jackson's work; ". . . it was my good fortune to have him at my side during all that season to help me solve many problems of composition. While learning a little from me, he was constantly putting in far more than he took out."

When the party reached the Grand Canyon of the Yellowstone, Moran remarked that the colors were "beyond the resources of human art." Still, he found it a fascinating challenge, and a subject he would return to often over the years. Now he made watercolor sketches from every angle and under varying light conditions, as well as careful line drawings of all rock structure and formation.

"So far as I am concerned, the great picture of the 1871 expedition was no photograph, but a painting by Moran of Yellowstone Falls," Jackson declared. "It captured, more than any other painting I know, the color and atmosphere of spectacular nature." As Hayden had hoped, Moran's dramatic paintings and Jackson's photographs were to provide the visual proof, and convince a hesitating Congress of the need to preserve this unique wonderland.

Before taking the finished painting of Yellowstone's Grand Canyon from the easel, Moran asked Dr. Hayden to inspect it for accuracy. Hayden found the foreground rocks so carefully depicted that any geologist could identify them. Yet it was not literal. "I place no value upon literal transcripts from Nature," Moran wrote. "My general scope is not realistic: . . . my tendencies are toward idealization."

The painting was hung in the Smithsonian galleries where it attracted crowds and received good press notices. It was then hung in the Speaker's office where it could be seen by congressmen, government officers, and visitors to the Capitol.

"It has created quite a sensation," Moran reported to Hayden. "Many of the members have expressed the opinion that Congress should purchase it."

That June when Congress voted ten thousand dollars to buy the painting, Hayden wrote Moran: "There is no doubt your reputation is made. Still you must do much to nurse it. . . . The next picture you paint must be the Tetons."

The doctor planned to return to northwestern Wyoming for the season of 1873, and arranged for a small party to go with

Moran to the Tetons. But trouble with the Sioux was imminent that summer, and Hayden shifted his survey to the Colorado Rockies. Moran did not go with him, but went instead with Major John Wesley Powell on an exploration of the Colorado River canyons.

Not until 1879 did Moran finally get to the Tetons.

One day during the third week in August of that year he and his younger brother Peter, a painter and etcher, arrived at Fort Hall. Thomas had with him a letter from the president of the United States, introducing him as a distinguished American artist and asking the commanding officer to extend the same "attentions and courtesies . . . he would extend to myself."

Captain Augustus Bainbridge immediately put himself on leave and organized an expedition to the Tetons. The recent Bannock War dictated a military escort, so on the morning of August 21 the Moran party set off with twenty soldiers, a number of teamsters and Indian hunters, two wagons, and several dogs. Of this first day's travels, Thomas's little pocket diary gives a sketchy report: ". . . very hot. Mirage. Dogs exhausted. Pete sick. Reached Taylors Bridge in late afternoon. 27 miles. Desolation. Abandoned town . . . Highway robber. Dismal camp. Furious wind all night driving sand everywhere. Almost blinding. Gray dismal morning. Black basalt. Abomination. Rushing river like Niagara Rapids."

The next day was little better: "Cold & windy with dust following & blinding us all the way." They did have their first sight of the Grand Teton, seventy miles off.

On August 23 he noted: "The Tetons are now plainly visible but not well defined owing to the mistiness of the atmosphere. They loom up grandly above all other mountains. An intervening ridge dividing us from the Teton Basin stretches for miles to the north, a beautiful pinkish yellow with delicate shades of pale cobalt, while the distant range is of an exquisite blue with but little definition of forms . . . "

Two days later they were on the top of the divide that cut them off from Pierre's Hole. From there, Thomas Moran saw the Tetons as perhaps the finest pictorial range in the United States or even North America. That afternoon he and his brother made sketches of them, "but the distance, 20 miles, is rather too far to distinguish the details, especially as it is very smoky from fires in the mountains on each side of the peaks. This evening is quite cold but we have a fine camp fire and the Cap. & Peter are broiling some venison ribs on willow sticks."

On the twenty-sixth they rode into Pierre's Hole, and after fording the stream, they noticed a tipi set up in the willows and a number of horses grazing nearby. It was Beaver Dick's camp, they found; he and a companion were trapping and had a good many skins stretched to dry. After a short visit with Dick the party moved on to set up camp in Teton Canyon. It was hot there, and so smoky that the peaks were at times entirely obscured: "sketching is out of the question & we spend our time working up some of our sketches made previously. As the sun goes down it gets quite cold but a roaring . . . fire gives warmth & cheerfulness to our camp & we all feel in the best of spirits."

The next morning, after "a substantial breakfast of venison," Moran, his brother, and Captain Bainbridge followed the trail up Teton Canyon for about six miles, then climbed to the top of a five-hundred-foot granite cliff. From there views of the mountains were "very magnificent . . . We remained on the cliff some 3 hours sketching and afterwards amused ourselves by rolling down great granite boulders over the precipice . . . & watching their descent as they went rebounding from rock to rock & crashing through the brush & dead timber at the base with a noise like the report of musketry. . . ."

On the way back to the valley they found "Red Raspberry & B. Currants plentiful," and ate their fill. They stopped to examine a large beaver dam that stretched across the canyon at one point. Moran admired the skill with which it had been engineered, and the beavers' industry in having cut the trees hundreds of feet above the stream and then brought them to the site.

By the time they reached camp he noticed that smoke from the forest fires had nearly obscured the Teton peaks. The sun sank that evening in fiery redness, and soon after, a strong, cold wind sprang up. During the night there was "a violent thunder storm." The party wakened at daybreak to find it raining coldly in the canyon and snowing on the peaks, and decided to break camp. After an uncomfortable breakfast prepared and eaten in a driving rain, they set off at six-thirty for the return to Fort

Hall. Looking back, Moran saw that the mountains were completely hidden in heavy storm clouds.

In spite of his intention to return to the Tetons, Thomas Moran never saw them again, except perhaps at a distance. Working conditions had been poor during his stay in Teton Canyon, yet he came away with enough impressions and watercolor sketches to enable him to paint two impressive landscapes in oil, *The Teton Range* and *Mount Moran,* which he considered among his most significant works.

XXIV
Six-Guns

Up from Texas came the first herds of longhorns to fatten on the rich grasses of the Wyoming prairies. Cattlemen were quick to realize the value of these natural pasturelands threaded by networks of sparkling streams. They soon picked out whatever ranges they wanted in this vast unsettled region and built ranch headquarters. Later, it was this same abundance of wild hay and ample water that attracted settlers to the Teton valleys.

In those early days of the open range, right after the Civil War, cattle stealing became a thriving business in Wyoming. To be successful, all a man needed was a rope horse, a running iron, and a couple of closemouthed and expert assistants. Encouragement of a kind was given rustlers by that unwritten law of the range which allowed any unbranded animal over a year old—a maverick—to be claimed and branded by the finder.

When large herds drifted over a hundred or more square miles, it was impossible to keep an accurate count of winter losses and depredations by wild animals. Most outfits did not even know the exact number of cattle they had. Stock which was driven off by thieves was usually never missed. If they were, little was done about it—in the beginning.

But just as soon as cattlemen began replacing longhorns with purebred stock, each animal came to have its value, and the attitude toward rustlers changed. Vigilance committees were formed, and men began disappearing mysteriously. Weeks, sometimes months later, their bodies might be found in some remote canyon or gulch, dangling from a cottonwood limb.

With the cattle industry's growth, the demand for horses increased. When the Wyoming grasslands were found to be equally suited to horse-raising, horse thievery became a popular occupation. It was easier than cattle rustling because horses travel faster and farther. For this reason, many a Wyoming outlaw served his apprenticeship stealing horses. Butch Cassidy was one of them. But there were others who built it into a full-time and profitable business.

Although it was considered a lower order of crime by the fraternity, in the eyes of men who were set afoot in a sparsely settled and sometimes arid country, the theft of a horse was akin to murder. The victims, as soon as they were mounted again, took off after the thieves, who were shot or hanged summarily upon capture. Rustling and horse thieving were not stopped by these stringent measures; they simply became more scientific. As a result, the total annual stealing of stock increased markedly.

As vigilantes, and later sheriffs and their posses, began closing in on them, the outlaws often found it imperative to disappear until the pursuit cooled. Jackson Hole became a favorite refuge, walling in the fugitive on four sides, almost without a break: ". . . every entrance lay through intricate solitudes. Snake River came in . . . through cañons and mournful pines and marshes, to the north, and went out at the south between formidable chasms. Every tributary . . . rose among high peaks and ridges, and descended into the valley by well-nigh impenetrable courses: Pacific Creek from Two Ocean Pass, Buffalo Fork from no pass at all, Black Rock from To-wo-ge-tee Pass—all these, and many more, were the waters of loneliness, among whose thousand hiding-places it was easy to be lost."

Horse Thief Pass, a rough trail known only to a few, followed the course of Bitch Creek through the Tetons to the west side. And there were others, remote and rugged: Death Canyon, Conant and Berry creeks—Indian trails that cut through the range and defied pursuit.

The noted outlaw Butch Cassidy is supposed to have been an occasional visitor to Jackson Hole, and to have buried some loot on Cache Creek. But Harvey P. Gleason alias William C. Jackson alias Teton Jackson established headquarters there in a stoutly built log cabin surrounded on three sides by marsh and backed by thick forest. It was claimed that he could hold it against almost anything except artillery.

Before turning outlaw, Jackson had worked as a scout and wagon-train driver for General George Crook's command. During the Sioux wars, he had discovered the almost impenetrable passes going into Jackson Hole and the narrow defiles leading out. Before getting his discharge, he made his first venture into his future profession by stealing a band of army mules. He was caught almost at once and put under guard, but made his escape by killing the two soldiers who had been detailed to watch him. Then, stealing a horse, he set off for Jackson Hole. Shortly he got together a gang of a dozen or so—Red Anderson, Blackie Marks, Big George Stevens, Frank Lamb, and Black Tom, to name some, hard cases all—and began horse thieving on a large scale.

During the early 1880s ranches in southeastern Oregon, Idaho, Utah, and Wyoming began losing hundreds of their choicest horses to Teton and his men. Driving them into the Hole, the outlaws would keep the animals there until they had collected eight hundred to a thousand head. Then, after they had changed the brands (doctoring them it was called), and allowed time for the new ones to heal, they put the horses on the trail— the old Indian trail that led over Two Ocean Pass, across the Divide, down Atlantic Creek to the Yellowstone's headwaters, through Sylvan Pass in the Absarokas, along the Shoshone River, and then across the Bighorn Basin to the Black Hills. There they sold them at high prices in Deadwood and other gold mining towns where horses were in demand.

On the return trip they reversed the process, stealing horses on the way back to headquarters, changing the brands, and selling them in the west, often to the very ranchers they had raided previously. It was a well-organized business that operated smoothly and lucratively for a number of years. No one was disposed to follow Teton to his hideout in Jackson Hole. The only way to catch him was on the trail, but he had strategically posted confederates who gave him timely warnings or managed expertly to send the pursuit astray.

Then one day Frank M. Canton, sheriff of Johnson County, Wyoming, received a telegram from Idaho lawman Billy Hosford, informing him that Teton had recently stolen fifty head of fine horses from two ranchers there, and these men, outraged, were demanding that something be done. Word had come in that Teton was heading toward Bighorn Basin, which was Canton's territory.

For a long time the sheriff had been waiting for a chance to capture Jackson. He suspected that an old trapper by the name of Lucas, who lived at the mouth of Paint Rock Creek Canyon, was one of Teton's allies. Taking with him two of his best deputies, Ed Loyd and Chris Gross, Canton left Buffalo "about dark" for the forty-mile trip across the Bighorn Mountains. By riding hard, they managed to reach Lucas' cabin about two hours before daylight.

They dismounted, tied their horses to some trees, and then stationed themselves within good shooting distance of the cabin. Just before daybreak a candle was lighted inside the house, and a few minutes later sparks began flying out of the chimney. Leaving his Winchester with the deputies, Canton ordered them to watch the single door and window and stop anyone who might try to escape. Then drawing his six-shooter, he stepped quietly into the cabin.

"I recognized Teton instantly by the description I had of him . . . He was about forty-five, over six feet in height, weight about a hundred and ninety, stubby beard, coarse features, flaming red hair, red face, and eyes as black as a snake's . . ." He was squatting in front of the fireplace, lighting his pipe with a splinter. He was only half dressed, and had not yet put on his six-shooter which was lying within reach, the belt full of cartridges. "I covered him at once with my revolver, and ordered my deputies to come in and handcuff him. Lucas was slicing venison for breakfast. . . . "

After they had eaten, Canton sent the trapper out with Loyd

and Gross, telling him that if he did not bring in every horse that Teton had hidden up the canyon, he would arrest him, too, and take him to Buffalo.

The sheriff was then alone with Teton. He had taken a seat about six feet away from the outlaw, covering him with his pistol. Teton soon began to complain that the handcuffs were cutting off his circulation, and that he was in great pain. If Canton would take them off, he would promise to keep quiet and not hurt him. "I told him I was not the least uneasy about his hurting me . . . that he was the one who was taking all the chances, for if he made the slightest move I would kill him. He said he understood . . . I then threw the keys over to him . . . he unlocked the handcuffs and pitched the keys and cuffs back to me."

Once free, Teton's attitude changed. He told Canton that even without his six-shooter, he, Teton, was the better man, and that the sheriff would never get him to Buffalo. Canton retorted that he was taking him there, dead or alive, it did not matter which, since he was worth as much one way as the other; and if he wanted to know the truth, he preferred to take his body because it would be "less trouble to handle." He then threw the handcuffs on the floor at Teton's feet and gave him ten seconds to put them on.

In about an hour the deputies returned with Lucas and the stolen horses. They mounted Teton on one, tied his feet under its belly, and set off for Buffalo.

While crossing a boggy meadow, Canton had a close call. In taking the lead, the herd had cut the turf so badly that the sheriff's horse broke through and mired. Jumping off, Canton sank into the mud and fell. Teton stopped to watch. By the time Canton got on his feet, his horse had pulled itself out and trotted up to Jackson's side.

"My Winchester was in the scabbard " Canton wrote, "and Teton . . . was just reaching for it when I called the deputies to look out. Ed Loyd drew his six-shooter just in time."

As the sheriff was mounting, Teton told him: "If I could have got that gun I would have settled with you anyway." But, as the lawman reflected, "an inch of a miss is as good as a mile."

That night they lodged Teton in the Buffalo jail. Billy Hosford rode over from Idaho and took him to Blackfoot for trial. He was given a long-term sentence for horse stealing and sent to the state penitentiary. The authorities were afraid his gang would rescue him if he was held at Blackfoot for the length of time it would take to gather evidence for the several murders he had committed. Three years later he knifed a guard and escaped. Some say he went back to his old headquarters in Jackson Hole and from there issued a challenge for the law to come and get him. Others say he was never heard of again. Traditionally Western badmen had a habit of reforming and becoming respected citizens—frequently bankers. A few hold that Teton Jackson was no exception.

While he was in jail his gang dissolved. Three of them were "sent to hell on a shutter," as the West termed it; several more were captured, and the rest left Jackson Hole for other parts. But that did not end the valley's use as a hideout. For years to come it remained "the most talked-of outlaw rendezvous in the world."

Things were as bad on the other side of the mountains. Pierre's Hole was a favorite resort for horse thieves. During the Civil War animals stolen from the garrison at Fort Hall were driven into the canyons that run back into the Tetons—deep, narrow gorges that were easily defended. Pursuit was hampered, for there was Blackfoot country to pass through, and the Indians, especially restive during those war years, were always on the lookout for troopers. The value of the horses was not considered worth the risk of battle.

But there came a time when depredations were too numerous to ignore—the cavalry was practically dismounted—so a party of soldiers was sent on the trail. They avoided trouble with the Blackfeet and tracked the stolen horses to Yamp Creek Canyon. Here, in the words of an early chronicler, they "executed swift vengeance by hanging the thieves to the trees under which they were sheltered." As an example to others, the bodies were left to hang until they became bundles of dry bones that rattled with the wind. But few were deterred, and horse thieves, especially those who raided the Montana ranches, continued to hide their stolen herds in Pierre's Hole.

Then there was the Cooper killing on Badger Creek. Robert Cooper was found dead in his cot one morning, with a bullet hole in his forehead. He and his two partners, prospectors, they said, had built a cabin beside the stream, and a corral farther up the canyon. But Cooper had not been discreet about that corral; he had hinted to a rancher that the horses they kept there were other men's horses. Before they left, his partners made sure he told no more tales.

The James brothers had been Edward Harrington's heroes ever since he was a small boy, and to emulate them became his life's ambition. As a result, he was constantly in trouble, although nothing serious until he came West with his wife and settled in Pierre's Hole. Then he changed his name to Ed Trafton, took in partners Jim Robertson and Columbus (Lum) Nickerson, and turned rustler and horse thief.

Harrington alias Trafton made his first mistake in May 1877, when he ran off with stock belonging to a neighbor, Hiram C. Lapham, who was the first homesteader in Pierre's Hole and a man of determination.

While Lapham was searching the Teton Canyons for his cattle, he came on a band of horses hidden in one of the gulches of Twin Creeks. They were hobbled and cross-hobbled, and their heads had been tied down. Lapham took note of their brands and descriptions. A little later he found his own stock in a ravine south of Leigh Creek, and that night he made a ride to Eagle Rock to get the sheriff. But the sheriff was off on business in another part of the county—it extended from Utah into Montana—however, deputy Sam Jones was willing to come. It was not hard to raise a posse since a number of ranchers in the area had recently had their horses stolen.

After an early breakfast that morning at Lapham's ranch, the party rode off on the trail. The following night they reached Lum Nickerson's cabin, built on an island in the Teton River. They surrounded it and called on the occupants to surrender. Jim Robertson and Lum were the only ones there for Trafton had left earlier that evening for Rexburg. As soon as the two came out, Robertson started to run. The deputy took aim and fired. Jim fell, mortally wounded. The stolen horses were recovered, and Nickerson was taken to the jail at Blackfoot.

Meanwhile, Trafton was arrested for robbing a store in Rexburg and soon joined his partner in the Blackfoot lockup. But they did not stay there long, for Lum's wife, Emma, paid him a visit: Hidden in her blouse was a revolver which she gave to Trafton. At gunpoint Bill High, the turnkey, unlocked the doors. In a matter of minutes the jail was empty, its four inmates making a wild break for freedom.

In a thicket at the edge of town Trafton and Nickerson found horses waiting for them, and were soon riding toward Eagle Rock. But the pair did not stay out of jail long either. While eating breakfast at a farmhouse along the way, they made a joking remark about their escape. The farmer overheard and gave the alarm. A posse soon caught up, and the two were cornered and held at bay overnight in the rush beds along the Snake's south fork. They had purposely taken this route, expecting their trail to be lost in the swamp, but were trapped when they found the river too high for fording. At dawn there was an exchange of gunfire, and Trafton was wounded in the foot. He and Lum were soon taken. This time Trafton received a twenty-five-year sentence, but was pardoned within four. His wealthy mother was said to have had a hand in this.

Ed Trafton had such a pleasant, friendly disposition and disarming smile that one could not hold things against him for long. He was one of a type of Western badmen described as "normal in everything except moral attitude toward horses, cattle, public vehicles, and bank safes." As he had promised to reform, he was awarded the contract to carry the United States mail into Pierre's Hole. After a time he grew bored and longed for the old life, more risky certainly, but also more interesting and exciting.

The high point in his career came on the morning of July 29, 1914. A party of one hundred and sixty-five tourists divided among thirty-five coaches was traveling through Yellowstone Park. As the first one came rolling up to Shoshone Point around ten o'clock, Trafton, his hat pulled low and his face masked with a handkerchief, stepped out from behind a large boulder and leveled his Winchester at the driver.

"Pull right off there, and stop!" he ordered, pointing to a wide place beyond.

"Now, all of you get out," he called to the passengers, "and hold up your hands. And you," he said to the driver, "don't you make any false moves because my podner in the timber has you covered with his gun."

Some accounts state that he was working alone; others that there was a confederate—that would have been Lum—who took up his position just down the trail and kept the coaches from going back to Old Faithful Inn to report the robbery.

"Line up, all of you," he told the passengers, "and march past me. As you go by, drop your cash—and cash only—into this sack. And don't any of you try to hide none."

They all did as they were told—except one man who was carrying a thousand dollars and managed to keep everything but the fifty-cent piece he dropped into the bag. Trafton then ordered the driver to pull his coach out of sight in a clearing beyond and instructed the passengers to follow. "Now just sit around and be comfortable," he is reported as saying. "None of you are going to get hurt if you behave." He felt reasonably safe since park rules prohibited drivers or passengers carrying weapons of any kind into the reserve.

A few minutes later the second coach—they were traveling about a mile apart—rolled up to the rock, and Trafton stepped out, stopped the driver, lined up the passengers, took their money, and sent the coach into hiding. He repeated the process until all thirty-five had been robbed.

Some of the passengers commented later on his "gentlemanly conduct." They told about one old lady, her coat and bonnet a little shabby, who in her excitement dropped her money. Trafton helped her pick it up, and handing it back, said:

"Here, ma'm, you keep this. You look as if you need it more than I do."

He even permitted those who had cameras to take pictures of the scene—after they had paid their tribute. Coolly he stuffed his saddlebag with the loot—twenty-thousand dollars according to some reports—then mounted his horse and galloped away.

It was a good hour before the lead coach reached Thumb Lunch Station to report the holdup. The telegraph wires to Yellowstone Park Hotel had been cut, so it was still longer until the alarm could be given. By then the trail of Ed Trafton and his partner (if he had one) was lost in the maze of mountains.

Riding south into Jackson Hole, he stopped for a few days in his hideout cabin near Colter Bay, then took one of the secret trails through the Tetons and made his way to his sister-in-law's house in Driggs, Idaho. There he stayed until he had grown a beard.

Up to the time the law caught up with him again and sent him to Leavenworth prison, Ed Trafton enjoyed a brief taste of fame and fortune. He went to Denver with his wife and spent money freely on clothes, jewelry, and "a costly touring car." He was no longer just a small-fry Western badman, he was the talk of the nation. Newspapers from coast to coast featured the story of the big stagecoach robbery. Even the *New York Times* considered it front-page news; the doings of Ed Trafton of Pierre's Hole were flanked by the latest reports on President Woodrow Wilson, the Czar, and the Kaiser.

Editorially, the *Times* chided him for having left the hold-up's immortalization to "amateur snapshotters." He should have made a contract with the "expert makers of moving pictures for an adequate—and profitable—reproduction of a romantic and interesting happening, pleasantly reminiscent of the good old days when highway robbery was in its prime."

When Trafton was finally arrested, he was reputedly at work on an armored car with which he intended to kidnap the president of the Mormon Church, and afterward hold him for ransom.

XXV
Taming the Hole

Jackson Hole's reputation as the place to lose one's identity as well as one's pursuer held through the end of the nineteenth century and well into the next one. Even among the homesteaders and ranchers who began settling the valley in the 1880s, there were some of whom no personal questions were ever asked, and a few whose real names were never learned.

In 1881 Robert R. Hamilton, a great-grandson of Alexander Hamilton, homesteaded on Jackson Lake, about eight miles from present Moran. A handsome, refined man who brought with him a large library of the classics, he had come to the Hole from New York City to escape unwelcome publicity following a love affair with an actress, a breach of promise suit, and a divorce by his wife. The next year he was joined by a partner, John D. Sargent, son of a distinguished New England family, and kin some said, to the painter John Singer Sargent. He brought with him his bride. The two men put up a ten-room log house and numerous outbuildings, and began raising purebred cattle and providing guide service for hunting parties.

One fine September day Hamilton, who was remembered as an enthusiastic sportsman, started off alone on a hunt. He rode along the Indian trail that skirted the lake, forded the Snake River a little below Moran, wound toward Timbered Mountain, and then led onto the plains near Deadman's Bar, where antelope grazed during this season. When he did not return to the ranch that night, a party went out to look for him. They agreed that anyone who found him or his trail would light a fire on the top of what was later called Signal Mountain.

On the third day the fire was lighted. Hamilton's body, with that of his horse, had been found in the Snake. It was concluded that he had tried to ford the river after dark, otherwise he would never have attempted to cross at such a treacherous point—a mile and a half below the regular ford. His horse, burdened with the extra weight of an antelope's hindquarters strapped to the saddle, had evidently waded out to where the water was deep, had started to swim but became entangled in the heavy growth of algae which choked the river there. Unable to go on, or back to the west shore, he drowned, and Hamilton with him. At least this was the deduction generally accepted.

There were a few people, however, who did not believe Hamilton's death was accidental. They said he had been instructed to cross the Snake at this particular spot. There were reasons for wanting Hamilton out of the way. Some said it was the pretty woman in the triangle. Others thought Sargent wanted all the profits from the lake property for himself.

Sargent continued to live at the ranch, which he took over from Hamilton's heirs, until 1898. At that time he was accused of having intentionally run over his wife with a cart and kept her injuries secret. When she died several months later from neglect, one account states that Sargent fled into the mountains at the north, hid out for a time, and then made his way into another state. Another report says that he was arrested and indicted for murder. Whichever happened, at the end of seven years he came back to his deserted house beside the lake, a bitter, brooding man. One August day, many months later, he was found dead in one of the empty rooms, a shotgun between his knees, the muzzle pointed at his head.

During the next decade the rustlers, horse thieves, poachers, and highway robbers began finding themselves nearly outnumbered by those men who came into Jackson Hole to wrest a living honestly from the land. They then moved their hideouts to the north end of the valley. There, in the remote and rugged wilderness they built their cabins and were able to hold their ground for many years more.

Jackson Hole was settled slowly because of its inaccessibility, its short season, and its long, cold winters. For many years the nearest railroad shipping point was St. Anthony, Idaho, a round trip of about one hundred and fifty miles and several days' travel. This not only made the marketing of products difficult, it also meant that all supplies had to be packed over the Tetons that distance.

An early resident wrote that in winter the entire Hole was buried under three to six feet of snow; that during this time cold spells often sent the mercury down to forty or fifty degrees below zero; and that the blizzards which swept across the flats made life uncomfortable even for the well-housed settler. Then hot rocks or heated flat irons were put in the children's beds to keep their feet from freezing. Save for a few well-packed roads where sleighs could be drawn, all other travel was limited to snowshoes. Except for those who trapped, "there was little to do but wait for spring," he recalled. Even after spring came, contact with the outside world remained limited, since many of the passes were blocked by snow until mid-June.

Not until 1884 were the first permanent homesteads established. That year trapper John Holland and a friend, John Carnes, took up adjoining land near Flat Creek. Each succeeding year brought in a few more settlers until by 1889 there were forty. That fall five Mormon families, all of the Wilson clan, came in by wagon over Teton Pass and swelled the population to sixty-four.

When a ranch wife, who came in as a bride, was asked what her first impressions were, she said that she had been thrilled by the beauty of the Tetons, and pleased at the abundance of elk, which was "grand to eat," until as a steady diet it began to pall. But she had to go on eating it because it was the only game that was easy to hunt. The streams were full of trout, which would have been a welcome change, but everyone was "too busy getting a start" to take the time to fish. Flour, cornmeal, dried apricots, black coffee, and elk meat were the staples. Wild gooseberries and currants were plentiful, she recalled, but these needed sugar, and sugar was scarce. As tired as they grew of eating elk, old settlers are all agreed that without it they would never have been able to stay in Jackson Hole during the years when they were proving their land.

In the beginning it was all hard work, and at times there was an overpowering sense of loneliness and isolation. However, once the house and barn were up, the wild hay cut, and the herd started, and, if there was a woman about the place, a garden put in, there came an awareness of belonging. Life began to take form along established patterns. Acquaintance was made among the neighboring ranchers, if only at first to discuss the mutual problems of mastering an unfriendly environment.

As more and more families came in, Thanksgiving, Christmas, and Fourth of July celebrations began to break the routine of endless ranch work. In some of the tiny settlements which sprang up throughout the valley, there were social halls where all-night dances were held, and local troupes put on plays or gave musical entertainments. Weddings, births, deaths, funerals, manhunts, and Indian scares also varied daily life and furnished topics of conversation for months to come.

A woman homesteader, describing a Thanksgiving wedding supper held at her cabin, wrote:

"Our dinner was a success, but that was not to be wondered at. Every woman for miles around contributed. Of course we . . . couldn't think of seating every one; so we set one table for twenty-four and had three other long tables, on one of which we placed all the meats, pickles, and sauces, on another the vegetables, soup, and coffee, and on the third the pie, cakes, ice-cream, and other desserts. . . . The people helped themselves . . . and hunted . . . a place to sit while they ate. Two of the cowboys from this ranch waited upon the table at which were the wedding party and some of their friends. Boys from other ranches helped serve . . . coffee, cake, and ice-cream. The tablecloths were tolerably good linen and we had ironed them wet so they looked nice."

By five o'clock the dishes were washed and everything cleared away, and the party was ready to set off in sleds and sleighs for the all-night dance in town.

Between events, little things in life assumed meaning and importance: taking the children into the woods to pick wild berries; the semiannual trips over the Tetons to St. Anthony; waiting impatiently for the seeds of favorite flowers, brought by women from the old home garden, to sprout in pots set in a sunny window; watching for those harbingers of spring—the robins, the buttercups, and the tiny, pink steershead; observing the Tetons' many moods, the changing seasons, and the weather.

For those living close to the land, weather is an integral part of existence. Skill is developed in forecasting, not by instruments but through reading those signs found in nature. Since in Teton country winter was the longest season, the harshest and most dreaded, it was important to know what to expect, and everyone began watching early for portents.

If the wild geese stopped to feed only briefly in the valley's marshes and streams in their southward fall flight then winter would be long and hard. If, however, they stayed a month or more, "carefree and happy," there would be "a nice mild winter of short duration." If blackbirds began to "bunch up" early in the fall, that was a sure sign of an early winter. When mice and wood rats took up quarters in cabins and barns, then a long, severe winter was on the way. Another infallible sign was the date when ground squirrels holed up: If they were still frisking about in late fall, then winter would be light, "for the squirrels always know." If the winter was mild with frequent rain, then a hot dry summer was expected. If elk and deer started moving to the hills before winter was over, spring was sure to be early and short.

For day-to-day forecasts there were other signs: A circle around the moon meant rain; the number of stars in the circle indicated the number of days before rain would fall. Rain was imminent if smoke drifted close to the ground, if leaves showed their undersides, and if birds flew low in flocks. Weather would be fair if smoke rose and crickets chirped loudly; but if smoke rose when it was cloudy, then snow was expected. Applying these observations gave the homesteaders a sense of mastery over the elements. It was part of the taming process.

Schools, ferries, toll bridges, wagon roads, churches, a newspaper (the *Jackson's Hole Courier*), and mail service of a sort—it came by rail to Victor, west of the Tetons, and was carried by horseback or snowshoe over the Pass, ferried across the Snake, then distributed throughout the Hole by volunteers—brought a semblance of civilization.

But it was to the advantage of many to keep the valley wild. Although hay and cattle raising continued to be the main occupations, a number of ranchers found it profitable to provide outfitting and guide service for those parties of wealthy eastern and European sportsmen and trophy hunters who had been coming to Jackson Hole since the 1870s, and would keep on coming only as long as the hunting remained prime and the area retained its wilderness character.

The largest and best equipped of these parties ever to go into Jackson Hole was that of the president of the United States Chester A. Arthur. He had been unwell, and his friends, urging a rest from state affairs and a complete change of scene, suggested Yellowstone Park. Arthur, who was a good outdoorsman and an enthusiastic angler, agreed. Further, he said, such a trip would enable him to enlarge his firsthand knowledge of the Indians, and of the geography of the Far West.

In the summer of 1883 the party went by rail to Green River, Wyoming, where they boarded stagecoaches, and their baggage was shifted to freight wagons. At the end of the stage line, the presidential party that included Secretary of War Robert Todd Lincoln, General Philip Sheridan, and United States Senator George Vest, an ardent conservationist, started off on the mountain trails by horseback. One hundred and seventy-five horses and mules were required to carry the men, provisions, and equipment on this three-hundred-and-fifty-mile trek through some of the wildest and most rugged areas in the West. A full troop of cavalry rode as escort. To keep the president in daily communication with the outside world, couriers were stationed with fresh relays at intervals of twenty miles.

There was a stopover at the Wind River Indian Reservation, where the president paid a formal call on Chief Washakie. The Shoshoni leader did not go with the other head men of his tribe to greet the president. Dressed in his best, Washakie waited in his lodge for Arthur to come to him. The Indians entertained their visitors with a war dance, and later in the day held a mock skirmish with the cavalry escort.

After hiring several Indian guides, among them the medicine

man Togwotee, the president's cavalcade moved on to the head of Wind River, along the old trail that led over the Divide and into Jackson Hole. Of their first sight of the Tetons, one of the party wrote that at the crest of a long hill "there burst upon our view a scene as grand and majestic as we had ever witnessed. Below us, covered with grasses and flowers, was a lovely valley. . . . Along the whole westerly edge of this valley . . . towered the magnificent Teton Mountains, their snowy summits piercing the air. . . ."

The trip north through Jackson Hole was unhurried. Six camps were set up there for the president to fish the lakes and streams. Some hunting was done to supply the party with fresh meat, but the emphasis was on angling and broiled trout dinners.

The dominant masculinity of cattle country prompted a cowboy to refer to it as "he country in pants." This was certainly true of Jackson Hole, where all the first settlers, except John Carnes, were bachelors. But it was not long before women began coming in to all parts of the range, first as ranchers' wives—who frequently brought with them unmarried sisters and cousins—then on their own as schoolteachers, homesteaders, and storekeepers. These women shared the work and hardships of frontier life in a harsh climate equally with the men. When Wyoming's first territorial government was organized, the founders recognized the women as peers and granted them the right to vote and hold office. This was the first state or territory to pass such a law, and the nation's attention was fixed on Wyoming. In March 1870, when a federal judge empaneled women to serve on grand and petit juries in the district court at Laramie, the attention became worldwide. Heads of European countries hastened to send their congratulations to President Grant on this most recent evidence of enlightenment, progress, and civil liberty in America. Newsmen from across the country flocked to the frontier town to report on women jurors at work. They were disappointed at finding the jurors all heavily veiled, and in revenge hinted that they were ancient, stern, and homely.

That same year the roaring gold camp of South Pass City elected a woman justice of the peace, claimed to have been the first woman in this country to ever fill such an office. Later,

Wyoming was to have the distinction of being the first state to elect a woman as governor.

In 1920 Jackson, one of the last strongholds of the rowdy Old West, became the first town in this country to elect an all-woman slate—mayor and council. At this same election a woman was voted into the office of sheriff. Before the second town meeting, the mayor and council had personally collected all delinquent taxes, swelling the treasury holdings from two hundred to over two thousand dollars. During their term they converted the narrow, crooked lanes into wide, graded streets, built sidewalks and crossings, planted cottonwood trees around the town square, designated a cleanup week in which all residents participated, made the start for a new water and irrigation system, replaced the steep, winding path to the cemetery with a good road—a project their predecessors had been putting off for years—and introduced so many other improvements and innovations that they were swept back into office at the next election.

Again the magazines and newspapers sent their staff writers to see for themselves and report. There was no doubt that Jackson Hole, once the most notorious outlaw rendezvous in the country, had, from the desperado's viewpoint, backslid and allowed itself to be tamed.

XXVI
Riders

To the Spaniards and Mexicans the American cowboy owed his vocation. For his character he was indebted to no one, observed a cowboy historian.

From the vaqueros of California and Texas he acquired all the tools of his trade, technic of his craft, even "the very words by which he designated his utensils, the very animals with which he dealt." The bronco he rode was descended from stock brought into Spain by the Moors, while the longhorns he herded were relatives of those animals bred by the Moors on the plains of Andalusia. The saddle, bridle, bit, spurs, lariat, branding iron, and such specialized apparel as chaps, were duplicates of what had been developed and used by generations of Spanish and Mexican herders.

Over the years the American cowboy made some adaptations—three types of saddle evolved between 1850 and 1880—and Americanized the terms. What had once been *la reata* became lariat; *jáquima*, hackamore; *chaparejos*, chaps; *cuerda* (or in Mexican, *cuarta*), quirt; *lazo*, lasso, and so on. Even buckaroo was of Spanish origin, for that was the way vaquero sounded to the cowboy, or at least the way he said it. American herders themselves came to be known variously as cowboys, cowpunchers, punchers, buckaroos, cowpokes, and cowhands. In Wyoming they preferred being called riders.

In Teton country, riders took the place of the mountain man as the picturesque and colorful frontier character. Like the mountain man's, the rider's era was also brief, but during that short time he was surrounded with an aura of romance that made him one of the most important figures in American folklore and literature.

The first ones rode up the long trail from Texas. Later they came in from nearly every state and from across the seas. From 1870 to the mid-1880s the Western cattle boom was on, and the craze to be a cowboy swept the country and drifted over the Atlantic. To adventurous young men in many walks of life, the mounted cowboy represented absolute freedom of spirit, while the land where he lived and worked promised high adventure.

So they came flocking West, but only the hardy and determined ones lasted. They soon discovered that it was a raw, isolated life that demanded stamina, resourcefulness, and courage at all times. It was a life that asked much of a man and gave little in return. The rider was expected to face death often, and usually alone. He once defined himself as "a man with guts and a horse." "The West demands you smile and swallow your personal troubles like your food," an old hand advised a tenderfoot. As a result, a carefully cultivated cheerfulness and an apparent nonchalance became a part of the cowboy's philosophy.

By the time the rider reached Teton country in the 1880s he was already wearing his distinctive uniform: the big hat, the colored neckerchief, the vest, the pointed, high-heeled boots, the chaps, the fringed gauntlets, the low-slung holster with its Colt—in the beginning always single-action—glamorous trappings in the eyes of his admirers. Yet it was usefulness, comfort, and convenience which had dictated the clothes. Although there was little deviation, individual tastes were often expressed in the matter of color, material, or cut. Cowboy artist Charles Russell maintained that every cow camp had its fashion leader, who went in for "fancy rigs."

From the start the hat was the most important article of dress; it came to be the first thing a cowman put on when he got up in the morning and the last thing he took off when he went to sleep at night. He didn't remove it often between times because Western etiquette allowed him to wear it at the dinner table and even on the dance floor.

He needed a hat that would hold its shape in all kinds of weather, would be heavy enough to stay on during the stiffest gale and roughest riding, shade the eyes, protect the head from the burning sun, keep rainwater from pouring down the back of the neck, be of use in putting out a grass fire, carrying water, or serving as a pillow. But until John B. Stetson began marketing such a hat in the late 1880s, the cowboy had to settle for whatever he could get. Within a short time the Stetson became the distinguishing article of the cowboy's dress and a synonym for Western headgear.

The cowpuncher soon developed a distinctive terminology that applied to his work, and a way of talking that was simple, direct, terse, rich in simile and anecdote, and often epigrammatic. His one rule for sentence-making was to "bobtail her and fill her with meat." So opposed was he to needless words he would often urge a verbose conversationalist outside the ranks to save his breath for breathing. This did not mean the average cowboy was not talkative; he was, but always with an economy of words.

His jargon, suggested by his work and the country around him, was interwoven with current slang, foreign phrases, gambling terms, and Indian words. So it came about that "hoof it" meant walk; "pound leather," ride; "beef," complain; "rope in," trick; "go over the range" or "no breakfast forever," die; "dry gulch," shoot a man in a waterless ravine. A man with "lead poisoning" was one who had been shot.

To "hit the hay" or "roll in" meant go to bed; "chassé" or "waltz" were synonyms for go, or happen on; a "buck" was a dollar; a "clodhopper," a farmer; "biscuit shooter," the camp cook; "prairie lawyers," coyotes; and "sky pilot," a preacher.

Poker's "busted flush" was applied to a plan fallen through; seven-up's "it's high, low, jack and the game" indicated success in an undertaking. A puncher described his preparations for a journey or enterprise as "making medicine"; depending on the outcome, this would be spoken of later as good or bad medicine.

He called his personal belongings his "plunder" or "dofunnies" and carried them in his "war sack" or "poke." He "post-age-stamped" his pony, which meant one didn't see daylight between him and his saddle. He referred to liquor as "snake juice" or "poison," and biscuits as "hot rocks." Many of his words and expressions were appropriated by those outside the calling and came into general use throughout the West.

Most of the cowboys' utterances were larded with profanity because, as someone defended them, they had to deal with the "incalculable idiocies" of cattle and horses. The manner of delivery and tone of voice determined the interpretation.

"Son-of-a-bitch" was the common greeting between friends, and used by them as a term of affection. But there were times when it was construed as a challenge, and the man so addressed "dug for his cannon" while the bystanders sent for the coroner. The phrase was subject to embellishments, and a man often fell into the category of "plain," "fancy," "natural-born," "self-made," or "pale pink" variety. In reserve for special revilement was "double distilled son-of-a-bitch net."

Some cowhands devoted much time and thought to compiling ingenious combinations of swear words, or to inventing them. They were known to ride miles to compete in what they called "cussing-matches," where the prize was usually a saddle.

As a raconteur, the cowboy was without match. The loneliness of the life gave ample time for thought. His calling, like the mountain man's, required him to be a keen and accurate observer of human nature as well as the country around him. Accounts of Indian ambuscades, encounters with cattle and horse thieves, trailing outlaws, horse races, grizzly bear attacks, stampeding cattle, and those remarkable horses he had known, were favorite subjects. Stories about the fierce and terrible "wouser" were reserved for the newcomer to the West. Although the animal's appearance, character, and family tree were left to each teller's imagination, the wouser was usually made a close relative of the grizzly bear. It resorted to ambush, attacked without warning, was most often rabid, and its favorite prey was man.

Cowboys were always anxious to tell about those ponies they had known who were "all horse," beasts that were extraordinarily sagacious, brave, and loyal; who countless times saved their riders from certain death, and sometimes killed themselves in the effort. Those highly trained horses that the puncher rode regularly he adopted into his family, and, claims an old hand, the horses adopted him into theirs. On long solitary rides cowboys talked to their mounts continuously. "However close-mouthed a man might be with . . . his fellow men, he imparted all his secrets to his horse." Although his expressions of affection "might be intermittant and be made in rough words or rude pats . . . they were sincere." The pony understood, and expressed loyalty and affection in his own way.

The cowboy's keen powers of observation contributed some valuable scientific data over the years: the locations of fossil beds, caves with unusual formations, petrified trees; the migration timetables of birds, and the sites of their way stations; the habits and ranges of certain wild animals; unusual Indian customs, and prehistoric archaeological sites and artifacts.

"Sings" as well as storytelling were part of an evening's entertainment around the campfire or in the bunkhouse. There was often a banjo, fiddle, or mouth organ as accompaniment. The favorite themes were doleful and full of longing, and the verses were many. "The Home I Ne'er Will Live to See," "I'm Thinking of My Dear Old Mother, Ten Thousand Miles Away," "I'm a Poor, Lonesome Cowboy" vied for popularity with "Bury Me Not on the Lone Prairie," which took a full ten minutes to get through. Among the riders in Jackson Hole it was remembered that "Home in the West" took its place with those other favorites.

"Nasal tones predominated, and the songs were rendered with very considerable seriousness of sound and facial expression," a cowboy recalled. "Variations in high notes were affectionately regarded, and notes long drawn out were deeply loved."

The more cheerful ballads were based on the daily experience of the range, and were marked by the strong rhythm of the trot, lope, or pace. Here again Teton country had preferences: "Pitch, You Piebally, Pitch," and "The Gol-Darned Wheel," a wheel being an unruly pony.

There were many opportunities for improvisation on the cattle drive, and the summer range, during the long hours of the graveyard stretch, or in solitary line camps. At these times cowboys recalled songs from boyhood, or those they had heard in dance halls and saloons. When these were exhausted, they made up verses for the old tunes. Hymns, because of their simple melodies, were easily remembered and most often used, although the inventive sometimes composed their own music.

On night herd the rider constantly chanted or crooned. "This serenading was done partly to hold the cattle under the compelling spell of the human voice, and partly to disabuse from the mind of any fearsome member of the herd the suspicion that either the puncher's silhouette against the sky-line or . . . the noise of his moving pony might represent a snooping dragon," an old hand explained.

For this reason, the rider was careful to avoid any sound or inflection that might startle and prompt a stampede. This shift, lasting from two to four hours, called for an inexhaustible repertoire. The cowboy, reaching his limit, would set to music or simply chant anything that came to mind—ribaldry, uncomplimentary opinions of the cattle, strings of swear words, or the texts of condensed milk and coffee can labels.

Books and periodicals were so scarce on the range that men in lonely camps took to reading the labels on cans of peaches, tomatoes, milk, and other prepared foods so often the words were automatically memorized. This "knowing your cans" led to a game called "Brand," which was played at table or around the campfire. It consisted of competitive recitations of the texts of various labels. There was a fine of five cents for every mistake in punctuation, and ten cents for each wrong word.

The average ranch library was composed of three or four well-thumbed mail-order-house and saddlers' catalogs, an almanac, parts of newspapers of ancient date and scattered locality, and a novel or two, one rider remembered; occasionally there was "a battered set of Shakespeare." He and his fellows lingered over the pictures and descriptions in the catalogs, avoided the novels, but "took a whirl" periodically in Shakespeare.

A hundred or more miles was never too far to ride for the dance that might be held after the roundup, or on Thanksgiving, Christmas, or New Year's. Since a woman was, in the cowboy's words, "a scanty thing" in Wyoming cattle country, some punchers at the dance would agree to be "heifer-branded," which meant wearing a white handkerchief tied around the upper arm, or putting on some ranch wife's ruffled apron. Then, with his hat securely fixed on his head, and spur rowels and chains jangling ("a cowboy moving across a board floor suggested the transit of a knight in armor," one of them observed), he would swing out with his partner for a night of dancing that was marked more by vigor and enthusiasm than grace.

The drunken cowboy has become a part of Western lore, which suggests he was in that state a good part of the time. But the very nature of his work, which demanded vigilance every minute, precludes this possibility. A cowboy habitually intoxicated would not have lasted long in the daily round. Those who knew him maintain he was no more prone to drunkenness than his contemporaries in other parts of the country, and that he was actually drunk less often because his opportunities for getting liquor were more limited. At the ranch there was usually nothing in the way of spirits except the carefully guarded bottle reserved for medicinal use. The town, then, was the principal source, and the puncher often went to town no more than twice a year. Admittedly, when he did get there after a six months' enforced abstinence, his first stop was likely to be the saloon. When he drank, he demanded the best. Bourbon whiskey, straight, was his invariable order. Mixed drinks were entirely foreign to cattle country.

Legend has the cowboy in his cups unlike any other man in his. But, writes one of them, this was not true: When he got drunk he did not do it "in any specialized way. He merely got drunk," and became as surly or quarrelsome or droll or maudlin as any easterner in the same condition. As to killing one another or shooting up the bar in their inebrity, it happened but it was not general. The first thing most punchers did on dismounting at the gambling saloon was to "peel off" their Colt's and holster and hang them over the saddle horn. "We boys didn't want any trouble. We came to town just for a change." But, as in any large group, there were always some men who were disposed to violence.

In the beginning, arms were carried only when the cowboy

thought he might need them in his work. Later they became standard equipment, pistols being considered as necessary a part of full dress—"full warpaint"—as chaps, boots, spurs, fancy vest (usually brown plush with wide black braid trim), and woven horsehair watch chain.

One cowboy admitted he had a liking for the girls, but complained that when he went to town they paid no attention to him. "Owen Wister hadn't yet written his book *The Virginian,* so we cowhands did not know we were so strong and glamorous as we were after people read that book."

The Virginian's cowboy hero immediately caught the public's fancy, and young women everywhere fell in love with him. He became the model for the cowboy folk figure—handsome, gentlemanly, fearless, reflective, and idealistic, with "conscience and trigger-finger accurate, quick, and in unison." The book became the prototype for the hundreds of Western stories and novels that followed.

In 1885 young Owen Wister, a grandson of the famed Shakespearean actress Fanny Kemble, went to Wyoming for his health. He had graduated from Harvard summa cum laude, was a composer and an accomplished pianist, had studied advanced musical composition in Europe (where he played one of his own works for Franz Liszt), and was now preparing to enter Harvard Law School.

Although he was admitted to the bar in 1890, those impressions gained during that first summer spent on the Major Wolcott ranch near Medicine Bow determined his career. After six trips to the West, he gave up the practice of law and became a writer of Western fiction.

"And so one Autumn evening of 1891, fresh from Wyoming and its wild glories, I sat . . . dining with a man as enamoured of the West as I was. This was Walter Furness," Wister wrote. "From oysters to coffee we compared experiences. Why wasn't some Kipling saving the sage-brush for American literature, before the sage-brush and all it signified went the way of the California forty-niner . . . the way of the Mississippi steamboat . . . the way of everything. Roosevelt had seen the sage-brush true, had felt its poetry; and also Remington. . . . But what was fiction doing, fiction, the only thing that has always outlived fact? Must it be perpetual teacups? . . .

"Walter, I'm going to try it myself!' I exclaimed . . . 'I'm going to start this minute.' "

Rushing upstairs to the library of the Philadelphia Club, where he and Furness had been having dinner, Wister started to work. He wrote most of the story of "Hank's Woman" that night, and when it was finished he sold it to *Harper's Magazine*. The setting is Teton country.

During those many trips West, Wister had not been intellectually idle. He was what he termed "a brilliant listener," and his eye missed nothing. Even the journal kept on his first trip is filled with detailed descriptions of the country and ranch life; with incidents that revealed the character of the frontier; with actual conversations, and vivid word pictures of the people he saw or met. It was as though he knew that he would one day write about the West.

On July 19, 1885, he entered in that first journal: "Got here at 5:30 this evening. . . . This place is called a town. 'Town' will do very well until the language stretches itself and takes a new word that fits. Medicine Bow, Wyoming consists of:

> 1 Depot house and baggage room
> 1 Coal shooter
> 1 Water tank
> 1 Store
> 2 Eating houses
> 1 Billiard hall
> 6 Shanties
> 8 Gents and Ladies Walks
> 2 Tool houses
> 1 Feed stable
> 5 Too late for classification
> _____
> 29 Buildings in all

". . . I have walked nearly two acres in order to carefully ascertain the exact details of this town. . . ."

When he came to write *The Virginian*, which is set in Wyoming, he included this early description of Medicine Bow.

On subsequent trips West he made it a point to get to know cowpunchers, ranch owners, saloonkeepers, trappers, rustlers, horse thieves, hunters, Indians, gamblers, and soldiers. In these journals he again recorded actual conversations and happenings, and made lists of Western expressions and figures of speech—"I'm feeling like a loaf of dough that hasn't risen"; "no more brains than a greased gimlet"; "double-triggered lightning"; "financially coon-failed" (dead broke); "I'd dealt him a misery"; "hard game" (badman); "his eyeballs jingled."

In writing about the West he was determined to be accurate. But when he put down life as it really was, using the actual language of the frontier, he ran afoul of censorship: "The plain talk in my Western tales published in *Harper's* . . . never got by the blue pencil of Henry Millys Alden liberal as he was. . . ." Once when the editor complained "your story is very bloody," Wister retorted: "You're not going to get much American Western adventure without blood."

His daughter, Fanny Kemble Wister, says he found "the pussyfooting vocabulary acceptable in conversation and the pasteurized prose in print" at the time "hard to endure." Even *The Virginian* was considered "daringly realistic."

Part of the action of *The Virginian* takes place in Pierre's Hole and Jackson Hole, and along the trails through the Tetons, which Wister saw first in the summer of 1887. Of his first view of those mountains he wrote on August 13:

"I looked down towards Jackson Hole and saw the ragged leavings of the thunder cloud prowling up the slopes of pine hill, beyond which the ice-sharp points of the Tetons glittered with snow and sunlight, and over the basin hung a golden cloud that swam in the rays. . . ."

And a few days later, in camp near Buffalo Fork, he wrote: "Over Snake River is a wide plain . . . and from it abruptly rise the Tetons grey and streaked with snow. They stood like steeples. The way in which they come up without any heralding of foot hills seems as though they rose from the sea. At sunset they turned lilac and all their angles swam together in a misty blue light . . . as if a veil had been thrown over them."

There were to be many more trips to Teton country to explore the lakes, the canyons, the streams and falls, and to ride the Indian trails that cut through the range from side to side.

In the Far West, the winter of 1845 was memorable for cold. Indians never tired of telling about the time when all their ponies froze or starved to death, and they recorded it on buffalo hide and rock with the picture of a prostrate horse. Trappers who were there have said that the temperature could have been no less than sixty degrees below zero, and they told of the thousands of buffalo which died, as well as antelope and elk.

The weather being cyclic, Wyoming experienced another winter of intense cold that came early and lasted long in the season of 1886-87. When spring finally came, ranchers found carcass piled on carcass. Their cattle had died by the thousands, and losses for individual owners ranged from thirty to one hundred percent. Many cattlemen were ruined, and many of the big land holdings were broken up. Cowboys drifted off to find work elsewhere, or turned to other callings.

In Jackson Hole some of those cattlemen who were not forced out of business turned to guest or dude ranching to help pay their way, on the premise that "dudes winter easier than cattle." The JY Ranch on Phelps Lake is said to have been the Hole's first dude ranch. There Owen Wister brought his wife and children to spend three months in 1911.

They came in from the north, through Yellowstone Park, camping along the way. When it was time to cross the Snake River to the west side of Jackson Hole, they took the ferry established nine years before by Bill Menor, a former cowboy who was tall and gaunt and wore a "drooping, sunburned mustache that had once been yellow." He had the only vegetable garden in the valley, and during the rest of that summer the Wister children would often ride over to call on him and buy his fresh peas.

Wister's daughter, Fanny Kemble, recalled that food at the JY was often scant, and not always the best. On those days "when a steer was shot for beef, we would have some of it for supper. . . . We ate dried, smoked, salted bear (like dark brown leather) from the year before; [and] fresh elk too tough to chew. . . . We frequently found dead flies between the flapjacks at breakfast, and we drank condensed milk."

All the children took lessons in dry-fly fishing from their father, who was a skilled angler, but only the oldest ones learned the technique. They spent most of their time riding: "I bareback for miles each day. Fording Snake River, loping through the sagebrush with no trail, we went into the foothills as far as our laboring horses could climb. We were not too young to be stunned with admiration by the Tetons, and we loved the acres of wild flowers growing up their slopes—the tremulous Hare-bell blue and fragile, the Indian Paint-brush bright red, and the pale, elegant Columbine. We were not awed by the wilderness, feeling that the Grand Teton was our own mountain and the most wonderful mountain in the world, and the Snake River the fastest, longest river in America. We would ride all day and never get past the Tetons. When we returned to the ranch in the later afternoon, we would ride up the brief slope and sud-denly Phelps Lake would appear in front of us. The mountains encircling it rose abruptly from the water, with Death Canyon at the far end. . . ."

They stayed in Jackson Hole until the first snows of Septem-ber. "We could not stand the thought of leaving. . . . No more smell of sagebrush, no more rushing Snake River, no more Grand Teton."

The next year they were back, this time with a ranch of their own. Owen Wister had taken up a hundred and sixty acres in a little valley west of Moose, now known as Wister Draw. They could not drive fast enough to get to it, Fanny remembered. When they came to the stone marking the boundary line be-tween Idaho and Wyoming, the children "yelled for joy. Every rock, every sage brush, every aspen tree was different and bet-ter because it grew in Wyoming. . . . There was no other such state."

They stayed at the JY while building their two-story cabin. Fanny recalled that the whole family worked on it, with no outside help at all, and that they moved in before it was finished.

Looking back over the years to those summer and fall months spent in the Tetons, Fanny felt that her father, in tak-ing his family there, was linking them with his youth, "mak-ing us in spirit next of kin to the country of his choice."

But the West he had known so well was already a vanished world. "No journeys, save those which memory can take, will bring it to you now," he wrote. "The mountains are there, far and shining, and the sunlight, and the infinite earth, and the air that seems forever the true fountain of youth,—but where is the buffalo, and the wild antelope, and where the horseman with his pasturing thousands? So like its old self does the sage-brush seem when revisited, that you wait for the horseman to appear.

"But he will never come again. He rides in his historic yesterday."

XXVII
The Changing Mountains

Constant change is in the order of things. All of Teton country's picturesque figures—Indians, hunters, trappers, traders, noblemen-adventurers, explorers, goldseekers, horse thieves, and highwaymen—ride in their historic yesterdays, and little beyond the memory of their presence remains.

Cattle and sheep raising, agriculture, lumbering, housing, resorts, ski lifts, roads, bridges, dams, levees, and an airport have altered the face of the Teton valleys. Only the mountains themselves appear to be the same. But this is deceptive, for those forces which first shaped the peaks are still at work ceaselessly modifying their form and character, while the stresses of inner earth are pushing them ever higher.

Eternity is not one of nature's laws. Everything inherently of this earth is within the cycle of creation, destruction, and rebirth. Continents and islands are slowly sinking or rising, while the restless seas trim them greedily on every side. Old mountains are being worn down, and new ones are rising. Rivers are growing ever longer or shorter, deeper or shallower, gaining new branches, shifting their courses, or disappearing altogether. Wherever they run steepest they tear away the

247

earth, and in the flat calm of their deltas deposit it to build land anew. Lakes become larger or smaller, or vanish entirely through that remarkable metamorphosis that turns them first into marshes, then into meadows, and finally forests. Ancient glaciers dwindle while new ones form in the cool shadow of peaks. Fresh canyons are cut by young streams; old canyons are filled by rock debris and their waters dammed to form new lakes. Ancient forest trees decay and fall, and seedlings spring up in their places. It is "as if Nature were ever repenting and undoing the work she had so industriously done," John Muir reflected.

In Jackson Hole there is a constant struggle to keep the Snake River from shifting to the west side of the valley as its floor continues to drop and tilt increasingly westward in response to action along the Teton fault. To the close observer there is evidence all about of the endless struggle between the forces which build and those which tear down. Minor earthquakes occur almost daily, and fresh faults break the valley floor and form numerous scarps along the Teton fronts. The talus heaps which cover the slopes below the higher peaks are ever enlarging. Rock glaciers advance along the slopes, and each year mud flows and landslides carrying rock and earth from the heights spread onto the valley floor. Surface rocks are bending and breaking as the earth's crust is being constantly raised, warped, tilted, dropped, and faulted.

The work of those erosive agents which ground out the Teton canyons and lake basins, carved their plain flanks, and boldly sharpened the peaks and crests is more pronounced and noticeable at the higher elevations where slopes are steep and unprotected, and daily temperature changes are extreme. These exposed areas are buffeted by tempests, struck by lightning, and pelted by sleet and hail. They are in turn buried in snow, drenched with sunshine, and chilled by frost. This cycle of heat and cold, expansion and contraction is, next to running water, the most powerful force at work, and gradually pries loose the sides of mountain faces, crags, and canyon walls, eventually causing them to collapse.

Among the peaks patches of snow lie throughout the year, and in the mellow warmth of summer or afternoon sunshine, they melt about the edges. This moisture trickles down the slopes and finds its way into the clefts of rocks. At night when intense cold grips the heights, the water freezes inside the cracks and expands them. With the coming of the sun again, the ice returns to water, and the crevices contract. Repetition of this process year after year causes the rock to finally split. All the Teton mountaintops have been shattered in this way and their summits strewn with fallen blocks. Many of the spires, once more needle-like than now, have through the centuries been blunted by this action.

Boulders are constantly tumbling from the upper slopes and bounding down the mountainsides. The underlying rock masses from which they break off are gradually weakened, and there comes a time when an entire peak face comes crashing down with a roar of such intensity that seven or eight minutes will pass before it begins to abate, and ten to twelve before it dies away. Lightning striking often triggers these falls. Then the rock mass, constantly gaining momentum and gathering debris, hurtles down, enveloped in a heavy cloud of dust. The slide is punctuated by thundering sounds that resemble intermittent cannonry—the impact of enormous boulders. Often these huge rocks strike with such force they are completely disintegrated. Occasionally, small lakes lying in their paths are totally extinguished by these avalanches.

After the collapse of a pinnacle face on Mount St. John, the entire mountain slope "appeared as though bombarded by artillery, hundreds of ragged holes marking the spots where rocks had struck. Fresh dirt and sod were strewn about, together with the wreckage of trees. Boulders previously lodged here were in many instances knocked out of position, shattered, or driven into the ground." The heavy dust cloud that formed rose sluggishly above the peak and hovered there, darkening the sky for half an hour.

Over the years, rocks of various sizes shed from the glaciated faces of peaks and canyon walls have slipped down the slopes and gathered on saddles or cols to form talus heaps. These have become home to marmots, and to conies, those tiny relatives of the rabbit who harvest flowers and grasses and cure them in little stacks for winter feeding; often they store as much as a cubic yard of dried plants in their rock shelters.

Encroachment by talus now threatens many of the Tetons'

alpine lakes and has, by its continual growth, caused a number to nearly disappear; some it has divided in two. In other places this debris has dammed streams and turned them into tarns, or ponds where water buttercups bloom, or wet meadows carpeted with white marsh marigolds—all the haunts of moose. With every major change there is an adaptation by plant or animal life. Nothing in nature is wasted, as Muir observed, but is "eternally flowing from use to use."

The sun beating on snowfields and icicles melts them and causes a network of rills to race down the slopes and feed the streams, swelling their volume hourly. The peak is reached in midafternoon, when they are so full they overflow their banks and flood those highland meadows close to their sources. Then the rush of brawling cascades and the thunder of falls is heard throughout the range. But with the drift of late afternoon shadows, the melt from the snow and ice lessens and finally stops. Like tides, the waters ebb from the alpine grasslands, and the tumult in the canyons quiets.

Snowslides also act as agents of change. After every heavy fall of snow the crash of avalanches echoes among the Teton peaks. When the mass first slips a dull rush and rumble is heard. This "increases with heavy deliberation, seeming to come nearer and nearer. Presently the white flood is seen leaping wildly over some precipitous portion of its channel with ever-increasing loudness of roar and boom, decked with long back trailing streamers . . . rushing through the air like the spray whorls and banners of a waterfall. Now it appears in an open spot, now . . . leaping from bench to bench, spreading and narrowing, throwing out fringes of rockets . . . airily draped with convolving, eddying gossamer spray. These cataracts of snow, however unlike those of water in duration, are like them . . . in form . . in voice and gesture. In the snowfalls we detect the same variety of tones, from the loudest low hollow thunderboom to the small voices in the highest key . . . we see the pearly whiteness with lovely gray tones in half-shadow, the arching leaps over precipices, the narrowing in gorges, the expansion into lacelike sheets upon smooth inclines, and the final dashing into up-whorling clouds of spray."

Passing the bounds of timberline, these snowslides will sweep away entire stands of trees, uprooting sound older ones that are often several feet in diameter, or snapping them off close to the ground. When repeated season after season, they destroy all chances for forest renewal by stripping the region of soil. Their protective covering of trees gone, new surfaces are laid bare to weathering and other erosive forces, and the mountain slope becomes radically changed. These avalanches sometimes overtake bighorn and moose, burying them deep beneath their debris.

Glaciers—Teton, Skillet, Falling Ice, Triple, and Middle Teton, the most familiar ones—are continually grinding and scouring, using as abrasives those rocks picked up from the masses shed by surrounding cliffs and from their own underlying beds. In their steady downward courses, they reshape the mountain peaks and walls, carve basins for new lakes, and gorges and hanging valleys for future streams and waterfalls.

Teton Glacier, the largest in the range, measures thirty-five hundred feet in length and eleven hundred in width. It fills the cirque between the two highest peaks and lies within the protective shadows cast by the Grand Teton and Owen. The central part of this river of compacted snowflakes is slipping over thirty feet a year, pushing before it a great mass of boulders and rock fragments.

Because the Tetons are the youngest of the Rocky Mountain ranges, they offer an unusual opportunity for the study of those complex interrelated forces which are responsible for the creation of mountain landscapes. How many thousands—or millions—of years more they will continue to push up, it is impossible to predict. That at some remote time their distinctive jagged peaks and sharp, clustering spires will be reduced to gently rounded domes is certain. The eons required for such a transformation are beyond man's concept of time.

With the changes, plants and animals will continue to adapt, just as streams will feel their way down fresh-cut courses, and melting snow will fill new lake basins. For man, the alterations in landscape will be almost imperceptible. For years to come, in following the trails through canyons and up peaks, he can count on finding thickets of thornapple in flower or fruit; white alpine avens blooming on bleak rock slopes, and clumps of deep blue gentian in bogs and on stream banks. He will hear the high, plaintive cry of the cony lookout, and come on the snowshoe hare, perhaps in his lustrous coat of winter white, nibbling at clumps of grass in the deep pine woods. He will listen to thrushes singing in groves, and watch beavers swim with arrow-shaped wakes across ponds and quiet river channels. He will trace the tracks of blue herons over the sands, and observe the stars lighting up the sharp-cut edges of the Grand Teton, blazing like "Indian signal fires in successive flashes, rising and dying out by hundreds as the hours pass." He will see the Tetons catch rainbows when thunderclouds break, and from spring until fall watch the ever-changing patterns of the melting snowfields on the heights. He will observe the varying colors which splash the lower slopes as aspen groves take on shades of green, yellow, gold, red, and when their leaves are dropped, turn silvery white.

He will follow the range's fleeting image projected on the floor of Jackson Hole each afternoon when the sun sinks at its back. At first the shadow peaks are low and rounded, but as their outline races across the plains toward the east, they grow higher. At the halfway mark they are in perfect proportion, each one recognizable. Then distortion begins again, and the broad peaks lengthen into slim spires as they race over the sagebrush flats and up the ridges beyond, and then vanish with startling suddenness when they meet the pale line of twilight sky.

He will observe a continuing round of seasons: the long, hushed sleep of winter, when even the rivers' voices are stilled; the awakening of spring whose rushing flow of life brims over into summer and brings with the warmth of lengthening days, a release of frozen waters, a vast bud and bloom, and myriad of wondrous smells; a series of births and nestings, and joyous choruses to every canyon, marsh, and grove. He will observe the mellow ripeness of fall with its urgency to reap, store, and sow as days shorten, frost starts to rime the meadow grasses, and ice to coat the edges of dwindling ponds and streams. Then he will be aware of chipmunks busily laying by provisions, beavers mending dams and lodges, birds flying southward in flocks and lines and wedges; and bear, deer, elk, and moose on the move, seeking the shelter of dry caves and protected canyons.

Teton country's cosmic cycle is completed with the coming

of those first heavy falls of snow which blanket the valleys and mountains and reduce the landscape to elemental forms. The deep drifts bring shelter from the blighting cold to those trees, flowering plants, and creatures which live on the alpine heights; protection to dormant roots and seeds on the lower slopes and in the valleys; warmth to the snug lodges of muskrats and beavers, and the burrows of badgers, voles, mice, and other ground-dwellers. Here in this vast covering of shimmering white lies the promise of rebirth.

Afterword
Saving the Tetons

A procession of fur trappers and traders, prospectors, big game and trophy hunters, cattle and sheep ranchers, horse raisers, lumbermen, and farmers went into Teton country over the years following its discovery by John Colter. Concerning themselves only with what could be turned to immediate profit or use, they killed the wildlife, converted the stands of pine, fir, and spruce into logs and lumber piles, and dammed and drained the lakes for irrigation projects. They displaced the native herds by ploughing up the herbage and feeding their stock on the wild grasses. Overgrazing by sheep stripped the Teton high country of much of its original beauty. By robbing the native bighorns of their food, men drove them ever higher among the peaks. There herbage was scarce and many starved. Domestic sheep transmitted to them their diseases and parasites which, in conjunction with the lack of forage, caused the bighorns to virtually disappear from these mountains.

The very presence of settlers in the Teton valleys disrupted the migration routes of moose, elk, buffalo, antelope, and deer. Fencing land, draining marshes, and felling trees further altered the habitat for these animals, and affected bears, beavers, muskrats, trumpeter swans, geese, songbirds, and nearly every other wild creature. Ranchers, resenting the indigenous grazers feeding on the natural hay, killed them ruthlessly. Swans, hunted for food or simply for sport were virtually exterminated. Poachers, living at the north end of Jackson Hole, preyed on the migrating elk who, in moving south each winter, left the protection of Yellowstone Park. Thousands of them were slaughtered.

Men searched the Teton canyons, slopes, and streams not for the beauty they might find there, but in the hope of striking a bonanza. They found enough gold along Trail and Moose creeks, in North Leigh and Whetstone canyons, and at the head of Bitch Creek to encourage them. In hunting for the mother lode, believed to be the source of the fine flakes they saw in nearly every stream, they discovered deposits of silver, copper, coal, asbestos, gilsonite, and lime, and near the mouth of Horseshoe Canyon, oil. So they blasted tunnels, dug prospect pits, built sluices, diverted streams, set up lime kilns, and formed companies to mine, drill for oil, irrigate, and lumber. On the west side, nearly every canyon had a sawmill.

In 1906, Jackson Lake was dammed so that its waters could be taken west to develop Idaho's semiarid Snake River Basin. Few were concerned that the contained and increased waters covered the historic Indian and trapper trail leading to Conant Pass, drowned ancient Indian artifacts and campsites along the shore—invaluable in the study of those people who first came into Jackson Hole—or that hundreds of conifers which ringed the natural lake were killed, leaving unsightly stands of bleached snags. Several years later, water storage rights were filed on Two Ocean and Emma Matilda lakes, and then on Jenny and Leigh, with plans to dam them and pipe their water west of the Tetons.

As early as 1897, Colonel S.D.M. Young, superintendent of Yellowstone Park, proposed to the secretary of the interior that the reserve's limits be extended south to include part of Jackson Hole, as a means of protecting the migrating elk from poachers. The next year, Charles D. Walcott, director of the United States Geological Survey, made a tour of Jackson Hole. He was so favorably impressed by everything he saw there, he suggested that a separate national park be created rather than an extension of Yellowstone. Both proposals were submitted to

Congress, but no legislative interest or support was aroused.

Throughout the West there were countless mountain ranges still not fully explored, their highest peaks unclimbed, and many yet unnamed. It was therefore difficult for senators, congressmen, and other government officials who had never seen the Tetons to understand why this one small group of peaks should be preserved. Although they were unlike any others in this country—they were already being called the Alps of America—it was impossible for them to compete in popular appeal with the novelty of Yellowstone's geysers, boiling lakes, bubbling mudpots, and roaring caves. Even John Muir found these thermal curiosities exciting and wrote enthusiastically about the wonders of Yellowstone, while giving the Tetons only passing mention. He saw these peaks only from a distance, and apparently made no effort to get any closer views, or explore them.

If the Hayden Surveys had been continued, the doctor's energies would have been doubtless directed next toward the creation of a Teton national preserve, for these were his favorite Western mountains. With William Henry Jackson and Thomas Moran to supply visual proof of their unique beauty, the reports of his specialists, the enthusiasm of Nathaniel Langford on the speaker's platform, and his own persuasiveness, the Tetons and possibly both east and west valleys would have been made into a park half a century earlier.

Wilderness areas were at this time still so plentiful in America they seemed inexhaustible to the average person. To most residents of the Teton valleys, so recently settled, and to their representatives in national government, wilderness was considered an obstruction to progress. Repeated efforts by conservationists to protect the Tetons and Jackson Hole from exploitation and commercialization failed. Years of education on the part of such men as Muir and John Burroughs were required to awaken in the public an appreciation of nature and an awareness of the necessity for preserving wilderness as a refuge from the stresses and demands of daily living.

By 1923 nearly all of the lakes and streams on the east side were threatened by irrigation projects. Rows of tourist cabins and a dance hall were spoiling the beauty of Jenny Lake's setting. Advertising billboards were disfiguring the sagebrush plains that form the Tetons' foreground and enhance their rugged sheerness. Gasoline stations and refreshment stands were lining the roadsides in Jackson Hole. The Forest Service, which by then had jurisdiction over the valley's timber stands, was proposing to license commercial lumbering at Jackson Lake, to allow a number of mines to operate in the north end of the Hole, and to open tracts for summer homes. Recently a proposal had been made to build a highway up through the wilderness along Pacific Creek and across historic Two Ocean Pass as an alternate route into Yellowstone Park.

That July a meeting of concerned residents (five in number), headed by author-dude rancher Struthers Burt, met in Maude Noble's cabin at the site of Menor's Ferry, to discuss the valley's future with conservationist Horace Albright. Albright was then superintendent of Yellowstone Park, and long an active advocate for extension of the park's boundaries south to include the Tetons and Jackson Hole.

The committee did not agree that the Tetons should be made a part of Yellowstone Park; they were in favor of some form of national recreation area that would allow cattle and horse raising, grazing, hunting, and dude ranching on a limited scale. They made an appeal for money among those wealthy eastern sportsmen who came regularly to Jackson Hole, but were unable to raise enough to buy the amount of land they had planned to included in the preserve. Congress was also approached, but proved unreceptive to that form of federal protection.

Horace Albright continued his campaign to save the Tetons. Whenever important or influential visitors came to Yellowstone, he talked to them about park extension and usually managed to take them to see the Tetons from Jackson Hole.

In the summer of 1926, John D. Rockefeller, Jr. brought his wife and three of their sons to Yellowstone Park. He had already seen a part of Jackson Hole but was anxious to see it all, and he readily accepted Albright's offer to drive him and his family there.

He and his wife were troubled by the sight of so many tourist cabins, refreshment stands, gas stations, dilapidated ranch buildings, and billboards—one stood directly in the foreground of the Grand Teton—which detracted from the overall beauty of the valley and mountains. After they had passed through this exploited area Rockefeller asked Albright to send him a map that would show the locations of these structures, and also an estimate of the value of the land on which they stood. Albright agreed.

While stopped at Hendrick's Point to look at the view, Albright told them about the meeting at Maude Noble's cabin, and the other plans and efforts to preserve the valley and protect the Tetons. The Rockefellers made no comment, he recalled, nor did he ask for their support or mention the subject again.

That winter Albright took the map, and the estimates to Rockefeller's New York office. After examining the map, Rockefeller told Albright that he had a much larger area in mind—in fact, all of that part of the valley which could be seen from Hendrick's Point. He wanted to acquire the entire northern section of Jackson Hole and eventually add it to Yellowstone Park. His two reasons for considering the project were "the marvelous scenic beauty of the Teton Mountains and the Lakes at their feet," which were seen at their best from Jackson Hole; and the fact that this valley was a natural feeding ground and necessary refuge for elk, deer, moose, and buffalo. It was an ideal project, he said, and he was only interested in ideal projects.

By February 1927 he was ready to act. To avoid unwanted publicity and inflated land prices, his name was kept out of the project. The Snake River Land Company, a Utah corporation, was organized, with New York lawyer Vanderbilt Webb as president, and Jackson banker Robert Miller as the resident purchasing agent.

Rockefeller made it clear that in buying the land his representatives were to pay fair value for it, and that in every case the owner's financial circumstances were to be appraised sympathetically. The company was to hold the acreage until it could be turned over to the federal government for inclusion in the park system or some other form of preserve that would benefit the general public. However, the ultimate disposition of the land was also to be kept secret.

On February 26, 1929, after thirty-two years of agitation, the conservationists scored a victory when President Calvin Coolidge signed a bill creating Teton National Park. The east face of the range from Webb Canyon south to Granite Canyon, and a narrow strip along the base that contained Leigh, Jenny, Bradley, Taggart, and Phelps lakes, were included in the park. The rest of Jackson Hole, except for that land held by Rockefeller, remained unprotected. The west side of the Tetons and Pierre's Hole had never been considered in this struggle for preservation.

There was little opposition to a park that consisted principally of high peaks. Only a few cattlemen objected, chiefly on principle, since their association had taken a stand against park extension.

In April 1930 the Snake River Land Company made its plans public, at the request of Wyoming's governor. When the people of Jackson Hole learned that the company's holdings were to be included in Teton National Park, the valley became embattled. Feelings ran high as everyone took sides, and many an old friendship was broken. One men's service club in Jackson passed resolutions against adding the Rockefeller lands to the park, while another took a vigorous stand in favor of it. The *Jackson's Hole Courier* was strongly pro-park, but it soon had a rival, the *Grand Teton,* established purposely to fight park enlargement. The bitterest opponents were the cattlemen who were convinced, in spite of assurances to the contrary, that their grazing rights would be abolished, and foresaw the end of all free enterprise in Jackson Hole.

Throughout this decade, frequent attemps were made to get congressional approval for inclusion of the Rockefeller lands, but every effort was frustrated by powerful lobbyist pressures. For nearly ten years, while he waited for the government to accept his gift, Rockefeller held around thirty thousand acres of taxable land. In November 1942, his patience wearing thin, he wrote to Harold Ickes, Secretary of the Interior, to say that if the government did not take advantage of his offer within a year, he intended to sell it on the open market.

In his reply Ickes assured him that the "great conservation project" which he had made possible would have been accepted long before, had it not been for "selfish local interests." He assured Rockefeller that he would do all he could to effect the inclusion of his lands within the park.

Certain that Congress would still resist park enlargement, Ickes drew up a proclamation that set aside 221,610 acres in Jackson Hole as a national preserve. On March 15, 1943, President Franklin Roosevelt, by executive order (allowed under the 1906 Antiquities Act), created Jackson Hole National Monument.

The entire state of Wyoming was outraged at what was regarded as an arbitrary act on Roosevelt's part. The proclamation seemed to indicate total indifference to popular opinion and disrespect toward their elected representatives in national government. Within four days Wyoming Congressman Frank Barrett had introduced a bill abolishing the monument. It passed both houses of Congress but was promptly vetoed by the president. In May, the state of Wyoming filed suit in the federal district court to prevent the government from taking control over the monument.

Throughout the 1940s the battle continued to wage locally and nationally, with most of the country's newspapers taking sides in the controversy. But by the beginning of the new decade much of the bitterness was tempered. On September 15, 1950, President Harry Truman signed a bill that included the monument in the Grand Teton National Park. Two of the most militant and vocal opponents of park enlargement, Senators Hunt and O'Mahoney of Wyoming, had introduced the measure.

It was the ambition of the early conservationists like Muir, Burroughs, Hayden, Langford, and Albright, to encourage as many people as possible to go to the national parks and forest reserves. "Wander here a whole summer, if you can, " urged Muir, "roaming . . . in rosiny pinewoods or in gentian meadows, brushing through chaparral . . . parting sweet, flowery sprays . . . jumping from rock to rock . . . panting in whole-souled exercise and rejoicing in deep, long-drawn breaths of pure wildness."

Naturally, none of these men could foresee the American public's present mobility, nor anticipate that the parks and reserves would ever be faced with the problems of overuse by tourists.

Three million people visit the Grand Teton National Park

each year, a number that will continue to increase as long as the people's mobility remains uncurbed. During the summer, the most popular season, picnic and campgrounds, lodges, dude ranches, scenic turnouts, lakeshores, and trails are crowded to excess. The noise of automobiles, motorcycles, and power-boats obtrudes on natural sounds—birdsong, aspen leaves rippling in the wind, the plop of feeding trout, the footfalls of small creatures in the woods, the drum of grouse, the drone of bees. Exhaust fumes from these vehicles overwhelm the delicate smells of dewy grass, lichen, pine needles warmed by the sun, bracken, and alder groves. The indigenous sounds and smells are as vital a part of the enjoyment of Teton country as are the peaks themselves. It is doubtful whether Muir, at least, would approve of the summer throngs. He once wrote: "Only by going alone in silence . . . can one truly get into the heart of the wilderness,"—comprehend its essence.

Those who agree with Muir must avoid the summer season. In doing so they will miss the finest displays of wildflowers and songbird choruses, and the sight of waterfalls and streams at their fullest. But they will discover other wonders, for there is no season in the Tetons without them.

The struggle to protect Jackson Hole from exploitation and commercialization still goes on. Business interests are continually agitating for enlargement of the airport to accommodate big jets, for the construction of more ski lodges and winter sports areas on the park's environs, the building of high-rise hotels in the town of Jackson to attract all-season tourists, and tract housing. The valley's future lies in the hands of planners who seek permanently effective ways to protect the Tetons' setting from encroachment by inappropriate and unwise land use.

John Muir was well aware that "the battle for preservation will go on endlessly. It is part of the universal battle between right and wrong." Fortunately, the most important victories in this battle for right have been won. The east side of the Teton Range, its forests, lakes, and wildlife, and the greater part of Jackson Hole are being held inviolable for present and future generations to enjoy.

"The clearest way into the Universe is through a forest wilderness," Muir observed. Because of the foresight of a few, and their unflagging labors in the realm of conservation, those who also wish to comprehend the macrocosm by way of a Teton wilderness may do so. They may also heed the injunction of that great naturalist—"climb the mountains and get their good tidings."

Notes and Sources Consulted and Quoted

I The Setting, pp. 13–20

Nature notes: firsthand observation during many exploratory trips into Teton country, starting in 1947. William Henry Jackson, in *Time Exposure,* recorded his estimate of the Teton Range. Mountain man Warren Ferris, *Life in the Rocky Mountains, a Diary of Wanderings on the Sources of the Rivers Missouri, Columbia, and Colorado from February 1830 to November 1835,* saw the peaks looming on the horizon, and gave their old name. Irving, *Astoria,* states that the name was in use as early as 1811-12. The explorer who likened the peaks to shark's teeth was Hayden, *Sixth Annual Report of the United States Geological Survey of the Territories . . . 1872.* Coulter, "Report," in Hayden, *ibid.,* found the purple saxifrage at 12,000 feet elevation on the Tetons' west face, in 1872. He also accounts for their survival by their being buried under deep snow. John and Frank Craighead, and Davis, *A Field Guide to Rocky Mountain Wildflowers,* give the theory of the saxifrage being carried south on the continental ice sheets. Muir, "The Yellowstone National Park," described the lodgepole pine. McClung, *Lost Wild America,* for information on the moose, elk (*wapiti*), buffalo, and pronghorn antelope. Muir, *The Mountains of California,* described the ouzel nest. Love and Reed, *Creation of the Teton Landscape;* Wright, "The Coming of the People," date approximately the first men in Jackson Hole. Shimkin, "The Wind River Shoshone Sun Dance," for prayers and rites. Dr. George C. Frison, Head, Department of Anthropology, University of Wyoming, for information regarding the making of tools, weapons, and bowls, and the locations of the Teton quarries. Wright gives their routes into the valley. Hyde, *Indians of the High Plains, from the Prehistoric Period to the Coming of the Europeans,* describes the Shoshoni retreat into the mountains. Accounts of John Colter's discovery of the Tetons in Chittenden, *The American Fur Trade of the Far West,* and *The Yellowstone National Park;* in Harris, *John Colter, His Years in the Rockies;* James, *Three Years Among the Mexicans and Indians.* Hunt, *Diary of an Overland Trip to Astoria in 1811-12,* used the Tetons to guide him and his party. Warren Ferris reported the distance at which the Tetons could be seen, and told about their fame as landmarks. Raynolds, *Report on the Exploration of the Yellowstone and the Country Drained by that River,* tells his own story and describes Hayden's findings, as does Hayden in *United States Engineer Department Geological Report of the Exploration of the Yellowstone and Missouri Rivers . . . 1859–60.* Reports of Hayden's party in Hayden, *Sixth Annual Report. . . .* Canton, *Frontier Trails, The Autobiography of Frank M. Canton;* Driggs, *History of Teton Valley, Idaho;* Kelly, *The Outlaw Trail;* David, *Malcolm Campbell, Sheriff,* provide background for post-Civil War outlawry in general and in the Tetons. Burt, *Diary of a Dude-Wrangler,* tells about the ghost riders and the old drift fence in Death Canyon. Owen Wister's unpublished diaries. Rollins, *The Cowboy;* Mora, *Trail Dust and Saddle Leather* for cowboy skills, dress, stories, songs, way of talking. Wolf Moon nights in Jackson Hole folklore, Writers' Program, WPA manuscripts.

II Genesis, pp. 21–24

Tetons' rate of growth in Love and Reed, *Creation of the Teton Landscape.* Origin of the Teton Range in Fritiof Fryxell *The Tetons, Interpretations of a Mountain Landscape;* Roald Fryxell, "Geology of the Teton Range." Hayden, *United States Engineer Department Geological Report of the Exploration of the Yellowstone and Missouri Rivers . . . 1859–60*, was the first geologist to report the range's westward tilt. Love and Reed (*op. cit.*) for the frequency of earthquakes. Bradley's report in Hayden, *Sixth Annual Report of the United States Geological Survey . . . 1872*; and St. John in Hayden, *Eleventh Annual Report of the United States Geological Survey . . . 1877*, write about that ancient sea responsible for the marine fossils. Hayden collected and catalogued the fossil marine plants and animals in Jackson Hole and the Tetons in 1860, doubtless the first scientist to do so. F. Fryxell, *The Tetons . . .*, for the erosive agents which shaped the Teton block, the successive ice ages, the work of the glaciers, and the final sculpturing of the peaks by Pinedale ice. In 1872 Frank Bradley and W. T. Taggart, geologists with the Hayden Survey for that year, recognized the glacial origin of the chain of lakes along the Tetons' east base, and enlarged on it in the *Sixth Annual Report*. F. Fryxell, *The Tetons . . .*; and Love and Reed, *Creation . . .*, locate some of today's glaciers and describe their action. Muir, "The Yellowstone National Park," described the landscape changes following the last glacial period. St. John in Hayden, *Eleventh Annual Report. . . .*, identified the Pre-cambrian crystallines. Muir on glaciers as a tool, *The Mountains of California*.

III The Mysterious West, pp. 25–33

Dunlap, letter of February 28, 1806, in *Diary of William Dunlap*, vol. 2, writes his wife about the amphibious, cowlike animal, the wondrous cavern, the lake that attracted stone, and the mysterious race with blue and gray eyes and light hair. Dunlap, a portrait painter, playwright, translator, biographer, and art historian, like many another of his learned contemporaries, gave credence to these tales about the wonders of the West. Mitchill, "Letters from Washington: 1801–1813," another highly literate man, also believed them, and reported on the volcanic eruptions along the Upper Missouri. The search for the Welsh Indians was a popular one. John Evans, a young Welshman, came to America in the early 1790s to look for them; after his death in 1799, the quest was continued by James Mackay. Mitchill writes in these letters about the formidable mountain range that was a barrier to reaching the Pacific Coast. Coutant, *History of Wyoming from the Earliest Known Discoveries,* gave the range's height, and quoted the reports about it being a single chain, or five ridges deep. He, and Chittenden, *The American Fur Trade of the Far West,* list the various names by which it was known. William Clark, in *Original Journals of the Lewis and Clark Expedition, 1804-1806,* records the Indians telling about the strange noises heard in the Rocky Mountains. Jefferson's interest in the West is reflected in his letters and other writings. His January 18, 1803, message to Congress, in brief in his letter of August 18, 1813, to Paul Allen; full text in Jackson, *Letters of the Lewis and Clark Expedition with Related Documents, 1783–1854.* Jefferson's estimate of Lewis' qualifications found in letter of February 27, 1803, to Dr. Benjamin Smith Barton; of February 28, 1803, to Drs. Caspar Wistar and Benjamin Rush; and the letter of August 18, 1813, to Paul Allen. The letters to the three doctors discuss those studies Lewis was undertaking in Philadelphia; they are in the Jefferson Papers, The Library of Congress, as are Rush's rules for maintaining health, and Clark's acceptance letter, July 18, 1803. Rush's questions for Lewis are in the American Philosophical Society. Jefferson's instructions to Lewis are found in Appendix, vol. 7, *Original Journals of the Lewis and Clark Expedition, 1804–1806,* edited by Thwaites. All quotations from the journals kept by Lewis and Clark are taken from the Thwaites edition unless otherwise stated. The expedition's movements and adventures are followed through the journals of both captains, as well as those of Charles Floyd, Joseph Whitehouse, and John Ordway. The journals of Floyd and Whitehouse are included in Thwaites; Ordway's journal was edited by Milo Quaife. For the meeting between Sacajawea and her brother, the Biddle edition of the Lewis and Clark journals was used since it gave more detail. Biddle had the advantage of being able to enlarge the often terse entries by the two captains with informatin obtained from them after their return, and from other expedition members.

IV Trail Through the Snow, pp. 34–41
Irving, *Astoria* (appendix), includes an early history of the fur trade in Europe and America. Lewis to Jefferson, September 23,

1806, in Appendix, vol. 7, Thwaites edition, *Original Journals of the Lewis and Clark Expedition, 1804–1806.* James, *Three Years Among the Indians and Mexicans* was one of the young men who flocked to the call for hunters and trappers, and described the enthusiasm. Lewis' journal for the meeting with trappers Dickson and Hancock. Clark told about Colter's discharge; and Ordway, *The Journals of John Ordway kept on the Expedition of Western Exploration, 1803–1806,* described the outfitting of Colter. James, *Three Years . . .* described his comrade, John Colter. Harris, *John Colter, His Years in the Rockies,* for biographical details. Brackenridge, *Journal of a Voyage Up the River Missouri Performed in Eighteen Hundred and Eleven,* told of Colter setting off alone with his pack, gun, and ammunition. Chittenden, *The American Fur Trade of the Far West,* and *The Yellowstone National Park,* thoroughly familiar with the country through which Colter traveled, has followed his trail minutely and lays it out convincingly. Father De Smet describes "Colter's Hell" in *Life, Letters and Travels of Father Pierre-Jean De Smet, 1801–1873;* he gives Jim Bridger as a source. Jones, *Report Upon the Reconnaissance of Northwestern Wyoming . . . Made in the Summer of 1873,* lists all of the Indian trails of the Bighorn Basin as well as those leading over the Wind River Mountains, across Togwotee Pass, into Jackson Hole, and north into Yellowstone country. Jones named Togwotee Pass for his Shoshoni guide, and stressed its easy passage. Grace Hebard, *Washakie,* learned from the Shoshonis that this was their chosen route. Raynolds, *Report on the Exploration of the Yellowstone and the Country Drained by that River (1859–1860),* found Union Pass "extremely difficult." The Indian trail over Togwotee Pass was much higher than the present road, so that from the summit Colter would have had all of Jackson Hole spread out below him, and much of the Teton Range on the horizon. Having followed the probable route of the Indian path to the crest, I am able to reconstruct Colter's impressions. Trapper Russell notes in his *Journal of a Trapper; or Nine Years in the Rocky Mountains, 1834–1843,* that the Shoshonis called the Tetons "hoary-headed fathers." Ferris, *Life in the Rocky Mountains, A Diary of Wanderings . . . February 1830 to November 1835,* calls the valley by its original name, Trou à Pierre. Dwight C. Stone,

Driggs, Idaho, descendant of pioneers, has hiked and ridden horseback over the Indian trails, up the Teton canyons and across the passes. He has made a study of Colter's route through Pierre's Hole (now Teton Valley), which he generously shared with me. He also furnished information about Colter's carving, the exact location of its discovery, and which passes Colter could have taken to cross the Tetons. Harris, *John Colter, His Years in the Rockies*, for details of the head Colter shaped. Personal observation for the flora of this area. Copies of William Clark's sketch maps in author's collection. Ferris, *Life in the Rocky Mountains . . .*, lived among the Indians for a number of years; he tells about their superstitions concerning the thermal regions. Chittenden, in his book on Yellowstone Park, believes they avoided the thermal regions because these were not good fishing or hunting grounds. Other mountain men agree with Ferris. Again, Chittenden in both his works, traces Colter's trail, as does Harris in *John Colter. . . .*

V "They Call Themselves Sho-sho-nies", pp. 42–53

Russell, *Journal of a Trapper; or Nine Years in the Rocky Mountains . . .* is the source for the chapter title. Hyde, *Indians of the High Plains, from the Prehistoric Period to the Coming of the Europeans*; and Trenholm and Carley, *The Shoshonis: Sentinels of the Rockies*, for the origin of the name, life in the Basin, the migration across the mountains, and life on the Plains. Personal observation of the wild fruit still found in abundance in the Teton valleys. Hamilton, *My Sixty Years on the Plains, Trapping, Trading, and Indian Fighting*, describes the Indian uses for berries; the Craigheads, and Davis, *Rocky Mountain Wildflowers*, list the Indians' use of seeds, roots, and leaves. Townsend, *Narrative of a Journey Across the Rocky Mountains to the Columbia, 1832–1834*, describes the Indian buffalo hunt, on foot. Hyde describes the Shoshonis as warriors. Ferris, *Life in the Rocky Mountains . . .*; and Lewis and Clark, *Original Journals . . .*, describe Shoshoni bows, and methods of making them. Ferris tells about their arrows. Russell, *Journal of a Trapper . . .*, the methods of poisoning arrow points. Lewis and Clark for the making of leather armor, and the important ceremony during which arrowproof properties were imparted to their hide shields. The Cree quoted in

Thompson, *David Thompson's Narrative of his Explorations in Western America, 1784–1812.* The Cree described fighting methods before and after the Shoshonis got horses. Lewis and Clark describe in great detail the Shoshoni dress and ornament. Trenholm and Carley tell about the powers of various feathers. Russell writes about their tipis; Lowie, *Indians of the Plains,* for further details of the Plains tipi. Lewis and Clark; and Ferris, for marriage customs. Shoshoni women's tasks cited by Ferris. Lowie describes the making of leather articles, and the painting; also men's occupations. Ferris watched the women play games and heard them singing. Lewis and Clark discussed the Shoshoni government, as does Shimkin, "The Wind River Shoshoni Sun Dance." Lowie; Shimkin; Trenholm and Carley, for games. Lowie, for storytelling; Trenholm and Carley for *NunumBi*; Jones, *Report Upon the Reconnaissance of Northwestern Wyoming . . . 1873,* heard the story of the spirits of Bull Lake from his Shoshoni companions. Shoshoni beliefs: Shimkin; Jones; and Ferris. Grass Hut's dream in Trenholm and Carley. Yellow Hand quoted in Shimkin. Shimkin is followed for the Shoshoni version of the Sun Dance. Voget, "Current Trends in the Wind River Shoshone Sun Dance," also consulted.

VI *The Wane of Shoshoni Power, pp. 54–58*

The Cree informant in Thomps(Î, *David Thompson's Narrative of His Explorations in Western America, 1784–1812,* told about the Blackfeet and their allies defeating the Shoshonis with guns. Irving, *Astoria,* says that the powerful Shoshonis were attacked, broken, and scattered by the Blackfeet who drove them into the Rockies and west of them, where they were subject to raids by these enemies. He also states that those who kept their horses also kept their organization and spirit. Irving's role as a serious historian has long been overlooked. Hyde, *Indians of the High Plains,* writes that what Irving has to say is "immensely important, more so than any ethnological study that can be made of Shoshoni today." Irving also quotes the fur trader who saw the Shoshoni lookouts on the hilltops. Ferris, *Life in the Rocky Mountains . . .,* rode with the Indians on their way to hunt buffalo. Hamilton, *My Sixty Years on the Plains,* told about making pemmican. Irving is once again the source for those Shoshonis who lived permanently in mountain caves and on remote cliff tops. For details on the Sheep Eaters: Hultkranz, "The Dukurika Indians," and "The Shoshones in the Rocky Mountain Area"; Russell, *Journal of a Trapper. . .*; W. A. Allen, *The Sheep Eaters*; and Frost, "The Sheep Eaters." Russell was a member of the trapping party which surprised the Sheep Eaters, and then made friends with them.

VII The Pilot Knobs, pp. 59–73

Chittenden, *The American Fur Trade of the Far West,* for the party that left Lisa's fort in March. James, *Three Years Among the Indians and Mexicans,* recalls Colter's stories of his encounters with Blackfeet; he noticed the skulls on the battle site. James went with Colter to look at the scene of his latest encounter, gave his own feelings as he heard the story, and Cheek's premonition of death. Chittenden, *ibid.* gives the history of the Henry-Menard expedition; he quotes the old chronicle. Letter of Pierre Menard to brother-in-law, Pierre Chouteau, April 21, 1810, in Chittenden. James writes about Colter again, and quotes him. He also describes Drouillard's death, the abandonment of the post, and establishment of Henry's Fort. Chittenden discusses the economic reasons for having to abandon the post. Irving, *Astoria,* tells about the three Kentuckians. Lindsley, "Major Andrew Henry," gives an account of the carved stones. Irving gives the history of Astor's Pacific Fur Company, and the description of Hunt. Brackenridge, *Journal of a Voyage Up the River Missouri . . .,* recorded the presence of fellow-passengers Sacajawea and Toussaint Charbonneau. Irving described Bradbury and Nuttall, and the latter's absorption with flora. Brackenridge also noted this enthusiasm, and recorded the voyageurs' opinion of the botanist. James is also a source for Colter's escape from the Blackfeet; he speaks of Colter's desire to accompany Hunt's party, as does Bradbury, who mentions his recent marriage. Irving tells of the meeting with the three Kentuckians and of their joining the expedition. Irving, *Astoria*; and Hunt, *Diary of an Overland Trip to Astoria in 1811–1812,* are relied on to follow the company. Bradbury took down one of the voyageurs' "most favorite songs" in French, then translated it to show its typical "frivolity." Irving writes about the feast held in honor of Hunt's arrival. In writing *Astoria*, Irving used primary source material entirely, and such firsthand accounts as Brackenridge and Bradbury. For a time he lived at Astor's home to enable him to talk with Astor and make use of his collection of papers, correspondence, and the letters and journals of men in his employ. Stuart's diary kept on his overland trip from Astoria in 1812–13, in *The Discovery of the Oregon Trail*, is used to follow this party eastward.

VIII Fortunes in Fur, pp. 74–79

Copy of *Missouri Gazette & Public Advertiser* in author's collection. Chittenden, *The American Fur Trade of the Far West*; and Dale, *The Ashley-Smith Explorations and the Discovery of a Central Route to the Pacific, 1822–1829*, describe the birth of Ashley's company. Ruxton, *Life in the Far West*; and Chittenden, tell of the beaver hunter as an explorer. Chittenden gives the place names for which the mountain men were responsible. Dale; and Chittenden, for biographical sketches of Ashley; Chittenden tells about Andrew Henry. Irving, *The Adventures of Captain Bonneville*, quotes Bonneville characterizing the mountain man. An account of the rendezvous system, and the history of Ashley's company, in Chittenden; and Dale. For Smith's travels, Sullivan, *Jedediah Smith, Trader and Trail Blazer*; and Morgan, *Jedediah Smith and the Opening of the West*. John Potts' description of Yellowstone Lake in Dale. For the history of Smith, Jackson & Sublette, Chittenden. *St. Louis Beacon* quoted in Sullivan.

IX Who They Were, pp. 80–95

Chittenden, *The American Fur Trade of the Far West*, tells about Lucien Fontenelle. Victor, *River of the West*, which is chiefly Joe Meek's story, gives his kinship to Polk. Coutant, *The History of Wyoming from the Earliest Known Discoveries*, for Jim Bridger's relationship to Tyler. Irving, *Astoria*, and *The Adventures of Captain Bonneville*; Garrad, *Wah-to-Yah and the Taos Trail*; and Chittenden, described the French Creole character, speech, and dress. Garrard heard their songs and noted their wonted cheerfulness. Ferris, *Life in the Rocky Mountains . . .*; listened to their stories. Irving in *Bonne-*

ville; Farnham, *Travels in the Great Western Prairies;* and Ruxton, *Life in the Far West,* all tell of the mountain man's adoption of Indian ways and dress. Bonneville recalled the compliment to the trapper in mistaking him for an Indian; Farnham noted the "wild, unsettled . . . expression of the eyes. . . ." Garrard wrote down the drinking song; Ruxton watched the trappers introduce Indian steps into their dances. Farnham saw how dark their skin was from exposure to weather. Irving, *ibid.,* noted the hair styles and the dress. Ruxton, himself a mountain man for a while, observed the many uses for fringe, and described the oversize Spanish spurs. Townsend, *Narrative of a Journey Across the Rocky Mountains to the Columbia River, 1832–1834,* told of the green capotes; Miller, *The West of Alfred Jacob Miller* (1837), wrote about the blanket poncho. Joe Meek, in Victor, talked about leggings, the shrinking of leather, and the popularity of tipi-cover moccasins. Dr. Townsend, who outfitted himself at a St. Louis store that catered to mountain men, bought the standard white wool hat. The artist Alfred Jacob Miller sketched the many kinds of headgear worn by trappers and traders, while on an expedition to the Rockies in 1837, and described them in notes contained in *The West of Alfred Jacob Miller.* Ruxton gave details of the trapper's outfit. Hamilton, *My Sixty Years on the Plains . . .,* described the coats of mail. Irving, *ibid.,* for the decorated rifles; Ruxton describes the Hawken. Free trappers and company men are described in Ferris; Irving in *Bonneville.* Joe Meek tells about their boasting. Ferris, and Irving for the freeman's horse. Meek, Ruxton, and Irving all tell about Indian wives and women. Townsend intimates that Bonneville was a squawman. Meek, and Townsend give the mountain prices. Meek describes the woman's horse; he and Hamilton give details of her dress and taste for finery. Ruxton wrote about the faithfulness of Indian women, and the attitudes of their white men. He also detailed the dangers in the trapper's life. Indians disguised as wolves crept into Hamilton's camp. Dr. Townsend told about those who were murdered by their fellow trappers and hunters; he also heard the accounts of atrocities committed against the Indians. James, *Three Years Among the Indians and Mexicans,* was one of those who had been turned against red men after seeing comrades hacked to pieces. Ruxton spoke of the need for constant vigilance, and described the mountaineer's skill in reading *sign*; also Meek; and Hamilton. The mountain man appeared solemn and taciturn to many early travelers; Farnham is the one used. Ruxton wrote about Old Bill Williams. Ferris; and Hamilton told about the numbers of grizzly bears, and the dangers. Sullivan, *Jedediah Smith, Trader and Trail Blazer,* for Smith's encounter with the grizzly. Ferris; and Larpenteur, *Forty Years a Fur Trader,* tell about the rabid wolves. Larpenteur was George Holmes' friend, and watched with anguish the fits of madness. Muir quoted in Wolfe, *John of the Mountains.* Ruxton observed the mountaineer's attitude toward life and death; Meek states it as a part of his philosophy. Garrard; Meek; Hamilton; Farnham; and Ruxton in *Life in the Far West,* and *Adventures in Mexico and the Rocky Mountains,* all discuss the mountain man's character. Hamilton recalled the prevailing honesty. Chittenden, *Fur Trade . . .,* writes about the mutual trust, and the crime rate. Ruxton, *Adventures . . .,* tells about the popularity of rifles at twenty paces. Hamilton; and Russell, *Journal of a Trapper . . .,* also told about men schooling themselves, and mentioned the favorite authors. Russell was a member of the Rocky Mountain College; he also wrote about storytelling. Artist Alfred Jacob Miller wrote down the audience's comments. The meteoric shower of November 12, 1833, was long remembered and often mentioned in contemporary accounts. Zenas Leonard, *Adventures of Zenas Leonard,* describes the consternation among Joe Walker's party, of which he was a member. Doane's journal, printed in *Battle Drums and Geysers,* records the uncanny echoes heard at Moran Bay. Ruxton, *Life . . .,* discussed the trapper's suspicion, and at times actual fear, of thermal regions; he also told about some mountaineers visiting them secretly to rid themselves of bad luck. Garrard heard Hatcher—"a small man, full of humor and good stories"—tell the story of his trip to hell. Accounts of the Phantom Horse are found in Kendall, *Narrative of the Texan-Santa Fe Expedition;* Dobie, *Tales of the Mustang;* and Gregg, *Commerce of the Prairies.* He was known also as The Pacing White Stallion; the White Mustang; the Ghost Horse of the Plains; and the White Sultan. The earliest account is found in Irving, *A Tour of the Prairies.* Chittenden, *The Yellowstone National*

Park, tells about some of Jim Bridger's most famous stories; Captain Raynolds, *Report on the Yellowstone and the Country Drained by that River,* heard Bridger tell his stories, but put them down in his own words rather than Bridger's. Ruxton, *Life . . .,* wrote out Harris' story in the mountain man's vernacular. Ruxton and Garrard were the only ones to record at length the colorful way of talking. Clyman, "Diaries and Reminiscences," told about the reporter overhearing Harris, and the St. Louis daily printing the account.

X Living Off the Land, pp. 96–102

Ruxton, *Life in the Far West;* Coyner, *The Lost Trappers;* Ferris, *Life in the Rocky Mountains . . .,* for the favorite meats. Although Coyner is mainly unreliable, he can be depended on limitedly. In contrast, Ruxton once wrote his publisher that *Life in the Far West* "is *no fiction.* There is no incident in it which has not actually occurred, nor one character who is not well known in the Rocky Mountains, with the exception of two whose names are changed. . . . With regard to the incidents of Indian attacks, starvation, cannibalism, &c., I have invented not one out of my own head. They are all matters of history in the mountains. . . ." For the relative merits of dog, Farnham, *Travels in the Great Western Prairies;* De Smet, *Life, Letters, and Journals . . .;* Garrard, *Wah-to-Yah and the Taos Trail;* and Jedediah Smith, letter of Dec. 24, 1829, in Sullivan, *Jedediah Smith, Trader and Trail Blazer.* Garrard was the victim who ate dog in the guise of terrapin. Ruxton noted in *Life . . .,* that most everything was eaten. Father De Smet's journal listed the variety of game in their diet. Ruxton, *Life . . .,* gives instances of cannibalism. Meek, in Victor, *River of the West,* recalled eating ants, and crickets, and bleeding horses and mules. Ruxton, *ibid.;* Farnham; Ferris, all described the delights of eating "fat cow." Dr. Townsend, *Narrative of a Journey Across the Rocky Mountains . . .,* reported on the amounts of buffalo they ate, and the number of meals a day. Ferris remarked on the fact that they never tired of buffalo meat. Meek; Farnham; Ferris; Hamilton, *My Sixty Years on the Plains . . .,* for the various ways of preparing buffalo for eating. Townsend; and Bourke, *On the Border With Crook,* ate the liver raw and warm, with a sprinkling of buffalo gall. Hamilton described *dépouille* and the methods of preparing and eating it. Ruxton, *ibid.;* and Garrard for the preparation of *boudins.* Farnham ate boudin sausages; Ferris, the buffalo meat dumplings. Ruxton, *ibid.,* gave details of the feast; he also wrote about kinnikinnick, and the effect of dogwood bark on the smoker. Sage, *Scenes in the Rocky Mountains and in Oregon, California, New Mexico, and the Grand Prairies;* Russell, *Journal of a Trapper . . .;* and *The Emigrant's Handbook* gave recipes for salves, cold cures, methods of stanching blood. Sage for the buffalo gall bitters and gunpowder treatment for rattlesnake bites. Clyman, "Diaries and Reminiscences," for his treatment of Jedediah Smith. Father De Smet received Bridger's classic reply.

XI Saturnalia in the Teton, pp. 103–107

Ruxton, *Life in the Far West,* described the trappers coming into rendezvous. Ferris, *Life in the Rocky Mountains . . .,* wrote about the famished Indian dogs; also the overland caravans. Meek in Victor, *River of the West,* also talked about the overland wagon trains, and what they brought; he described the almost immediate transformation of a wilderness valley into a bustling settlement. Dr. Townsend, *Narrative of a Journey Across the Rocky Mountains . . .,* told about the bedlam in camp. Larpenteur, *Forty Years a Fur Trader,* likewise a newcomer to the mountain rendezvous, also reported the noise and confusion, and the opening of the saloons. Ruxton, *ibid.,* described Turley's alcohol; Turley had a distillery not far from Taos, New Mexico. Ruxton, *ibid.;* and Irving, *The Adventures of Captain Bonneville,* wrote about the buying sprees. Russell, *Journal of a Trapper . . .,* recorded the rate of profit. Ruxton, *ibid.,* for cheating the Indians. Russell reported on the pastimes, making no mention, however, of women. Ruxton, *ibid.;* Townsend; Meek; Larpenteur, all enlarged on the drunkenness and brawling. Townsend recorded the gouging, stamping, and attempts to shoot each other. The gamblers, in Ruxton, *ibid.* Parker, *Journal of an Exploring Tour Beyond the Rocky Mountains,* was an eyewitness to the Shunar-Carson duel. The Indian girl in question was Waa-nibe, whom Carson subsequently married. Carson, *Kit Carson's Autobiography,* for his own account. Meek told about what the traders were doing mean-

while. Leonard, *Adventures of Zenas Leonard; and* Chittenden, *The American Fur Trade of the Far West,* discussed the
mountain man's improvidence. The French trapper told his
story to Ruxton, *Adventures in Mexico and the Rocky Mountains.*

XII Pilgrim's Progress, pp. 108–116

Meek, in Victor, *River of the West,* gave the mountain man's
opinion of Jedediah Smith. The friend was William Waldo,
quoted in Chittenden, *The American Fur Trade of the Far
West.* Dale, *The Ashley-Smith Explorations and the Discovery
of a Central Route to the Pacific, 1822–1829;* Sullivan, *Jedediah Smith, Trader and Trail Blazer;* Sanborn, *The American:
River of El Dorado,* for Smith's character. Trapper Hugh Glass,
quoted in Sullivan heard the moving prayer. Both Sullivan, and
Dale cover Smith's ride to Henry's post. Sullivan describes
Smith's appearance, and furnishes biographical data. His travels are followed in Dale, and in Sullivan. Smith's report to
William Clark, dated July 17, 1827, in Dale; his diary quoted in
Sullivan. Joe Meek explained the trapper's seeming indifference to the death of his comrades. Smith's letter to his brother,
dated December 24, 1829, in Sullivan, who also recounts Jedediah's activities after his return to St. Louis, and his decision to
enter the Santa Fe trade. The final journey is covered in Dale;
and Sullivan. Warner, "Reminiscences of Early California from
1831–1846," was with the party. He wrote about the lack of
water, of Smith's death, and about the traders bringing Jedediah's rifle and silver-mounted pistols to Santa Fe; he also gave
the reasons for the Indians wanting to sell them. For further details on his death, Austin Smith's letter of September 24, 1831,
to his brother Ralph, quoted in Sullivan.

XIII The Battle of Pierre's Hole, pp. 117–124

Participants' accounts of the battle in Irving, *The Adventures
of Captain Bonneville;* in Ferris, *Life in the Rocky Mountains . . .;* Meek, in Victor, *River of the West;* in Nidever, *The
Life and Adventures of George Nidever;* in Leonard, *Adventures of Zenas Leonard;* in Wyeth, *The Correspondence and
Journals of Captain Nathaniel J. Wyeth, 1831–6.* Dwight C.
Stone, Driggs, Idaho, identified Pine Creek Pass for the author.

Leonard gave the reasons for covering only eight miles the first day. Mr. Stone has plotted the Indians' route; he also described the stone structure on Bald Hill, in which he played as a boy. Leonard remembered the British flag. *The Adventures of Captain Bonneville* is used for the act that precipitated the battle. Mr. Stone, as a child, lived near the battle site, and explored it often with his grandfather, Charles Stone, a pioneer settler in Pierre's Hole (Teton Valley). The Indian breastworks were still visible at that time; he recalled seeing mounds in the area, which he was told were graves of Indians killed in the fight. His familiarity with the site enabled him to point it out to the writer, with exactness. Ferris gave the fort's size; Leonard was aware of the "destructive fire." Meek gave the mountain man's motto. Irving, *Bonneville*, describes Sinclair's death, and the wounding of William Sublette. Wyeth recalled the deadly crossfire. The warrior is quoted in *Bonneville*. Meek remembered the haste with which they departed for the main camp. Leonard recalled the fury of those who considered it a ruse; he described the fort as it appeared the following day, and the discovery of Fitzpatrick's horses. Ferris, who knew and admired the Horn Chief, describes him. Ferris gives the first version of his death; the second is found in *Bonneville*. Driggs, *History of Teton Valley, Idaho*, gives the site of the main camp as Teton Creek. Leonard described Indian style burials. John Wyeth, *Oregon; or A Short History of A Long Journey from the Atlantic Ocean to the Region of the Pacific By Land*, recounts the attack on Stephens, More, and Foy. Ferris was the diarist who recorded the return of the survivors. Leonard noted the cause of Stephens' death; Ferris was present at his burial. Irving describes Sublette's caravan in *Bonneville*. Bird's appearance observed by Maximilian, Prince of Wied, quoted in Chittenden, *Fur Trade*. . . . Townsend, *Narrative of a Journey Across the Rocky Mountains* . . ., gives biographical notes on Bird, and recounts the story of revenge.

XIV Sacajawea's Son, pp. 125–132

All quotations from Lewis or Clark are from the Thwaites edition, *Original Journals of the Lewis and Clark Expedition*. Hebard, *Sacajawea*, says Pomp is a customary Shoshoni name. This spelling of Pompy's Pillar is Clark's, diminutive of Pomp.

Letter of August 20, 1806, from William Clark to Toussaint Charbonneau, in *Original Journals*. . . . Letter of June 5, 1925, from Stella M. Drumm to Senator Nelson A. Mason, gives the time of Charbonneau's arrival in St. Louis, his acquisition of land, and its sale. Miss Drumm was Librarian of the Missouri Historical Society from 1913 until 1943, and a historian, author, and editor. Luttig, *Journal of a Fur-Trading Expedition on the Upper Missouri*. There are two versions of Sacajawea's death: one, that she eventually made her way to the Wind River Reservation in Wyoming, where she died at an advanced age; the other supports Luttig's report of her death. Even after the discovery of Clark's notebook in 1955, with its record of her death, many still subscribed to the other version. As early as 1925, Miss Drumm, in her letter to Senator Mason, presents a most convincing case in favor of Sacajawea's early death. One must recall that Brackenridge in his diary entry in 1811 notes that Sacajawea was then "sickly." It is very reasonable to suppose that she died in 1812 as the result of complications following the birth of Lizette. Again it must be recalled the difficult labor with her first child, recorded by Meriwether Lewis in his journal. Clark's accounts in American State Papers; copies in Grace Raymond Hebard Collection. Duke Paul Wilhelm, *First Journey to North America in the Years 1822 to 1824*, tells about meeting young Charbonneau and arranging for him to go to Germany. Correspondence between Dr. Hebard and German historians concerning Baptiste's position in the duke's household, and his schooling, in Hebard Collection. Facsimile of W. M. Boggs' handwritten description of Baptiste, at Bent's Fort, in Hebard Collection. Other mentions of him are found reported by Meek, in Victor, *River of the West*; Ferris, *Life in the Rocky Mountains* . . .; Ruxton, *Life in the Far West*; Nathaniel Wyeth, *The Correspondence and Journals of.* . . . Hebard suggests that Baptiste may have gone back to Europe after 1833. Frémont writes of his stay with "Mr. Charbonard" in his *Report of Exploring Expedition to the Rocky Mountains in the Year 1842*. Sage, *Scenes in the Rocky Mountains*. . . . Duke Paul's reference to Sutter's Indian reminding him of Baptiste, in his *Early Sacramento, Glimpses of John Augustus Sutter, The Hok Farm, and Neighboring Indian Tribes*. This version of his remarks about the Indian, translated by the author, from the entry in German in the Duke's daybook, found in Hebard Collection. Kennerly, *Persimmon Hill, A Narrative of Old St. Louis,* gives an account of Stewart's pleasure party to the Rocky Mountains, and reflects his attitude toward Baptiste. Griffin, "A Doctor Comes to California. The Diary of John S. Griffin, Assistant Surgeon with Kearny's Dragoons, 1846–47," tells about Baptiste Charbonneau starting out with Kearny, and then being sent back to guide Philip St. George Cooke, future father-in-law of the dashing cavalry officer "Jeb" Stuart. Cooke describes Charbonneau in his books *Conquest of New Mexico and California,* and *Journal of the March of the Mormon Battalion.* Bancroft, *History of California,* vol. V, gives the mission alcalde's duties. Letter of Colonel J. D. Stevenson to Governor Richard B. Mason, July 24, 1848, concerning complaints against Charbonneau, California State Library. Beckwourth, *The Life and Adventures of James P. Beckwourth.* Description of James Marshall, and of the American River mining camps in Sanborn; *The American: River of El Dorado.* The U.S. Census of Placer County, 1860, lists J.B. Charbonneau age fifty-seven, with residence at Secret Ravine; Steele, Bull, and Houston, *Directory of Placer County, 1861,* give his occupation as clerk at the Orleans Hotel in Auburn. Account of Baptiste's final journey and his death in *The Placer Herald,* July 7, 1866; microfilm in Auburn, California, Public Library. Death notice in *Butte Record,* July 14, 1866; Oroville, California, Public Library.

XV Peregrinating Peers, pp. 133–144

Biographical details on Duke Paul in Butscher, "A Brief Biography of Prince Paul Wilhelm of Württemberg (1787–1860);" and Bauser, "Biographic Facts Regarding Duke Paul of Württemberg." Photocopy of Paul's letter of May 5, 1823, to William Clark, in Hebard Collection. Paul describes his travels and discusses his interests and collections in *First Journey to North America in the Years 1822–24* (Bek translation); and, *Travels in North America 1822–1824* (Nitske translation). Photocopy of letter of December 23, 1829, from William Clark to the secretary of war, in Hebard Collection. Paul's "An Account of Adventures in the Great American Desert" is the source for his visit to the Tetons and other Wyoming mountains; for the date of his reaching the Rocky Mountains, and the strong possibility that he was present at the rendezvous of 1830. Copies of the Fort Union records in Hebard Collection. Paul writes of his meeting with Tom Fitzpatrick in "An Account of Adventures. . . ." Chittenden, *American Fur Trade . . .*, maps out the fall hunt of 1830. Bauser, "Biographic Facts Regarding Duke Paul . . .," for the solo trip in the pirogue. Clipping from an old, undated German newspaper, concerning Paul's penchant for collecting people; in Hebard Collection. Father De Smet's meeting with Paul recorded in his *Life, Letters, and Travels.* . . . "An Account of Adventures . . ." which includes contributions by Paul's companion, Heinrich Balduin Möllhausen, whose stirring depictions of American Indian and pioneer life gave him a reputation as "the German Cooper," gives the story of the 1851 trip to Fort Laramie and back. Biographical material on William Drummond Stewart, in De Voto, *Across the Wide Missouri*; in detail in Porter and Davenport, *Scotsman in Buckskin, Sir William Drummond Stewart and the Rocky Mountain Fur Trade*; and Stewart's novel *Altowan; or Incidents of Life and Adventure in the Rocky Mountains*, which is semiautobiographical. Baltimore artist Alfred Jacob Miller, who accompanied Stewart to the Rockies in 1837, described his patron's outfit in his notes, in *The West of Alfred Jacob Miller (1837)*. Ruxton, *Life in the Far West*, listed Stewart's stock of comestibles and gave a picture of his appearance. Miller wrote that Stewart was something of a martinet; he also noted his popularity with the mountain men. Miller described Jim Bridger's present as "a full suit of armor," and also as a "coat of mail." What Miller sketched appears to be a metal cuirass, worn over a coat of mail, and greaves. Miller states that this was the uniform of the Life Guards. A careful review of the history of the Life Guards of the British Army discovers no such outfit, suggesting this may have been a composite. ". . . Joe Meek, not to be outdone, arrayed himself in a suit of armor belonging to Captain Stuart [sic] and strutted about the encampment; then mounting his horse, played the part of an ancient knight, with a good deal of *éclat*," writes his biographer, Frances Fuller Victor, in *River of the West*. Order for McKenzie's coat of mail, in Chittenden, *ibid*. Finerty, *War-Path and Bivouac, or The Conquest of the Sioux*, saw the helmet that may well have been Bridger's. Letters of December 17, 1828, and November 26, 1839, from William Drummond Stewart to William Sublette, Sublette Papers, Missouri Historical Society; photocopies in author's collection. Miller's notes; and a letter to his sister, quoted in Porter and Davenport, described Antoine Clement, and Stewart's quarters. Kennerly, in *Persimmon Hill, A Narrative of Old St. Louis*; Chittenden, *ibid.*, describes Audubon's deception of the inspector. There have been some statements that Miller made paintings of the Tetons. Professor Robert C. Warner, University of Wyoming, long a student of Alfred Jacob Miller, and foremost authority on the artist's life and work, has found no indication that Miller ever visited the Tetons or painted them.

XVI End of an Era, pp. 145–150

Joe Meek in Victor, *River of the West*, gives a good account of the fierce rivalry between the companies, as does Chittenden, *The American Fur Trade . . .*; and Irving, *The Adventures of Captain Bonneville*. Meek, who was with Bridger and Fitzpatrick, tells about the attempts to fool their rivals and lead them astray; he is also the source for the decision to cure them of dogging their trail. Ferris, *Life in the Rocky Mountains . . .*, was riding with Vanderburgh and Drips, and gives their side. He saw Vanderburgh killed and was himself badly wounded. William Drummond Stewart's letter describing the Crow attack, reprinted in Chittenden, *ibid.*, who enlarges on the rivalry and what it led to. Meek is the source for Fitzpatrick being robbed along the road; he also talked about the penalty for luring men away, and for succumbing to the inducements. Chittenden quotes the terms of sale and describes the organization of the new partnership, as well as its dissolution. Meek told about the scarcity of beaver, and the fur trade's decline. Russell, *Journal of a Trapper . . .*, recorded the discontent at the rendezvous of 1838. Dr. Wislizenus, *A Journey to the Rocky Mountains in the Year 1839*, noted the scarcity of beaver furs, and the trappers' subdued behavior. Ruxton, *Life in the Far West*, quoted the old trapper's reasons for not returning home. Jim Bridger's letter describing his post, reprinted in Chittenden.

XVII *Washakie, pp. 151–165*

Background: Wissler, *Indians of the United States;* Hebard, *Washakie;* Trenholm and Carley, *The Shoshonis: Sentinels of the Rockies.* Osborne Russell, *Journal of a Trapper . . .,* told about the Blackfoot fear of Washakie. Hebard had many interviews with Washakie's sons, which enabled her to include much personal data about the chief. Lowe, *Five Years ('49–'54) a Dragoon and Other Adventures* on the Great Plains, described the Indian encampment, the arrival of the Shoshonis, and the Sioux threat. Trenholm and Carley give the reasons for removal of the meeting place, and record Washakie's disappointment at being unable to take part in the council. Larpenteur, *Forty Years a Fur Trader,* gave the results of the treaty. Hebard; Trenholm and Carley, for the Battle of Crowheart Butte. Reynolds, "The Redskin Who Saved the White Man's Hide," quotes Washakie's answer as to whether he ate the Crow's heart. Hebard states there were eyewitnesses to Washakie dancing with a heart impaled on his lance. Reynolds names them: Burnett, the government agricultural instructor, and Yarnell, the government scout. Father De Smet, *Life, Letters, and Travels . . .,* observed the smoothness of the overland trails. E. N. Wilson, *The White Indian Boy,* was adopted as a child by Washakie; he gives details of his life as a member of the chief's family, as well as an excellent picture of Shoshoni life. He recalls the seasonal moves. Hebard, for Washakie riding off to test his powers as a warrior. Washakie's reaction to the treaty of 1868, quoted in Trenholm and Carley. Bourke, *On the Border With Crook;* and Finerty, *War-Path and Bivouac or The Conquest of the Sioux,* both wrote about the Shoshonis riding into Crook's camp. Search by the Navy and Old Army Branch, Military Archives Division, National Archives and Records; and Indian Records, Civil Archives Division, National Archives and Records, indicates that Washakie was not present at the Battle of the Rosebud, and that he did not join General Crook until July 11, 1876. Finerty wrote about the scouts discovering the Sioux. Charles King, *Campaigning With Crook,* thought of the Rebel yell when he heard the Shoshonis. Indian Agent James Irwin, quoted in Hebard, in regard to Washakie's usefulness as a military adviser. The army's movements are followed through the writings of Crook's staff officers, and war correspondent John Finerty. King listed General Terry's impedimenta. The saddle presentation in Hebard; she also quotes opinions of Washakie by his white friends, and his familiarity with French phrases. Governor John Hoyt's account of his meeting with Washakie, and Washakie's speech in Hebard; and Wissler. His death, the official orders, and account of the funeral in Hebard. After Washakie's death the office of chief was abolished by the federal government, and a council of six leading tribesmen was substituted.

XVIII Continental Tea, pp. 166–176

This chapter is based entirely on Raynolds' journal contained in his *Report on the Exploration of the Yellowstone and the Country Drained by that River.* The captain's reasons for giving the name Union to the peak and pass, are usually attributed to "patriotic zeal." His journal reveals that the name suggested itself because of the union of waters on the peak he fixed as the topographical center of the continent. On his return to Washington, all botanical specimens were given to Dr. George Engelmann, while the zoological collection was put into the hands of Dr. Spencer Fullerton Baird, of the Smithsonian Institution.

XIX The Great Surveys, pp. 177–185

Biographical data on Dr. Hayden, as well as his Sioux name, in Clarence Jackson, *Picture Maker of the Old West;* and William Henry Jackson, *Time Exposure.* Further biographical material on Hayden, and James Stevenson, in Jesse V. Howell Collection, and Fritiof M. Fryxell Collection. W. H. Jackson remembering Hayden on horseback, and his first meeting with the Doctor; he also wrote about the party's equipment. The roster of the first party to explore the Tetons, in Hayden, *Sixth Annual Report of the United States Geological Survey of the Territories . . . 1872.* Langford, "The Ascent of Mount Hayden," gave the approach to the Tetons from Fort Hall. Letter of March 8, 1899, from Beaver Dick Leigh to Dr. Penrose, reprinted in Murie and Murie, *Wapiti Wilderness,* tells about his father and grandfather, his coming to Philadelphia, and service in the Mexican War. Chittenden, *The Yellowstone National Park,* tells how Leigh got his nickname. Langford, Mss., for

Dick's accomplishments as a guide, and for a description of Pierre's Hole. Jackson tells about the abundance of game in *Pioneer Photographer*. Hamp, "Diary of Sidford Hamp," gives the Leigh children's names, and tells about playing with them. Langford, "The Ascent . . .," decribes the beaver dinner. C. Hart Merriam's "Report," in Hayden, *Sixth Annual Report . . .*, lists the mammals and birds; John Coulter's botanical discoveries in his report, in Hayden, *Sixth Annual Report. . . .* Frank Bradley, on the geology of the Teton Range and the valley, in his report, also in Hayden's *Sixth Annual Report.* Jackson reports on the activities of the "Photographic Corps" in *Time Exposure*. Langford in his manuscripts and in "The Ascent of Mount Hayden" tells about preparations for the climb.

XX Conquering the Giant, pp. 186–192

Langford's manuscript notes; his article, "The Ascent of Mount Hayden"; Bradley's report in Hayden, *Sixth Annual Report*; Hamp's diary, and his letter of August 16, 1872, to his mother, are the sources for the climb. Robert Adams was the climber who had been in the Alps. Langford described Bechler's fall, in his article; also the frozen lake. Bonney and Bonney, *Guide to the Wyoming Mountains and Wilderness Areas*, give a history of the Owen-Langford-Stevenson controversy which went on for years; they also discovered Dr. Kieffer's letter and map of his route to the summit of the Grand Teton, and are the sources for Owen having failed to acknowledge Kieffer's climb or make it public. Dr. Hayden's error in reporting that the Inditress below the summit, was built on the top of the Grand Teton is doubtless responsible for the controversy starting. Members of the Hayden Survey Party for that year did not express any doubt that Langford and Stevenson reached the summit. William Henry Jackson, in *Time Exposure*, states that when Franklin Spalding "led a small party to the top, he took with him a certain gentleman who later announced that Langford and Stevenson were frauds—since he found at the top no evidence to prove that anyone had been there twenty-six years earlier! A realist of high order, and with political influence as well, this gentleman still later succeeded in having himself acclaimed—by joint resolution of the Wyoming legislature—as the first man ever to scale the peak."

XXI *Mystery of the Grand Teton, pp. 193–198*

Frances Densmore quote in Alexander, *The World's Rim*. Langford, "The Ascent of Mount Hayden," and his manuscript notes, are the sources for his and Stevenson's discovery of the stone enclosure on the spur, and the questions it aroused. Captain Jones' discussion of the stone works, and his scale drawings of them, in *Report Upon the Reconnaissance of Northwestern Wyoming . . . 1873*. Eddy, "Astronomical Alignment of the Bighorn Medicine Wheel," describes its form. Dr. George C. Frison, Head, Department of Anthropology, University of Wyoming, who has done archaeological work on the Bighorn "wheel," stated in interview that the central cairn is older than the spokes. He is also of the opinion that the form may not be a wheel, but was intended to be the form of the so-called shield seen in petroglyphs. At that time he did not agree with Dr. Eddy on astronomical alignments of cairns. See also, Frison and Wilson, "An Introduction to Bighorn Basin Archeology." In 1977 Dr. Eddy published the results of his further investigations of the Bighorn and other wheels; these, in conjunction with the findings of Drs. Forbis and Kehoe, seem to uphold the theory of astronomical alignments of cairns. These findings, in "Probing the Mystery of the Medicine Wheels." Dr. Frison believes that the stone enclosure on the Grand Teton could have been used for vision quest, basing this statement on descriptions of such structures in ethnographic literature. Lowie, *Indians of the Plains,* discusses the importance of dreams and visions; customs pertaining to them; visionary patterns, and an account of guardian spirits. Alexander writes about the Youth Vigil, and also the various approaches to the vision quest. Lowie describes the relationship between guardian and protégé; the unsuccessful vision-seeker. Eddy, "Probing the Mystery . . .," writes of archaeologist Forbis and colleagues discovering artifacts in the central cairn of the Majorville wheel in Alberta, indicating when its construction was started. Dr. Dorothy Dunn, *American Indian Painting of the Southwest and Plains Areas,* states that through the arts it becomes obvious that there were connections between various basic cultural areas in the United States with Middle America. Some studies point out mass migration from Mexico; others simply trade, and transmission of cultural elements. Astronomical knowledge could have come through these same channels. Dr. Dunn also stresses how little is known about our earliest inhabitants. In 1977, man's entry into the New World was confirmed at "at least forty thousand years ago—nearly twice the previously accepted estimate. . . ." *Science News* (March 26, 1977).

XXII *The Other Side of the Mountains, pp. 199–209*

Frank Bradley, "Report," in Hayden, *Sixth Annual Report,* told about the plans for travel, and Beaver Dick's objections. Sidford Hamp's letter of August 16, 1872. Langford, "The Ascent of Mount Hayden" for the description of Sawtelle, and an account of the horse thieves. Jackson, in *Pioneer Photographer,* tells about getting lost. Hamp records in both his diary and the letter of August 16, 1872, the uncomfortable night without food, water, or blankets. Langford, "The Ascent . . ." for the clues they found to Hayden's trail. Jackson, *Pioneer . . .,* recalled the meeting and its purpose. W. H. Holmes, in Random Records, Jesse V. Howell Collection, Western History Research Center, for information about William Blackmore. Langford's article tells about his proposal to rename the Grand Teton. Bradley's report is followed for the party's discovery of the Snake's sources, and their travels into Jackson Hole; his observations included flora, mammals, weather, fall coloring, and views of the Tetons. W.H. Holmes' versatility to be found in biographical data in Random Records, Jesse V. Howell Collection. Bradley reported the answer to the Snake River's diversion from its natural course, the discovery of the lakes, the conclusions as to their formation by glaciers, and the naming of them. He also observed the antelope and chipmunks. C. Hart Merriam in his report in Hayden, *Sixth Annual Report . . .,* wrote about the trumpeter swans, listed the other birds he found, and described the water ouzel. Coulter, in *Sixth Annual Report . . .* described the flora of the east side and valley, and made observations on the differences in the forests on each slope. Jackson, *Pioneer . . .,* remembered the stage ride and the road agents. Dr. Hayden to the secretary of the interior, in *Eleventh Annual Report of the United States Geological Survey . . . for the Year 1877.* Jackson writing about the 1878 survey in *Time Exposure.* Wilson reported on the failure to reach the summit of the Grand Teton, and the Indian attack, in Hayden, *Eleventh Annual Report. . . .* Jackson, *ibid.,* told about the early winter, their route out of the mountains, and breaking the ice to look for the division of waters on Two Ocean Pass; he also told about the formation of the new survey, and what the results meant for him. James Stevenson's *Ceremonial of Hasjelti Dailjis* is classic. Matilda Coxe Stevenson's most distinguished contribution is a monumental monograph of over six hundred folio pages, and hundreds of illustrations on the Zuñi, with whom she lived for many years.

XXIII *Immortalizing the Tetons, pp. 210–215*

W. H. Jackson, "With Moran in the Yellowstone," tells about Moran illustrating Langford's 1871 article; about Dr. Hayden hearing Langford lecture, and his decision to make Yellowstone country his field of exploration. Clarence Jackson, *Picture Maker of the Old West*, writes about the storm of protest over Langford's article. After deciding to take his survey into Yellowstone, Hayden invited Langford to join the party; Langford introduced Hayden and Moran. Wilkins, *Thomas Moran, Artist of the Mountains*, for the Turner influence. Moran's rail and stage trip, described in Moran File, Jesse V. Howell Collection, Western History Research Center. W. H. Jackson recalling Moran's ignorance of Western ways in *Time Exposure*; Moran's jaunty appearance, in "With Moran in the Yellowstone"; as a wilderness cook, *Time Exposure*—also the source for Moran's broad knowledge. Wilkins tells about him being self-educated and self-taught in art. Moran's interest in photography, and Jackson's estimate of his painting, in *Time Exposure*. Moran on literal transcripts, quoted in Wilkins, who also reprints the Moran-Hayden correspondence. Fryxell, "Thomas Moran's Trip to Tetons," is a transcription of Moran's entire diary, kept on that journey in 1879. Dr. Fryxell prefaces the diary with a detailed account of the artist's trip, and includes a quotation from Dr. Hayden's letter to Moran encouraging him to paint the Tetons.

XXIV *Six-Guns, pp. 216–225*

Philip Ashton Rollins, *The Cowboy*; Struthers Burt, *Powder River, Let 'Er Buck*, for the ease with which early-day rustling was accomplished. Burt tells about the change in attitude after purebred cattle were introduced. Rollins, for turning thieving into a science, and the increase in stealing. Owen Wister, thoroughly familiar with the Tetons, described Jackson Hole as the ideal hideout, and named the secret passes in *The Virginian*. Butch Cassidy, in Kelly, *The Outlaw Trail*. Teton Jackson's story in Canton, *Frontier Trails*. Driggs, *History of Teton Valley, Idaho*, for outlaw activities on the west side of the Tetons. Driggs, a descendant of pioneer settlers in Pierre's Hole (Teton Valley), with firsthand knowledge of other early families there, states that Edward Harrington was his real name, and Ed Trafton, his alias. Driggs' account of Trafton's career is followed. The number of coaches and tourists held up varies, as does the amount of loot. Driggs states that there were 19 coaches and 147 passengers; Burt, *Diary of a Dude-Wrangler*, says 18 coaches; the *New York Times*, 165 travelers and 35 coaches. The present account of the robbery based on Driggs, and the *New York Times* in both news reports and editorial. The record is confused because Trafton had repeatedly held up the Yellowstone Park coaches before his big day. Burt, *ibid.*, is the authority for Trafton's plans for his next crime.

XXV Taming the Hole, pp. 226–233

Material on Hamilton and Sargent in Simpson, "Talks with J. Pierce Cunningham;" and Burt, *Diary of a Dude-Wrangler*. Watson, "History of Jackson's Hole Before the Year 1907," recalls the inaccessibility and the long, hard winters. Interview with Mrs. Elizabeth (Lizzie) Woolstenhulme, Driggs, Idaho, described her life as a child of pioneer settlers; she also remembered the cold winters. Pioneer ranch wife's recollections, Writers Program, Jackson Hole Collection. Burkes, "History of Teton County," recounts the march of civilization into Jackson Hole. Chittenden, *The Yellowstone National Park;* and Tilden, *Following the Frontier with F. Jay Haines*, for accounts of President Arthur's elaborate party. Hebard, *Washakie*, writes about the president's call on Washakie. Rollins, *The Cowboy*, for the lack of women in cattle country. Larson, *History of Wyoming;* and Stone, *Uinta County, Its Place in History*, discuss Wyoming's recognition of women's rights and tells about those women who held office in Jackson Hole, and elsewhere in the state. Stone for the accomplishments of the women mayor and council in Jackson. Genevieve Parkhurst, on assignment from *The Delineator,* interviewed Jackson's women in office and wrote the fairest and most comprehensive article. The men's reports were frequently scoffing.

XXVI Riders, pp. 234–246

Rollins, *The Cowboy;* and Mora, *Trail Dust and Saddle Leather,* give excellent accounts of the evolution of the American cowboy, his adaptation of the dress, equipment, and terminology. Owen Wister, "The Evolution of the Cowpuncher," quoted in Wister, *Owen Wister Out West,* writes of the appeal of the cowboy's vocation, of the young men who flocked West, and what the job demanded of them. Rollins quotes the cowboy's definition of himself, and Andy Downs, the old hand, who gave advice. Russell, *Trails Plowed Under,* describes the cowboy fashion plate. Nordyke, "Boss of the Plains," gives the history of the Stetson. Rollins, a former cowboy, is relied on for the puncher's way of talking, his expressions, his profanity, his abilities as a storyteller, for the subjects of those tales, for his devotion to his horses, his powers of observation, and his singing. Elinore Stewart, *Letters of a Woman Homesteader,* wrote about the songs she heard Wyoming cowboys singing and gave the titles. Jackson Hole favorites were found in Writers' Program, Jackson Hole Collection. Rollins explained the reason for the rider constantly singing or crooning on night herd. He also told about improvisation, about the scarcity of reading material; "Brand"; and cowboy dances. The Virginian in Wister, "Hank's Woman," speaks of a woman being "a scanty thing" in cattle country. Rollins, for the cowboy and drink. Cowboy Harry Williams, in interview, Writers' Project, Jackson Hole Collection, told of leaving the Colt's outside the saloon. Cowboy Bruce Sieberts quoted in Larson, *History of Wyoming,* on the rider's recognition socially before and after the publication of *The Virginian.* Fanny Kemble Wister, *Owen Wister Out West,* comments on the popularity of *The Virginian,* and its influence on Western fiction. Rollins, for a characterization of the cowboy folk figure. Fanny Kemble Wister for biographical data on her father. Owen Wister telling how he came to write Western fiction, in *Roosevelt, The Story of a Friendship.* Owen Wister's journals kept on his trips West are in the Western History Research Center. Wister describes his difficulty with censorship, in *Roosevelt*. . . . Coutant, *The History of Wyoming from the Earliest Known Discoveries*, wrote about the record cold winter of 1845, and quoted trapper Jim Baker who was there. Jack Eynon, pioneer cattleman, gave the opinion that "dudes winter easier than cattle." Burt, *Diary of a Dude-Wrangler*, tells about the JY Ranch; he described Bill Menor (pronounced Meaner), whom he knew well, in *Powder River*. . . . Fanny Wister tells of getting fresh peas from Menor, of the poor food at the JY, and of riding all day along the Tetons; she is also the source for their joyous return to Jackson Hole, and the building of their own cabin. Owen Wister wrote movingly of the vanished cowboy in his preface to *The Virginian*.

XXVII The Changing Mountains, pp. 247–253

Muir's reflection on nature undoing her work, in "The Yellowstone National Park." Fryxell, *The Tetons, Interpretations of a Mountain Landscape*, speaks of the continuing work of the erosive agents. Personal observation of a lightning-triggered rock slide. Fryxell witnessed the slide following the collapse of the pinnacle face on Mount St. John (named for Hayden Survey geologist Orestes St. John). Personal observation of cony. Fryxell describes talus encroachment on the lakes. Muir, *The Mountains of California*; Fryxell, *ibid.*, and personal observation for the swell and ebb of mountain streams. Muir described the snow avalanche in *Our National Parks*. Dr. Fryxell in his work; and Love and Reed, *Creation of the Teton Landscape*, for today's glaciers. Love and Reed name the most important ones, and give the size of Teton Glacier. Fryxell is the authority for the statement that the Teton peaks and spires will eventually be worn down. Nature notes compiled from personal observation. Lieutenant Doane, in Bonney and Bonney, *Battle Drums and Geysers: The Life and Journals of Lt. Gustavus C. Doane, Soldier and Explorer of the Yellowstone and Snake River Regions*, watched the stars lighting up the Grand Teton, one December night in 1876.

Afterword, Saving the Tetons, pp. 254–262

Fryxell, *The Tetons, Interpretations of a Mountain Landscape*, tells about the destruction by sheep; Murie and Murie, *Wapiti*

Wilderness, for transmission of disease to bighorn. Tom Reinecker, supervisor, Idaho Department of Fish and Game, in correspondence, described the disruption of migration routes by settlement. Driggs, *History of Teton Valley, Idaho,* for the discovery of mineral deposits and oil. Mrs. Woolstenhulme, Driggs, Idaho, in interview, remembered sawmills in nearly every west side canyon. Murie and Murie; Saylor, *Jackson Hole, Wyoming;* and Burkes, "History of Teton County," part 2, tell about damming Jackson Lake, and the other water projects in the area; Burkes, for the early attempts to extend Yellowstone Park; also Saylor. Exploitation of the valley—waterworks, tourist cabins, billboards, etc.—in Burkes, *ibid.;* Saylor; the Muries. All three write about the meeting at Maude Noble's cabin. Albright's account of his trip through Jackson Hole with the Rockefellers, in Fosdick, *John D. Rockefeller, Jr., a Portrait.* Rockefeller's reasons for wanting to back the project, in Fosdick. History of the project in Burkes, *ibid.;* Fosdick. Rockefeller-Ickes correspondence in Fosdick. For the reactions of the residents of Jackson Hole, Murie and Murie, who were living there at the time. Muir, *Our National Parks.*

Bibliography

Books

Alexander, Hartley Burr. *The World's Rim*. Lincoln: University of Nebraska Press, 1967.

Allen, W. A. *The Sheep Eaters*. New York: The Shakespeare Press, 1913.

Alter, J. Cecil. *Jim Bridger*. Norman: University of Oklahoma Press, 1962.

Bancroft, Hubert Howe. *History of California*, Vol. V. San Francisco: The History Co., 1882–1890.

―――. *History of Nevada, Colorado, and Wyoming, 1540–1888*. San Francisco: The History Co., 1890.

Bauser, Friedrich. "Biographic Facts Regarding Duke Paul Wilhelm of Württemberg." *South Dakota Historical Collections*, Vol. XIX, 1938.

Beckwourth, James. *The Life and Adventures of James P. Beckwourth*. T. D. Bonner, ed. Reprint of 1856 edition. New York: Arno Press, 1969.

Bonney, Orrin H., and Bonney, Lorraine. *Battle Drums and Geysers: The Life and Journals of Lt. Gustavus C. Doane, Soldier and Explorer of the Yellowstone and Snake River Regions.* Chicago: The Swallow Press, 1970.

——. *Guide to the Wyoming Mountains and Wilderness Areas.* Denver: Sage Books, 1960.

Bourke, John G. *On the Border With Crook.* New York: Charles Scribner's Sons, 1896.

Brackenridge, Henry M. *Journal of a Voyage Up the River Missouri; Performed in Eighteen Hundred and Eleven,* in R. G. Thwaites, ed., *Early Western Travels 1748–1846.* Cleveland: The Arthur H. Clark Co., 1904.

Bradbury, John. *Travels in the Interior of America in the Years 1808, 1810, and 1811,* in R. G. Thwaites, ed., *Early Western Travels 1748-1846.* Cleveland: The Arthur H. Clark Co., 1904.

Bradley, Frank. "Report," in Hayden, *Sixth Annual Report of the United States Geological Survey of the Territories Embracing Portions of Montana, Idaho, Wyoming, and Utah . . . for the Year 1872.* Washington: Government Printing Office, 1873.

Bryant, Edwin. *What I Saw in California: Being the Journal of a Tour in the Years 1846, 1847.* New York: D. Appleton & Co., 1848.

Burt, Struthers. *Diary of a Dude-Wrangler.* New York: Charles Scribner's Sons, 1924.

——. *Powder River, Let 'Er Buck.* New York: Farrar & Rinehart, Inc., 1938.

Canton, Frank M., *Frontier Trails, The Autobiography of Frank M. Canton.* Edward Everett Dale, ed. Boston and New York: Houghton Mifflin Company, 1930.

Carson, Christopher. *Kit Carson's Autobiography.* Milo M. Quaife, ed. Chicago: The Lakeside Press, 1935.

Chichester, Henry Manners, and Burges-Short, George. *The Records and Badges of Every Regiment and Corps in the British Army.* London: Gale & Polder, Ltd., 1900.

Chittenden, Hiram Martin. *The American Fur Trade of the Far West.* 2 vols. Stanford, CA: Academic Reprints, 1954.

――――. *The Yellowstone National Park.* Cincinnati: The Robert Clarke Co., 1895.

Clarke, Charles G. *The Men of the Lewis and Clark Expedition.* Glendale: The Arthur H. Clark Co., 1970.

Cooke, Philip St. George. *Conquest of New Mexico and California, An Historical and Personal Narrative.* New York: G. P. Putnam's Sons, 1878.

――――. *Journal of the March of the Mormon Battalion, 1846–1847,* in *Exploring Southwestern Trails 1846–1854.* Ralph P. Bieber and Averam B. Bender, eds. Glendale: The Arthur H. Clark Co., 1938.

Coulter, John M. *Manual of Rocky Mountain Botany.* Chicago: Ivison, Blakeman, Taylor & Co., 1890.

――――. "Report," in Hayden, *Sixth Annual Report of the United States Geological Survey of the Territories Embracing Portions of Montana, Idaho, Wyoming, and Utah . . . for the Year 1872.* Washington: Government Printing Office, 1873.

Coutant, C. H. *The History of Wyoming from the Earliest Known Discoveries.* 3 vols. Laramie: Chaplin, Spafford & Mathison, 1899.

Coyner, David H. *The Lost Trappers.* Reprint of 1850 edition. Glorieta, NM: The Rio Grande Press, 1969.

Craighead, John J., Craighead, Frank C., Jr., and Davis, Ray J. *A Field Guide to Rocky Mountain Wildflowers.* Boston: Houghton Mifflin Company, 1963.

Dale, Harrison C. *The Ashley-Smith Explorations and the Discovery of a Central Route to the Pacific 1822–1829.* Cleveland: The Arthur H. Clark Co., 1918.

David, Robert B. *Malcolm Campbell, Sheriff.* Casper, Wyoming: Wyomingana Inc., 1932.

De Smet, Pierre-Jean. *Life, Letters, and Travels of Father*

Pierre-Jean De Smet, S.J., 1801–1873. Hiram Martin Chittenden and Alfred Talbot Richardson, eds. 4 vols. New York: Francis P. Harper, 1905.

De Voto, Bernard. *Across the Wide Missouri.* Boston: Houghton Mifflin Company, 1947.

Dobie, J. Frank. *Tales of the Mustang.* Dallas: The Book Club of Texas, 1936.

Drannan, W. F. *Thirty-one Years on the Plains and in the Mountains.* Chicago: Rhodes, 1900.

Driggs, B. W. *History of Teton Valley, Idaho.* Caldwell, Idaho: The Caxton Press, 1926.

Dunlap, William. *Diary of William Dunlap,* Vol. 2. New York: New York Historical Society, 1930.

Dunn, Dorothy. *American Indian Painting of the Southwest and Plains Areas.* Albuquerque: The University of New Mexico Press, 1968.

The Emigrant's Handbook. Although title page is missing, internal evidence indicates it was published in 1843.

Estergreen, M. Morgan. *Kit Carson, A Portrait in Courage.* Norman: University of Oklahoma Press, 1962.

Ewers, John C. *Artists of the Old West.* Garden City, NY: Doubleday & Co., 1965.

Farnham, Thomas Jefferson. *Travels in the Great Western Prairies.* London: Richard Bently, 1843.

Ferris, Robert G. Series ed., *Prospector, Cowhand, and Sodbuster.* The National Survey of Historic Sites and Buildings. Washington: U.S. Department of Interior, National Park Service, 1967.

Ferris, Warren A. *Life in the Rocky Mountains, A Diary of Wanderings on the Sources of the Rivers Missouri, Columbia, and Colorado from February 1830 to November 1835.* Paul C. Phillips, ed. Denver: The Old West Publishing Co., 1940.

Finerty, John F. *War-Path and Bivouac, or The Conquest of the Sioux.* Chicago: Donahue & Henneberry, 1890.

Fosdick, Raymond B. *John D. Rockefeller, Jr., A Portrait.* New York: Harper & Brothers, 1956.

Frémont, John C. *Report of the Exploring Expedition to the Rocky Mountains in the Year 1842. . . .* Washington: Government Printing Office, 1845.

Fryxell, Fritiof. *The Tetons, Interpretations of a Mountain Landscape.* Berkeley and Los Angeles: University of California Press, 1953.

Fryxell, Roald. "Geology of the Teton Range," in Leigh Ortenburger, *A Climber's Guide to the Teton Range.* San Francisco: The Sierra Club, 1956.

Garrard, Lewis H. *Wah-to-Yah and the Taos Trail.* Reprint, Ralph P. Bieber, ed. Glendale: The Arthur H. Clark Co., 1938.

Gilbert, E.W. *The Exploration of Western America, 1800–1850,* New York: Cooper Square Publishers, 1966.

Gregg, Josiah. *Commerce of the Prairies.* Max L. Moorhead, ed. Norman: University of Oklahoma Press, 1954.

Hamilton, William. *My Sixty Years on the Plains, Trapping, Trading, and Indian Fighting.* E. T. Sieber, ed. New York: Forest and Stream Publishing Co., 1909.

Harris, Burton J. *John Colter, His Years in the Rockies.* New York: Chas. Scribner's Sons, 1952.

Hart, John L. J. *Fourteen Thousand Feet.* Denver: The Colorado Mountain Club, 1925.

Hayden, F. V. *Sixth Annual Report of the United States Geological Survey of the Territories Embracing Portions of Montana, Idaho, and Wyoming . . . for the Year 1872.* Washington: Government Printing Office, 1873.

———. *Ninth Annual Report of the United States Geological Survey of the Territories Embracing Colorado and parts of Adjacent Territories for the Year 1875.* Washington: Government Printing Office, 1877.

————. *Tenth Annual Report of the United States Geological Survey of the Territories Embracing Colorado and Parts of Adjacent Territories for the Year 1876.* Washington: Government Printing Office, 1878.

————. *Eleventh Annual Report of the United States Geological Survey of the Territories Embracing Idaho and Wyoming . . . for the Year 1877.* Washington: Government Printing Office, 1879.

————. *Twelfth Annual Report of the United States Geological Survey of the Territories for the Year 1878;* Part II. Washington: Government Printing Office, 1882.

————. *United States Engineer Department Geological Report of the Exploration of the Yellowstone and Missouri Rivers . . . 1859–60.* Washington: Government Printing Office, 1869.

Hebard, Grace Raymond. *Sacajawea.* Glendale: The Arthur H. Clark Co., 1933.

————. *Washakie.* Cleveland: The Arthur H. Clark Co., 1930.

Hendricks, Gordon. *Albert Bierstadt, Painter of the American West.* Harry N. Abrams, Inc., in association with the Amon Carter Museum of Western Art, 1973.

Hodge, Frederick Webb. *Handbook of American Indians.* Smithsonian Institution, Bureau of American Ethnology; *Bulletin 30,* Part I. Washington: Government Printing Office, 1912.

Hoffman, W. J. "Stone Circles and Signals," in Hayden, *Tenth Annual Report of the United States Geological Survey of the Territories . . . for the Year 1876.* Washington: Government Printing Office, 1878.

Holmes, William H. "Report," in Hayden, *Twelfth Annual Report of the United States Geological Survey of the Territories for the Year 1878;* Part II. Washington: Government Printing Office, 1882.

Horan, James. *Desperate Women.* New York: G. P. Putnam's Sons, 1952.

Howard, Harold P. *Sacajawea*. Norman: University of Oklahoma Press, 1971.

Hunt, Wilson Price. *Diary of an Overland Trip to Astoria in 1811–12*. Translated from *Nouvelles Annales des Voyages*. Paris: 1821; in Philip Ashton Rollins, ed., *The Discovery of the Oregon Trail, Robert Stuart's Narratives of his overland trip eastward from Astoria in 1812–13*. New York and London: Charles Scribner's Sons, 1935.

Hyde, George E. *Indians of the High Plains, from the Prehistoric Period to the Coming of the Europeans*. Norman: University of Oklahoma Press, 1959.

Irving, Washington. *The Adventures of Captain Bonneville*. New York: J. B. Miller & Co., 1885.

———. *Astoria, or Anecdotes of an Enterprise Beyond the Rocky Mountains*. Philadelphia: Carey, Lea & Blanchard, 1836.

Jackson, Clarence. *Picture Maker of the Old West, William Henry Jackson*. New York and London: Charles Scribner's Sons, 1947.

Jackson, Donald, ed. *Letters of the Lewis and Clark Expedition with Related Documents, 1783–1854*. Urbana: University of Illinois Press, 1962.

Jackson, William Henry, and Driggs, Howard R. *Pioneer Photographer*. Yonkers: World Book Co., 1929.

———. *Time Exposure*. New York: G.P. Putnam's Sons, 1940.

James, Thomas. *Three Years Among the Indians and Mexicans*. Reprint of 1846 edition. Philadelphia and New York: J. B. Lippincott Co., 1962.

Jones, William A. *Report Upon the Reconnaissance of Northwestern Wyoming including Yellowstone National Park made in the Summer of 1873*. Washington: Government Printing Office, 1875.

Kelly, Charles. *The Outlaw Trail*. New York: Devin-Adair, 1959.

Kendall, George Wilkins. *Narrative of the Texan Santa Fe Expedition.* 2 Vols. New York: Harper & Brothers, 1844.

Kennerly, William Clark. *Persimmon Hill, A Narrative of Old St. Louis and the Far West.* Norman: University of Oklahoma Press, 1948.

King, Charles. *Campaigning With Crook.* Norman: University of Oklahoma Press, 1964.

La Farge, Oliver. *A Pictorial History of the American Indian.* New York: Crown Publishers, Inc., 1956.

Langford, Nathaniel P. "Report," in Hayden, *Sixth Annual Report of the United States Geological Survey of the Territories . . . for the Year 1872.* Washington: Government Printing Office, 1873.

Larpenteur, Charles. *Forty Years a Fur Trader.* Elliott Coues, ed. Minneapolis: Ross & Haines, Inc., 1962.

Larson, T. A. *History of Wyoming.* Lincoln: University of Nebraska Press, 1965.

Lawson, Cecil C. P. *History of the Uniforms of the British Army.* Vol IV. London: Norman Military Publications, 1940.

Leonard, Zenas. *Adventures of Zenas Leonard, Fur Trader.* John C. Ewers, ed. Norman: University of Oklahoma Press, 1959.

Lewis, Meriwether, and Clark, William. *The Journals of the Expedition under the command of Captains Lewis and Clark to the sources of the Missouri, thence across the Rocky Mountains and down the river Columbia to the Pacific Ocean, performed during the Years 1804–5–6 by order of the Government of the United States.* Nicholas Biddle and Paul Allen, eds. First published in 1814. New edition, 2 Vols. New York: The Heritage Press, 1962.

––––––. *Original Journals of the Lewis and Clark Expedition 1804–1806.* 9 Vols. Reuben G. Thwaites, ed. New York: Dodd, Mead & Co., 1904.

Love, J. D., and Reed, John C., Jr. *Creation of the Teton Land-*

scape. Reprint by Grand Teton Natural History Association. Moose, Wyoming: 1975.

Lowe, Percival G. *Five Years a Dragoon ('49–'54) and Other Adventures on the Great Plains.* Kansas City, MO: The Franklin Hudson Publishing Co., 1906.

Lowie, Robert H. *Indians of the Plains.* Garden City, NY: The Natural History Press, 1963.

Luttig, John. *Journal of a Fur-Trading Expedition on the Upper Missouri.* Stella M. Drumm, ed. St. Louis: State Historical Society of Missouri, 1920.

McClung, Robert M. *Lost Wild America.* New York: William Morrow & Co., 1969.

Merriam, C. Hart. "Report " in Hayden, *Sixth Annual Report of the United States Geological Survey of the Territories . . . for the Year 1872.* Washington: Government Printing Office, 1873.

Miller, Alfred Jacob. *The West of Alfred Jacob Miller (1837).* With an Account of the artist by Marvin C. Ross. Norman: University of Oklahoma Press, 1951.

Miller, Olive Thorne. *A Bird-Lover in the West.* Boston: Houghton Mifflin Co., 1894.

Mora, Jo. *Trail Dust and Saddle Leather.* New York: Charles Scribner's Sons, 1950.

Morgan, Dale C. *Jedediah Smith and the Opening of the West.* Lincoln: University of Nebraska Press, 1953.

Muir, John. *John of the Mountains.* Linnie Marsh Wolfe, ed. Boston and New York: Houghton Mifflin Co., 1938.

———. *The Mountains of California.* 2 Vols. Boston and New York: Houghton Mifflin Co., 1913.

———. *Our National Parks.* Boston and New York: Houghton Mifflin Co., 1901.

———. *Travels in Alaska.* Boston and New York: Houghton Mifflin Co., 1915.

————. *The Wilderness World of John Muir.* Edwin Way Teale, ed. Boston and New York: Houghton Mifflin Co., 1954 .

Murie, Margaret, and Murie, Olaus. *Wapiti Wilderness.* New York: Alfred A. Knopf, 1966.

Murphy, Robert William. *Wild Sanctuaries.* New York: E. P. Dutton & Co., 1968.

Nelson, John Young. *Fifty Years on the Trail, A True Story of Western Life as described to Harrington O'Reilly.* Reprint. Norman: University of Oklahoma Press, 1963.

Nidever, George. *The Life and Adventures of George Nidever.* William Henry Ellison, ed. Berkeley and Los Angeles: University of California Press, 1937.

Ordway, John. *The Journals of John Ordway Kept on the Expedition of Western Exploration.* Milo M. Quaife, ed. Madison: The State Historical Society of Wisconsin, 1916.

Parker, Samuel. *Journal of an Exploring Tour Beyond the Rocky Mountains . . . Performed in the Years 1835, '36, and '37.* Reprint of 1838 edition. Minneapolis: Ross & Haines, 1967.

Paul Wilhelm, Duke of Württemberg. *Early Sacramento, Glimpses of John Augustus Sutter, The Hok Farm, and Neighboring Indian Tribes.* Louis C. Butscher, trans. The Sacramento Book Collectors Club, 1973.

————. *First Journey to North America in the Years 1822 to 1824.* William G. Bek, trans.; with *Supplementary Material Relating to the Prince.* South Dakota Historical Collection, Vol. XIX, 1938.

————. *Travels in North America 1822–1824.* W. Robert Nitske, trans., Savoie Lottinville, ed. Norman: University of Oklahoma Press, 1973.

Peterson, Roger Tory. *A Field Guide to Western Birds.* Boston: Houghton Mifflin Co., 1941.

Porter, Mae Reed, and Davenport, Odessa. *Scotsman in Buck-*

skin, Sir William Drummond Stewart and the Rocky Mountain Fur Trade. New York: Hastings House, 1963 .

Raynolds, William F. *Report on the Exploration of the Yellowstone and the Country Drained by that River.* Senate Executive Document No. 77; 40th Congress, 1st Session. Washington: Government Printing Office, 1868.

Rollins, Philip Ashton. *The Cowboy.* New York: Charles Scribner's Sons, 1936.

Russell, Charles. *Trails Plowed Under.* Garden City, New York: Doubleday & Co., Inc., 1948.

Russell, Osborne. *Journal of a Trapper, or Nine Years in the Rocky Mountains, 1834–1843.* Boise, Idaho: The Syms-York Co., 1921.

Ruxton, George F. *Adventures in Mexico and the Rocky Mountains.* London: John F. Murray, 1847.

———. *Life in the Far West.* New York: Harper & Brothers, 1849.

Sage, Rufus B. *Scenes in the Rocky Mountains and in Oregon, California, New Mexico, and the Grand Prairies.* Philadelphia: Cary and Hart, 1846.

St. John, Orestes. "Report," in Hayden, *Eleventh Annual Report of the Geological Survey of the Territories . . . for the Year 1877.* Washington: Government Printing Office, 1879.

Sanborn, Margaret. *The American: River of El Dorado.* New York: Holt, Rinehart & Winston, 1974.

Saylor, David J. *Jackson Hole, Wyoming: In the Shadow of the Grand Tetons.* Norman: University of Oklahoma Press, 1970.

Schiel, Jacob H. *Journey Through the Rocky Mountains and the Humboldt Mountains to the Pacific Ocean.* Thomas N. Bonner, trans. and ed. Norman: University of Oklahoma Press, 1959.

Shaw, Richard J. *Plants of Yellowstone and Grand Teton National Parks.* Salt Lake City: Wheelwright Press, 1974.

Shimkin, D. B. "The Wind River Shoshone Sun Dance." *Anthropological Papers,* No. 41. Smithsonian Institution, Bureau of American Ethnology, *Bulletin* 151, 1947.

Steele, R. J., Bull, James P., and Houston, F. I. *Directory of Placer County, 1861.* San Francisco: C. F. Robbins, 1861.

Stewart, Elinore P. *Letters of a Woman Homesteader.* Lincoln: University of Nebraska Press, 1961.

Stewart, William Drummond. *Altowan; or Incidents of Life and Adventure in the Rocky Mountains.* 2 Vols. J. Watson Webb, ed. New York: Harper & Brothers, 1846.

Stone, Elizabeth Arnold. *Uinta County, Its Place in History.* Glendale: The Arthur H. Clark Co., 1924.

Stuart, Robert. *The Discovery of the Oregon Trail. Robert Stuart's Narratives of his overland trip eastward from Astoria in 1812–13.* Philip Ashton Rollins, ed. New York and London: Charles Scribner's Sons, 1935.

Sullivan, Maurice S. *Jedediah Smith, Trader and Trail Blazer.* New York: Press of the Pioneers, Inc., 1936

Thompson, David. *David Thompson's Narratives of His Explorations in Western America, 1784–1812.* Toronto: J.B. Tyrrell, ed. Champlain Society, 1916.

Tilden, Freeman. *Following the Frontier With F. Jay Haines.* New York: Alfred A. Knopf, 1969.

Townsend, John Kirk. *Narrative of a Journey Across the Rocky Mountains to the Columbia River, 1832–1834.* Philadelphia: Henry Perkins, 1838.

Trenholm, Virginia Cole, and Carley, Maurine. *The Shoshonis: Sentinels of the Rockies.* Norman: University of Oklahoma Press, 1964.

Victor, Frances Fuller. *The River of the West. Life and Adventures in the Rocky Mountains and Oregon . . .* Hartford: Columbian Book Co., 1870.

Voget, Fred W. "Current Trends in the Wind River Shoshone Sun Dance." *Anthropological Papers,* No. 42. Smithsonian

Institution, Bureau of American Ethnology, *Bulletin 151,* 1947.

Wedel, Waldo R. *Prehistoric Man on the Great Plains.* Norman: University of Oklahoma Press, 1961.

Wilkins, Thurman. *Thomas Moran, Artist of the Mountains.* Norman: University of Oklahoma Press, 1966.

Wilkinson-Latham, Robert and Christopher. *Cavalry Uniforms, Including Other Mounted Troops of Britain and the Commonwealth.* New York and London: The Macmillan Co., 1969.

Wilkinson, Frederick. *Battle Dress.* Garden City, NY: Doubleday & Co., Inc., 1970.

Wilson, A. D. "Report," in Hayden, *Eleventh Annual Report of the United States Geological Survey . . . for the Year 1877.* Washington: Government Printing Office, 1879.

Wilson, E. N., and Driggs, Howard R. *The White Indian Boy.* Yonkers, NY: World Book Co., 1926.

Wilson, Gilbert Livingstone. "Hidatsa Eagle Trapping." *Anthropological Papers of The American Museum of Natural History.* Vol. XXX, Part IV. New York, 1928.

Wislinzenus, F. A. A. *A Journey to the Rocky Mountains in the Year 1839.* St. Louis: Missouri Historical Society, 1912.

Wissler, Clark. *Indians of the United States.* Garden City, NY: Doubleday & Co., Inc., 1946.

Wister, Owen. "Hank's Woman," in *The Jimmyjohn Boss and Other Stories.* New York: Harper & Brothers, 1900.

————. *Owen Wister Out West: His Journals and Letters.* Fanny Kemble Wister, ed. Chicago: University of Chicago Press, 1958.

————. *The Virginian, A Horseman of the Plains.* New York: The Macmillan Co., 1911.

Wyeth, John B. *Oregon; or a Short History of a Long Journey from the Atlantic Ocean to the Region of the Pacific by*

Land, in R. G. Thwaites, *Early Western Travels 1748–1846.* Cleveland : The Arthur H. Clark Co., 1905.

Wyeth, Nathaniel J. *The Correspondence and Journals of Captain Nathaniel J. Wyeth, 1831–6.* F. H. Young, ed. Eugene, OR: University Press, 1899.

Periodicals

Bell, William Gardner. "Frontier Lawman." *The American West,* Vol. I, No. 3, Summer 1964.

Burkes, Glenn R. "History of Teton County." *Annals of Wyoming,* Vol. 44, Nos. 1 and 2. Spring 1972; Fall 1972.

Butscher, Louis C. "A Brief Biography of Prince Paul Wilhelm of Württemberg (1797–1860)." *New Mexico Historical Review,* Vol. XVII, No.3, July 1942.

Clyman, James. "Diaries and Reminiscences." Charles L. Camp, ed. *California Historical Society Quarterly,* Vol. IV, No. 2, June 1925.

Craighead, Frank, and Craighead, John. "Cloud Gardens in the Tetons." *The National Geographic,* Vol. XCIII, No . 6, June 1948.

Eddy, John A. "Astronomical Alignment of the Big Horn Medicine Wheel." *Science,* Vol. 149, June 7, 1974.

———. "Probing the Mystery of the Medicine Wheels." *The National Geographic,* Vol. 151, No. 1, January 1977.

Frison, George C., and Wilson, Michael. "An Introduction to Bighorn Basin Archaeology." *Wyoming Geological Association Guidebook, 1975.*

Frost, Nedward M. "The Sheep Eaters." *Wyoming Wildlife,* Vol. 8, August 1941.

Fryxell, Fritiof. "Thomas Moran's Journey to Tetons." Reprint from *Augustana Historical Publications,* 1932; in *Annals of Wyoming,* Vol. 15, No. 1, January 1943.

Goosman, Mildred. "Old Gabe of Her Majesty's Life Guards." *The American West,* November 1969.

Griffin, John S. "A Doctor Comes to California. The Diary of John S. Griffin, Assistant Surgeon with Kearny's Dragoons, 1846–47." George Walcott Ames, Jr., ed. *California Historical Society Quarterly*, Vol. XXI, No. 3, September 1942.

Hamp, Sidford. "Diary of Sidford Hamp." Herbert Oliver Brayer, ed. *Annals of Wyoming*, Vol. 14, No. 1, October 1942.

Hultkranz, Ake. "The Dukurika Indians." *Annals of Wyoming*, Vol. 29, No. 2, October 1957.

———. "The Shoshones in the Rocky Mountain Area." *Annals of Wyoming*, Vol. 33, No1, April 19 61.

Huth, Hans. "Yosemite: The Story of an Idea." *Sierra Club Bulletin*, Vol. 33, No. 3, March 1948.

Jackson, William Henry. "With Thomas Moran in the Yellowstone." *Appalachia* (no date).

Langford, Nathaniel P. "The Ascent of Mount Hayden." *Scribner's Monthly*, Vol. VI, No. 2, June 1873.

Lindsley, Margaret H. "Major Andrew Henry." *Scenic Idaho*, Vol. X, 1955.

Mitchill, Samuel Latham "Letters From Washington: 1801–1813." *Harper's New Monthly Magazine*, Vol. LVIII, December 1878–May 1879.

Moran, Thomas. *Diary*, transcribed by Fritiof Fryxell, in "Thomas Moran's Journey to Tetons." Reprint from *Augustana Historical Publications*, 1932; in *Annals of Wyoming*, Vol. 15, No. 1, January 1943.

Muir, John. "Wild Parks and Forest Reservations of the West." *Atlantic Monthly*, Vol. 81, January 1898.

———. "The Yellowstone National Park." *Atlantic Monthly*, Vol. 81, April 1898.

Nordyke, Lewis T. "Boss of the Plains." *The Saturday Review of Literature*, Vol. XXV, No. 20, May 16, 1942.

Paul Wilhelm, Duke of Württemberg. "An Account of Adventures in the Great American Desert." Louis C. Butscher, trans. *New Mexico Historical Review,* Vol. XVII, Nos. 3 and 4, July and October 1942.

Reynolds, Sidney O. "The Redskin Who Saved the White Man's Hide." *American Heritage,* Vol. XI, No. 2, February 1960.

Science News, March 26, 1977. "Early Man Confirmed in America 40,000 Years Ago."

Warner, J. J. "Reminiscences of Early California from 1831–1846." *Historical Society of Southern California Quarterly,* Vol. 7, 1906.

Wright, Gary A. "The Coming of the People." *Naturalist,* Vol. 27, No. 1, Spring 1976.

Newspapers

Butte Record, Oroville, California, July 14, 1866. Death notice, Jean Baptiste Charbonneau.

Le Courrier, New Orleans. December 13 and December 20, 1830. "Suite du voyage du prince de Würtemberg." Two-part article by Duke Paul Wilhelm of Württemberg on his experiences among the Iowa Indians.

Missouri Gazette & Public Advertiser, St. Louis. February 13, 1822, p. 3. William Ashley's advertisement for recruits.

New York Times, July 30, 1914, p. 1; July 31, 1914, p. 8; August 4, 1914, p. 18. The Yellowstone Park stagecoach robbery.

The Placer Herald, Auburn, California. July 7, 1866. Obituary article on Jean Baptiste Charbonneau.

Wyoming State Journal, Lander, Wyoming. July 14, 1889, p.1. Account of the lynching of "Cattle Kate" Watson and Jim Averill.

Manuscripts and Other Unpublished Sources

Charbonneau, Jean Baptiste. Correspondence, research notes, and other material relating to, in Grace Raymond Hebard

Collection, Western History Research Center, The University of Wyoming.

Drumm, Stella M. Letter of June 5, 1925 to Senator Nelson A. Mason, in above collection.

Hamp, Sidford. Letters of July 18, July 27, and August 16, 1872, to his mother. The State Historical Society of Colorado, Denver.

Hayden, F. V. Correspondence of and pertaining to; biographical and other material relating to, in Jesse Howell and Fritiof Fryxell Collections, Western History Research Center, The University of Wyoming.

Hazeltine, Harry (donor). "Mother's Journal of a Trip Through Yellowstone Park and the Tetons, June–October 20, 1901." Yellowstone Library and Museum Association, Yellowstone National Park, Wyoming.

Holmes, William H. "Random Records," in Jesse Howell Collection, Western History Research Center, The University of Wyoming.

Jackson, William Henry. Material relating to, in Jesse Howell Collection, Western History Research Center, The University of Wyoming.

Langford, Nathaniel P. Diary of his trip to the Tetons and Yellowstone Park with the Hayden Survey of 1872. Yellowstone Library and Museum Association, Yellowstone National Park, Wyoming.

———. "Hayden Party Under Stevenson," unpublished article, in above archives.

Leigh, Richard (Beaver Dick). Diaries, correspondence, and other related material in Edith Thompson Collection, Western History Research Center, The University of Wyoming.

———. Letters (1896–1898) to Lieutenant Lindsley. Yellowstone Library and Museum Association, Yellowstone National Park, Wyoming.

———. Further papers and correspondence concerning Leigh,

material,in Jesse Howell Collection, Western History Research Center, The University of Wyoming.

Moran, Thomas. Biographical notes, correspondence, and other material, in Jesse Howell Collection, Western History Research Center, The University of Wyoming.

Mushback, J.R. Diary of his trip into Jackson Hole with the Hayden Survey of 1878, in above collection.

Paul Wilhelm, Duke of Württemberg. Correspondence, research notes, and other material in Grace Raymond Hebard Collection, Western History Research Center, The University of Wyoming.

Sacajawea. Correspondence, research notes, and other material in the above collection.

Simpson, Milward L. Material concerning Robert R. Hamilton and John D. Sargent, in "Talks with J. Pierce Cunningham." W. O. Owen Collection, Western History Research Center, The University of Wyoming.

Smith, Jedediah S. Letter of July 12, 1827, to General William Clark. Copy in National Archives and Records.

Stewart, William Drummond. Letters of December 17, 1838, and November 26, 1839, to William Sublette. Sublette Papers, Missouri Historical Society, St. Louis.

Watson, Walcott. "History of Jackson's Hole Before the Year 1907." Yellowstone Library and Museum Association, Yellowstone National Park, Wyoming.

Wister, Owen. Western Journals, Frontier Notes, and correspondence. Owen Wister Collection, Western History Research Center, The University of Wyoming.

————. Correspondence with F. M. Fryxell in Fritiof Fryxell Collection, Western History Research Center, The University of Wyoming.

Writers' Program of WPA. State of Wyoming, Jackson Hole Collection. Wyoming State Archives and Historical Department, Cheyenne.

Interviews and Correspondence

Subject: *Alfred Jacob Miller and William Drummond Stewart:* Professor Robert C. Warner, The University of Wyoming; Marvin C. Ross, formerly staff, The Walters Art Gallery; Mildred Goosman, Curator, Western Collections, Joslyn Art Museum; Marie E. Keene, Assistant Librarian, Thomas Gilcrease Institute of American History and Art; Margaret P. Davis, *Woodlawn Plantation.*

Subject: *Teton geology:* C. N. Savage, Associate Chief, Idaho Bureau of Mines and Geology.

Subject: *Teton wildlife count; migration patterns, and disruption of through settlement:* Tom Reinicker, Supervisor, Region 6, Idaho Department of Fish and Game.

Subject: *Indian petroglyphs, pictographs, and dwelling caves on the west side of the Tetons:* Dr. B. Robert Butler, Curator, Archaeology Museum, Idaho State University.

Subject: *Indian stone circles; medicine wheels; possible astronomical alignment of cairns; Plains Indian culture; Indian quarry sites in the Tetons:* Dr. George C. Frison, Head, Department of Anthropology, The University of Wyoming.

Subject: *Lepus bairdii; Dr. C. Hart Merriam, and Dr. Josiah Curtis' identification of:* Dr. Henry W. Setzer, Curator of Mammals, National Museum of Natural History, Smithsonian Institution.

Subject: *Chief Washakie:* Elaine C. Everly, Navy and Old Army Branch, Archives Division, National Archives and Records Service; Richard S. Maxwell, Natural Resources Branch, Civil Archives, Indian Records, National Archives and Records Service.

Subject: *Robert R. Hamilton, and John D. Sargent:* Elizabeth Wied Hayden, Jackson, Wyoming.

Subject: *Teton botany:* John T. Howell, Curator Emeritus, Botany Department, California Academy of Sciences.

Subject: *Sheep Eater Indians in Tetons:* Illa Jane Bucknall, Librarian, Yellowstone Library and Museum Association, Yellowstone National Park.

Subject: *Paul Wilhelm, Duke of Württemberg:* Dr. Wolfgang Irtenkauf, Handshriftenabteilung, Württemberger Landesbibliotek, Stuttgart.

Subject: *William Henry Jackson:* Alice Susong, Librarian, Yellowstone Library and Museum Association, Yellowstone National Park; Catherine T. Engel, Reference Librarian, Documentary Sources, The State Historical Society of Colorado; Irene Moran, The Bancroft Library; Judith Reis, Archives of American Art; Jean R. McNiece, Manuscripts and Archives Division, New York Public Library.

Subject: *Jackson Hole and Teton history:* William H. Williams, Director, Wyoming State Archives and Historical Department, Cheyenne; William H. Barton, Research Historian, Wyoming State Archives and Historical Department, Historical and Publications Division; Dr. Gene M. Gressley, Director, Western History Research Center, The University of Wyoming; David Crosson, Research Historian, Western History Research Center, The University of Wyoming.

Subject: *Recollections of pioneering in Pierre's Hole, (Teton Valley):* Elizabeth (Lizzie) Woolstenhulme, Driggs, Idaho.

Subject: *Site of the Battle of Pierre's Hole; Indian trails throughout Teton country; Togwotee Pass; Indian structure on Bald Hill; John Colter's route through Pierre's Hole and his crossing of the Tetons; early history of Pierre's Hole (Teton Valley): pioneering in Pierre's Hole:* Dwight C. Stone, historian, Driggs, Idaho.

Absaroka Mountains, 41, 218
Albright, Horace, 257, 258, 260
Alden, Henry Millys, 243
Altowan, 142
American Fur Company, 63, 128, 135, 145, 147, 148
American River, 111, 131
Amphitheater Lake, 189
Antelope (Pronghorn), 16, 19
Arapaho Indians, 51, 153, 196
Arikara Indians, 67, 108, 135
Arkansas River, 115
Arthur, Chester A., 231, 232
Ash Hollow, 137
Ashley River, 75
Ashley, William H., 74, 75, 76, 77, 109, 115, 138, 145, 148; revolutionizes fur trade, 76–77
Assiniboin Indians, 54
Astor, John Jacob, 63, 69, 71, 128, 145, 146, 148
Astoria, Oregon, 32, 63, 71, 72
Atlantic Creek, 218
Atlantic Ocean, 170, 235
Audubon, John James, 142, 143
Avalanche Canyon, 23

Backwourth, James (Jim), 75, 84, 131
Badger Creek, 221
Bainbridge, Captain Augustus, 213, 214
Baird's rabbit, (Rocky Mt. snowshoe hare), 170, 252
Bannock Indians, 40, 86, 103, 155, 158
Bannock Trail, 40
Barrett, Frank, 260
Barton, Dr. Benjamin Smith, 27
Basin Culture, 46, 48, 57
Bear, grizzly, 16, 47, 61, 62, 78, 81, 84, 88, 89, 115, 188, 194, 197, 237
Bear River, 75, 103
Bechler, Gustavus R., 181, 187, 188
Beecher, Henry Ward, 160
Bent and St. Vrain, 129
Bent, William, 84
Benton, Thomas Hart, 76
Bent's Fort, 128

Berry Creek, 218
Beverage, Philo P., 184
Bierstadt, Albert, 168
Bighorn Range, 50, 155, 195, 219
Bighorn River, 37, 38, 67, 90, 103, 139; 168, 218, 219
Bighorn sheep, 16, 19, 57
Big Robber, Chief, 155, 156
Bird, 124
Birnham Wood, 137
Bismarck, North Dakota, 28
Bitch Creek, 40, 218, 255
Bitterroot Mountains, 31
Black, Arthur, 112, 113
Blackfoot, Idaho, 221, 222
Blackfoot Indians, 17, 54, 59, 61, 62, 64, 65, 66, 67, 76, 78, 81, 87, 88, 117, 118, 119, 120, 121, 122, 123, 124, 140, 146, 147, 152, 172, 221
Black Hills, 45, 53, 162, 218
Blackmore, William, 202
Black Mountain, 156
Black's Fork, 75, 149
Blacktail Butte, 204
Bonneville, Captain Benjamin L. E. de, 84, 145
Boone, Daniel, 36, 123
Bourke, John G., 159, 160
Bozeman Trail, 158
Brackenridge, Henry M., 38, 63, 64, 67, 127
Bradbury, John, 63, 64, 66, 69, 101,
Bradley, Frank H., 181, 183, 184, 187, 188, 189, 200, 202, 203, 204, 205,
Bradley Lake, 23, 204, 259
Bridger, James (Jim), 18, 75, 80, 84, 93, 102, 103, 129, 136, 137, 140, 145, 146, 148, 149, 153, 154, 167, 168, 169, 170, 171, 172, 173, 174, 175, 176, 208
Buffalo, Wyoming, 219, 220
Buffalo Fork, 62, 202, 203, 208, 217, 243
Bull Lake, 49
Burroughs, John, 256, 260
Burt, Struthers, 257

Cache Creek, 19, 218

312

Cache Valley, 77
Caldron Linn, 70, 72
California, 26, 92, 110, 111, 112, 129, 130, 131, 132, 150, 156, 234, 241
Cambrian sea, 22
Cameahwait, Chief, 31, 55
Campbell, Charles, 184
Campbell, Robert, 119, 120, 123
Canton, Sheriff Frank M., 219, 220
Carnes, John, 228, 232
Carson, Christopher (Kit), 18, 84, 103, 106, 150, 153; duel, 106
Cascade Canyon, 23, 204
Cassidy, Butch, 19, 217, 218
Catlin, George, 135
Cattle rustling, 216, 217
Charbonneau, Jean Baptiste (Pomp), 29, 103, 125–32, 135, 136, 142
Charbonneau, Lizette, 127
Charbonneau, Toussaint, 29, 31, 63, 125, 126, 127, 128, 135, 136
Cheek, 60
Cheyenne Indians, 36, 153, 159
Chicago Times, 140, 158
Chicago, University of, 203
Chimney Rock, 75
Cimarron River, 115
Clappine, Antoine, 70
Clark, Jefferson, 130, 142
Clark, William, 27, 28, 29, 30, 31, 32, 33, 35, 36, 37, 39, 40, 59, 62, 64, 110, 113, 126, 127, 128, 130, 134, 135, 138, 142, 143
Clatsop Indians, 32
Clearwater River, 32
Clement, Antoine, 141, 142
Clyman, James, 75, 101, 102
Colorado, 150
Colorado River, 77, 112, 213
Colter, John, 35, 36, 37, 38, 39, 40, 41, 59, 60, 61, 62, 64, 65, 66, 78, 254; death, 66; discovers Tetons, 38
Colter Bay, 224
Colter's Hell, 37
Colter's River, 39
Colter Stone, 39, 62
Colt's Revolver, 235, 240
Columbia River, 16, 26, 31, 32,

33, 63, 67, 68, 70, 79, 113, 134, 135, 167
Comanche Indians, 45, 50, 55, 79, 116
Conant Creek, 218
Conant Trail, 40, 218, 255
Cooke, Col. Philip St. George, 131
Coolidge, Calvin, creates Teton National Park, 258–59
Cooper, Robert, 221–22
Coral reefs in Tetons, 22
Corcoran Gallery, 203
Coulter, John Merle, 181, 183, 184, 205
Council Bluffs, 135
Cowboy, 234–46; dress, 20, 235, 236, 241; drunken, 240; adopts equipment, skills of Spanish-Americans, 20, 234; as folk hero, 235, 241; jargon, 236–37, 243; other names for, 235; keen observers, 238; and pony, 237–38; profanity, 237; readers, 239; songs, 238–39; as storyteller, 237; in Teton country, 20, 235
Crazy Horse, Chief, 159, 160
Cree Indians, 45, 54
Crook, General George, 140, 158, 159, 160, 161, 218
Crooks, Ramsay, 70, 71, 72
Crowheart Butte, Battle of, 155–56
Crow Indians, 17, 36, 37, 40, 51, 59, 60, 62, 147, 153, 155, 158, 159, 162, 195
Curtis, Dr. Josiah, 181
Custer Massacre, 160

Darby Creek, 118, 119
Dartmouth College, 80
Day, John, 71
Deadman's Bar, 227
Deadwood, South Dakota, 218
Death Canyon, 19, 23, 218, 245
Densmore, Frances, 193
Denver, Colorado, 225
Dickson, Joseph, 35
Dorion, Pierre, 63
Driggs, Idaho, 225
Drips, Andrew, 145, 150

Drouillard, George, 59, 61
Drummond, Idaho, 62

Elk, (*wapiti*), 16, 19, 200
Ellicott, Andrew, 27
Emma Matilda Lake, 255
Evans, Robert, 111

Falling Ice Glacier, 251
Ferris, Warren, 149
Field, Matthew C., 142, 143
Finerty, John, 140, 158, 160
Firehole River, 200, 201
Fitzpatrick, Sublette and Bridger, 148
Fitzpatrick, Thomas (Tom), 75, 77, 78, 103, 113, 115, 117, 121, 136, 137, 145, 146, 147, 148
Flat Creek, 228
Flathead House, 113
Flathead Indians, 17, 55, 103, 113, 118, 152
Flathead River, 113
Fontenelle, Lucien, 80, 84, 145
Fort Clatsop, 32
Fort Hall, 124, 181, 205, 213, 221
Fort Laramie, 94, 134, 137; Indian council at, 153–55
Fort Mandan, 29, 125
Fort Manuel, 127
Fort Nonsense, 145
Fort Recovery, 135
Fort Union, 136
Fort Vancouver, 110, 112, 113
Fox Creek Pass, 118
Foy, John, 123
Fraeb, Henry, 78, 117, 148
Frémont, John C., 129
French Creoles, 80, 81, 84, 99, 138
Furness, Walter, 241

Gallatin Range, 40
Gallatin River, 30, 167
Garnet Canyon, 23
Gens du Serpent (Snake Indians), 42
Gervais, Jean Baptiste, 78, 148
Glacier Creek, 184
Gleason, Harvey P. (alias Teton Jackson), 218

Gobel, Silas, 111, 112
Godin, Antoine, 118, 124
Gordon, Alexander, 142
Grand Teton, 23, 172, 176, 181, 184, 185, 186, 188, 189, 190, 191, 192, 193, 196, 198, 199, 202, 205, 213, 251; first ascent by white men, 181, 186–92; second ascent, 191; Indian structure on, 193–98; as landmark, 18, 67, 70
Grand Teton, 259
Grand Teton National Park, creation of, 260
Granite Canyon, 259
Grant, Ulysses S., 162, 232
Grass Hut, 50, 52
Gray, Asa, 206
Great Basin, 42, 43, 46, 48, 57
Great Falls of the Missouri, 29
Great Salt Lake, 77, 110, 135, 136
Green River, 55, 103, 139, 141, 144, 149, 152, 168, 206
Green River Mountains, 138
Green River Valley, 17, 50, 67, 72, 77, 129, 138, 140, 143, 145, 148, 169
Gross, Chris, 219, 220
Gros Ventre Indians, 17, 118
Gros Ventre River, 169, 170, 173, 189
Gulf of California, 79, 168, 169
Gulf of Mexico, 168, 169, 170

Hamilton, Alexander, 226
Hamilton, Bill, 201
Hamilton, Robert R., 226, 227
Hamp, Sidford, 186, 187, 188, 189, 190, 191, 201, 202
Hancock, Forrest, 35
"Hank's Woman," 242
Harper's Monthly Magazine, 242, 243
Harrington, Edward, (alias Ed Trafton), 222–25
Harris, Moses (Black), 18, 91, 93, 94, 95, 103; story, 94–95
Harvard College, 64, 80, 122, 206, 241
Hatcher, John, 92, 93; story, 92–3
Hawken rifle, 83

Hayden, Dr. Ferdinand V., 19, 167, 170, 171, 175, 176, 177, 178, 179, 180, 191, 199, 200, 201–02, 205, 206, 207, 208, 209, 210, 211, 212, 213, 256, 260
Hayden Surveys, 177–85; 186–92; 199–209, 256; name lakes in Jackson Hole, 204
Hayden Valley, 40
Heart Mountain, 38
Hendrick's Point, 258
Henry, Andrew, 59, 61, 62, 64, 76, 77, 109
Henry, Captain Guy, 160
Henry's Fork, 40, 113, 199, 203
Henry's Fort, 62, 68, 69, 70, 78
Henry's Lake, 40, 157, 200, 207
Hering, Rudolph, 181
Herring, Valentine (Rube), 18, 91, 103, 150
Hidatsa Indians, 31, 55
Hidden Falls, 204
Hoback, John, 61, 62, 66, 67, 68, 69, 72
Hoback River, 68, 110
Holland, John, 228
Holmes, George, 90
Holmes, William Henry, 203
Hooker, Sir Joseph Dalton, 206
Horn Chief, 121–22
Horse Creek, 75, 138, 148
Horse stealing, 217, 218–21
Horsethief Pass, 40, 217–18
Hosford, Billy, 219, 220–21
Hoyt, John, 163, 164
Hudson's Bay Company, 77, 99, 113, 124, 149, 178
Hunt, Wilson Price, 63, 66, 67, 68, 69, 70, 71, 72, 127

Ice ages, effect on Tetons, 22, 23, 24
Ickes, Harold, 259, 260
Idaho, 218, 221, 245
Independence, Missouri, 104
Independence Rock, 75
Irving, Washington, 123–24

Jackson, David, 13, 74, 77, 78, 91, 103, 110, 113, 114, 115

Jackson, William Henry, 14, 178, 179, 180, 181, 184, 185, 200, 201, 203, 205, 206, 208, 209, 211, 212, 256; makes first photographs of Teton peaks, 184–85
Jackson, Wyoming, 233, 258, 259
Jackson Hole (Jackson's Hole), 13, 20, 21, 22, 37, 39, 40, 41, 57, 62, 67, 72, 75, 78, 91, 103, 110, 113, 123, 144, 167, 173, 189, 199, 203–5, 206, 217, 218, 219, 221, 226, 227, 228, 229, 230, 231, 232, 233, 243, 244, 245, 248, 252, 255, 256, 257, 258, 259, 260, 261; first red men there, 17; first white men, 18, 39; battle for preservation, 254–62; tilt, 21, 248
Jackson Hole National Monument, 260
Jackson Lake, 23, 40, 92, 202, 203, 204, 205, 206, 226, 255, 257
Jackson Lake Dam, 255
Jackson, Teton, 218–21
Jackson's Hole Courier, 230, 259
Jackson's Little Hole, 75, 205
Jefferson River, 30, 60, 64, 65, 136, 157
Jefferson, Thomas, 26, 27, 28, 29, 30, 33, 34, 63
Jenny Lake (Jennie's Lake), 23, 204, 255, 256, 259
Jessaume, René, 125
Jones, Captain William A., 194, 195, 196, 208
JY Ranch, 244, 245

Kearny, Col. Stephen W., 130
Kemble, Fanny, 241
Kennerly, William Clark, 130, 142–43
Kieffer, Dr. Charles H., 191
King, Charles, 161–62
Kiowa Indians, 135–36

Ladd, A. C., 206, 207
La Jornada, 115
Lamar River, 41
Langford, Nathaniel P., 181, 182,

185, 186, 188, 189, 190, 191,
192, 193, 194, 196, 200, 201,
202, 210, 260; makes first as-
cent of Grand Teton, 186–92
Lapham, Hiram C., 222
Laramie, Wyoming, 232
Laramie River, 154
Lebret, Dr. Johann, 134
Leidy, Joseph, 205
Leigh, Jenny, 181, 203, 204
Leigh, Richard (Beaver Dick),
181, 182, 186, 199, 203, 204;
nickname, 182
Leigh Canyon, 23
Leigh Creek, 23, 40, 222
Leigh Lake, 204, 255, 259
Leland, Richard, 112
Les Trois Tetons, 15
Lewis, Meriweather, 26, 27, 28,
29, 30, 31, 32, 33, 34, 35, 55, 59,
62, 64, 125, 126
Lewis and Clark Expedition
(Corps of Discovery), 26–33,
36, 39, 59, 64, 67, 109, 127;
significance of work, 33
Lewis Lake, 40
Lexington, Missouri, 115, 123
Lincoln, Robert Todd, 231
Lisa, Manuel, 36, 59, 76, 84
Lisa's Fort, 36, 37, 41, 59, 62, 66,
67
Liszt, Franz, 241
Lodgepole pine, 15–16
Lost Tribes, 25, 27
Louisiana, 80
Louisiana Purchase, 27
Lovett, Lance Corporal, 173, 174
Lowe, Percival, 153, 154
Loyd, Ed, 219, 220
Luttig, John, records death of Sa-
cajawea, 127

McClellan, Robert, 70, 71
McKenzie, Donald, 70, 71
McKenzie, Kenneth, 140
McLoughlin, Dr. John, 113
Macbeth, 137
Madison River, 30, 60, 146
Madoc, Prince, 25
Malade River, 129
Mammoth Hot Springs, 40, 207,
211

Mandan Indians, 28, 29, 125, 135
Mandan villages, 28, 63, 126, 135
Manton rifle, 138, 139, 140
Marshall, James, 131
Medicine Bow, Wyoming, 242
Medicine Bow Mountains, 135
Medicine Mountain, 195, 198
Medicine wheels, 193–98
Meek, Fielding Bradford, 177
Meek, Joseph (Joe), 18, 75, 80, 84,
85, 89, 91, 103, 114, 129, 140,
149, 175; Shoshoni wife, 85
Menard, Pierre, 59, 60, 61
Menor, Bill, 244
Menor's Ferry, 244, 257
Merriam, C. Hart, 181, 183,
204–5
Merritt, General Wesley, 161
Meteoric shower of November
12, 1833: 92, 94
Mexican War, 130, 150, 181
Middle Teton, 188
Middle Teton Glacier, 251
Miller, Alfred Jacob, 140, 141,
144
Miller, Joseph, 69, 72
Miller, Robert, 258
Mississippi River, 25, 26, 27, 241
Missouri, 107, 123, 149
*Missouri Gazette & Public Ad-
vertiser*, 74
Missouri River, 25, 26, 28, 29, 30,
31, 33, 35, 36, 63, 74, 76, 94,
127, 134, 135, 176
Mojave Indians, 112
Mojave River, 77
Möllhausen, Balduin, 137
Montana, 221, 222
Monterey, California, 112
Moose Creek, 118, 255
Moran, Peter, 213, 214
Moran, Thomas, 14, 202, 210–15;
256; paints Teton Range, 14,
213–15
Moran, Wyoming, 226
More, Joseph, 122
Mountain men, 18, 74–79, 80–95,
96–102, 103–7, 108–16, 117–
24, 145–50; character, 83–4,
90–1; classes of, 83–4; crime
among, 91; dangers to, 86, 87,
88, 89, 90; dress, 81–2; as ex-

plorers, 75, 110, 115; food, 96, 97, 98, 99; honesty, 91; and horses, 84; and Indians, 86–7, 118; adopt Indian characteristics, 81, 87–8; Indian wives and women, 84, 85, 86; as readers and students, 91; remedies, 100, 102; at rendezvous, 103–7; as storytellers, 91, 92, 93, 94, 95, 176; types, 80; masters of woodcraft, 87, 88
Mount Hayden (Grand Teton), 202
Mount Leidy, 205
Mount Moran, 23, 205
Mount Owen, 251
Mount St. John, 249
Muir, John, 16, 23, 24, 90, 248, 250, 256, 260, 261, 262
Murthly Castle, Perthshire, 137, 141

Napoleon I, 27
National Gallery of Art, 203
Nevada, 110, 111
New Fork Lakes, 139, 143
New Orleans, 114, 128, 141
New Orleans Picayune, 142
New York Times, 225
Nez Perce Indians, 17, 103, 120
Nicholson, William, 181
Nickerson, Columbus (Lum), 222, 223, 224
Noble, Maude, 257, 258
Nodowa River, 63
Nudd, William, 123
NunumBi, 49
Nuttall, Thomas, 63, 64, 67

Oberlin College, 177
Ogden's Hole, 136
Oregon, 32, 117, 123, 132, 149, 156, 218
Ouzel, water (dipper), 16–17
Owen, W. O., 191–92
Owl Creek Mountains, 38
Owyhee River (Oregon), 132

Pacific Coast, 26, 29, 63, 66, 103, 110, 136
Pacific Creek, 39, 217, 257
Pacific Fur Company, 63

Pacific Ocean, 26, 32, 110, 135
Paleozoic Period, 22
Patterson, Dr. Robert, 27
Paul Wilhelm, Duke of Württemberg, 133, 134, 135, 136, 137, 138
Peale, Albert Charles, 206
Peale, Charles Wilson, 206
Pennsylvania, University of, 178
Persimmon Hill, 144
Pettis, Spencer, 76
Phantom Horse, 93
Phelps Lake, 23, 182, 204, 244, 245, 259
Philadelphia, 27, 63, 181
Pierre's Hole, Battle of, 18, 117–124, 129, 146
Pierre's Hole (Trou à Pierre), 39, 40, 41, 57, 62, 68, 72, 77, 78, 89, 103, 113, 117–123, 136, 167, 175, 182, 183, 199, 206, 213, 214, 221, 222, 223, 243, 259
Pilot Knobs (the three Tetons), 67, 68, 71, 73
Pine Creek Pass, 117
Pinedale glaciation, 22, 23
Plains Culture, 43, 44, 46, 50, 57
Plateau Culture, 46, 55
Platte River, 129
Polk, James Knox, 80
Pompy's (Pompey's) Pillar, 126
Popo Agie River, 168
Portneuf River, 124
Potts, John, 64, 65
Powder River, 67, 129
Powell, Major John Wesley, 213
Provost, Etienne, 74–75
Pryor's Creek, 37, 41

Raynolds, Captain William F., 19, 166–76, 194
Remington, Frederic, 241
Rendezvous, 76, 77; of 1824, 77; of 1825, 77; of 1826, 77–78; of 1829, 113–14; of 1830, 78; of 1832, 117–24, 145; of 1833, 138; of 1834, 148; of 1837, 139–40; of 1838, 140; of 1839, 148–49
Rexburg, Idaho, 222
Reznor, Jacob, 61, 62, 66, 67, 68, 69, 72

Roberts, Rev. John, 165
Robertson, Jim, 222
Robinson, Edward, 61, 62, 66, 67, 68, 69, 72
Rockefeller, John D., Jr., 257, 258, 259; reasons for preserving Jackson Hole, 258
Rocky Mountain College, 91
Rocky Mountain Fur Company, 78, 129, 145, 148; rivalry with American Fur Company, 145–50
Rocky Mountain fur trade, 18, 33, 35, 36, 63, 74–79, 80–95, 98, 103–7, 132; decline, 145–50, 153
Rocky Mountain snowshoe hare (Baird's rabbit), 170, 252
Rocky Mountains, 21, 25–26, 35, 76, 89, 92, 93, 97, 128, 129, 136, 141, 142, 144, 149, 157, 181, 194, 251; other names for, 25; strange noises in, 26, 30
Rogers, Harrison, 113
Roosevelt, Franklin D., creates Jackson Hole National Monument, 260
Roosevelt, Theodore, 241
Rose, Edward, 84
Rush, Dr. Benjamin, 27
Russell, Charles, 235

Sacajawea, 29, 30, 31, 32, 63, 125, 126, 127, 130; death, 127
Sage, Rufus B., 129–30
St. Anthony, Idaho, 230
St. Helena, 129
St. Louis, 28, 33, 35, 36, 37, 61, 63, 66, 72, 74, 75, 77, 79, 81, 83, 93, 95, 109, 114, 122, 123, 126, 127, 128, 134, 135, 136, 138, 140, 141, 142, 144
St. Louis Beacon, 79
Salt Lake City, 153
San Diego, California, 131
Santa Fe, 114, 115, 116, 129, 131, 149
Sargent, John D., 226, 227
Sawtelle, Gilbert, 200
Saxifraga oppositifolia (purple saxifrage), 15
Scott's Bluffs, 75

Scribner's Magazine, 210
Shakespeare, 91, 239
Sheep Eater Indians (Takadükas), 17, 38, 56–58, 195
Shenandoah Valley, Virginia, 36
Sheridan, General Philip, 231
Shoshone River (Stinking Water), 37, 41, 218
Shoshoni Indians, 17, 29, 30, 31, 36, 38, 40, 42–53, 54–58, 67, 68, 69, 85, 103, 121, 125, 139, 141, 143, 151–65, 173, 195; arts, 48, 57; characteristics, 49; and children, 49; dress, 42–43, 46–7; food, 42, 43–44, 55; games, 49; government, 48–49, 152; get horses, 45; housing, 43, 47, 56, 58; hunting, 31, 42, 44, 56, 57; men's role, 48, 49; power decline, 54–58; storytelling, 49–50; Sun Dance, 50–53; warfare, 43, 45, 56, 152, 154, 155–66; weapons, 44, 45, 58; women's role, 47–8
Shunar, 106
Sierra Madre Mountains, 135
Sierra Nevada Mountains, 110 111
Signal Mountain, 23, 206, 227
Simons, Dr. Titus Gordon Vespasian, 109, 114
Sinclair, Alexander, 117, 119, 120
Sinclair, Pruett, 120
Sioux Indians, 63, 135, 137, 143, 153, 154, 157, 158, 159, 160, 161, 177, 213, 218
Sitting Bull, Chief, 161
Skillet Glacier, 251
Smet, Pierre-Jean de, 137
Smith, Austin, 114, 115, 116
Smith, Jackson and Sublette, 77, 78, 109, 114
Smith, Jedediah S., 18, 74, 77, 78, 79, 89, 101, 102, 103, 108–16; death, 79, 115–16; as explorer, 77–78, 110–13, 115, and grizzly, 89, 101–12
Smith, Peter, 114, 115
Smith, Ralph, 114, 116
Snake Indians, (see Shoshoni Indians)
Snake River, 16, 17, 32, 39, 40,

41, 62, 63, 67, 69, 70, 71, 78, 92, 167, 173, 174, 175, 189, 199, 202, 203, 204, 227, 245, 248, 255; sources, 202
Snake River Land Company, 258, 259
South Pass, 72, 110, 143, 144
South Pass City, 232
Spalding, Rev. Franklin, 192
Spencer, Charles, 188, 189, 190
Stanley, John Mix, 168
Stephens, Alfred K., 122, 123
Stetson, John B., 236
Stevenson, James, 177–78, 180, 181, 185, 188, 189, 190, 191, 192, 193, 194, 196, 199, 202, 208, 209; makes first ascent of the Grand Teton, 186–92
Stevenson, Matilda Coxe, 209
Stewart, Sir William Drummond, 95, 133, 137–44; gives armor to Jim Bridger, 140; described, 139
Stinking Water River (Shoshone River), 37, 41
Stuart, Robert, 71, 72
Sublette, Milton, 74, 78, 84, 103, 117, 119, 122, 148
Sublette, William, 18, 74, 77, 78, 103, 113, 115, 117, 119, 120, 123, 138, 141, 142
Sun Dance *(Dogoo Winode)*, 50–53
Sutter, John A., 130
Swan Valley, 205
Swans, trumpeter, 16, 204, 255
Sweetwater River, 75, 77, 143
Sylvan Pass, 218

Taggart, W.T., 181, 183, 204, 205
Taggart Lake, 175, 204, 259
Taghee, Chief, 155
Tam Apa, 195
Taos, 128
Targhee Pass, 200
Terminal moraines, 204
Terry, General Alfred, 161, 162
Teton block, erosive forces shape, 22–24
Teton Canyon, 182, 183, 184, 186, 199, 214; birds indigenous, 183
Teton Creek, 183, 184, 185

Teton fault, 21, 248
Teton Glacier, 23, 251
Teton Pass, 39, 68, 72, 166, 175, 199, 205, 228, 231
Teton Range, age, 21; calcareous algae, other fossils, 22; and Pinedale glaciation, 22–23; proposal to include in Yellowstone Park, 255, 257; rising, 21; tilt, 21, 176
Teton River, 72, 222
Texas, 20, 216, 234, 235
Texas Placer Herald, the, 132
Three forks of the Missouri, 30, 46, 59, 60, 64, 103, 136, 139, 146, 167
Tigee, 160
Tillamook Indians, 113
Timbered Mountain, 227
Tivanitagon, Pierre, 39
Togwotee, 38, 58, 195, 231–32
Togwotee Pass, 38, 62, 67, 208, 217
Tower Fall, 40
Trafton, Ed, 222, 223, 224, 225
Trappers, free, 81, 83, 84, 85, 107
Trappers, hired, 83, 106, 107
Triple Glacier, 251
Truman, Harry S., creates Grand Teton National Park, 260
Turley's distillery, 104
Turner, John 112
Turner, Joseph M.W., 210
Two Ocean Lake, 255
Two Ocean Pass, 208, 217, 218, 257
Tyler, John, 80

Umatilla Indians, 152
Umpqua River, Oregon (Smith River), 112
Union Pass, 38, 67, 169
Union Peak, 169
United States Geological Survey, origin, 208–09
Utah, 110, 111, 218, 222, 258
Utah Lake, 77, 110
Ute Indians, 17, 43, 136, 158
Uto-Aztecan Family, 42

Vanderburgh, William, 145, 146, 147; death, 147

Vest, George, 231
Vigilance committees, 217
Virgin River, 77
Virginia City, Montana, 202, 211
Virginian, The, 241, 242, 243
Vision quests, 193–98

Walcott, Charles D., 255
Walker, Joe, 84, 91, 92, 103
War of 1812, effect on fur trade, 72–73
Washakie, Chief, 49, 58, 151–65; appearance, 152, 153, 160, 163; birth and youth, 152–53; as civil leader, 151–52, 153, 155, 158, 163; death, 164–65; at Fort Laramie council, 153–55; friendly to whites, 152, 158, 159; and fur trade, 153; as orator, 152, 157, 163–64; as military leader and warrior, 152, 153–54, 155–56, 157, 160, 161, 162; rise to power, 151–52; resentment toward, 157; and reservation, 157, 158; white opinion of, 162
Washake Needles, 38
Washington, D.C., 27, 164, 179, 208
Washington, George, 163, 206
Webb, Vanderbilt, 258
Webb Canyon, 259
Webster, Daniel, 163
Welsh Indians, 25
West Point (U.S. Military Academy), 80, 146, 166
White House, the, 26
Wilderness areas unappreciated, 256
Williams, Old Bill, 18, 80, 84, 91, 92, 103
Wilson,, A.D., 206, 207, 208; attacked by Chief Joseph's Nez Perce, 207–8; fails to reach summit of Grand Teton, 206–7
Wilson, Woodrow, 225

Wind River, 38, 67, 137, 148, 155, 167, 195, 232
Wind River Indian Reservation, 157–58, 163, 231
Wind River Mountains, 72, 81, 135, 137
Wind River Shoshonis, 53, 152, 165
Wistar, Dr. Caspar, 27
Wister, Fanny Kemble, 243, 244, 245
Wister, Owen, 20, 241, 242, 243, 244, 245–46; describes the Tetons, 20, 243; sets fiction in Teton country, 242, 243; homesteads in Jackson Hole, 245
Wister Draw, 245
Wolf Moon, 20
Wyeth, Dr. Jacob, 122
Wyeth, Nathaniel, 103, 118, 119, 120, 121, 122, 123, 124
Wyoming, 13, 21, 138, 163, 178, 179, 194, 195, 212, 216, 217, 232, 233, 240, 241, 242, 244, 245; and women's rights, 232, 233
Wyoming Shoshonis, 55

Yamp Creek Canyon, 221
Yellow Hand, 50, 51
Yellowstone country, 41, 57, 78, 92, 93, 144, 176, 210
Yellowstone Lake, 40, 78, 202
Yellowstone Park, 16, 37, 167, 181, 191, 199, 208, 223, 244, 255, 256, 257
Yellowstone Park stage robbery, 223–25
Yellowstone River, 28, 36, 37, 40, 59, 78, 103, 126, 136, 161, 166, 171, 200, 212, 218
York, 29
Young, Col. S.D.M., 255
Yount, Harry, 206, 207, 208
Youth Vigil, 196